Working the System

Crossings: Asian Cinema and Media Culture

Editors: Po-Shek Fu (University of Illinois, Urbana-Champaign) and Man-Fung Yip (University of Oklahoma)

The series "Crossings" publishes books in English and Chinese that investigate Asian cinema and media from cross-disciplinary and cross-methodological perspectives. It situates Asian cinema and media within a global or regional framework and explores different dimensions of transnationality in relation to production, distribution, and reception. It also entails transmedial interrogations of past and present media culture, looking into the complex interactions of media forms and how they have shaped aesthetic and social practices. Wide-ranging in scope and method, the series places special emphasis on cutting-edge scholarship that draws on careful archival research or derives from vigorous, insightful theoretical study.

Books in the series:

Chinese Cinema: Identity, Power, and Globalization
Edited by Jeff Kyong-McClain, Russell Meeuf, and Jing Jing Chang

Malaysian Cinema in the New Millennium: Transcendence beyond Multiculturalism
Adrian Yuen Beng Lee

Remapping the Sinophone: The Cultural Production of Chinese-Language Cinema in Singapore and Malaya before and during the Cold War
Wai-Siam Hee

Screening Communities: Negotiating Narratives of Empire, Nation, and the Cold War in Hong Kong Cinema
Jing Jing Chang

Working the System: Motion Picture, Filmmakers, and Subjectivities in Mao-Era China, 1949–1966
Qiliang He

Working the System

Motion Picture, Filmmakers, and Subjectivities in Mao-Era China, 1949–1966

Qiliang He

Hong Kong University Press
The University of Hong Kong
Pokfulam Road
Hong Kong
https://hkupress.hku.hk

© 2023 Hong Kong University Press

ISBN 978-988-8805-60-0 (*Hardback*)

All rights reserved. No portion of this publication may be reproduced or transmitted in any form or by any means, electronic or mechanical, including photocopying, recording, or any information storage or retrieval system, without prior permission in writing from the publisher.

British Library Cataloguing-in-Publication Data
A catalogue record for this book is available from the British Library.

Digitally printed

To all filmmakers in Mao-era China,

who worked hard to make their audience laugh, cry,
and soar on the wings of new ideas

Contents

List of Illustrations	ix
Acknowledgments	x
Introduction	1
The Relationship between the Party and Artists in Mao-Era China	3
Beyond the Resistance/Accommodation Paradigm	6
Filmmaking as a Subjectivizing Practice	8
Chapter Design	15
1. Wu Xun, Song Jingshi, and Lin Zexu: Cinema and Historiography in Mao's China (1949–1966)	18
The Wu Xun Film and New Historiography in the PRC	22
Song Jingshi: The Integration of the Class View and Historicism	26
The Disputes between Dogmatists and Historicists: The 1960s	33
History as a Public Realm of Communication	39
Conclusion	41
2. From Wu Xun to Lu Xun: Film, Stardom, and Subjectivity in Mao's China	43
To Survive: Zhao Dan and *The Life of Wu Xun*	47
To Thrive	48
To Survive: Zhao Dan's Confessions as a Survival Tactic	61
Conclusion	64
3. "Putting New Wine into Old Bottles": Sun Yu's Filmic Career in Post-1949 China	66
The Storyline	69
The Production of the Film	70
Criticisms and Reevaluation	74
Putting New Wine into Old Bottles	79
Sun Yu in the Early 1960s	87
Conclusion	88

4. Wu Yonggang: Opera Film, the Cinematic Cold War, and Artistic Autonomy	90
The Second-Generation Directors in Mao-Era China	93
The Cinema of Attractions	96
The Cinematic Cold War	98
The Jade Hairpin, a Yue Opera Film	103
Conclusion	113
5. The Making of Xie Jin in the PRC: Womanhood, Melodrama, and Co-authorship	114
Woman Basketball Player No. 5	116
Red Detachment of Women	120
Stage Sisters	126
The Xie Jin Mode Reconsidered	131
Conclusion: The Making of Xie Jin	136
Conclusion	138
Bibliography	143
Index	166

Illustrations

Figure 1.1: Scenes of the Qing court from *Song Jingshi* — 30
Figure 1.2: Battles in *Song Jingshi* — 31
Figure 1.3: The final part of *Lin Zexu* — 37
Figure 3.1: "Oliver Hardys" — 81
Figure 3.2: Young women's bodies in *Queen of Sports* and *Brave the Wind and Waves* — 84
Figure 4.1: The protagonist's horizontal movement in *The Jade Hairpin* — 112
Figure 5.1: The furnishings in *Woman Basketball Player No. 5* — 121
Figure 5.2: The reunion in *Red Detachment of Women* — 125

Acknowledgments

This book is an outgrowth of my endeavor to work on film history in the past several years. I call attention to the studies on film not as texts or textual relations but as a cultural institution and a contested zone where different parties negotiate or conflict with one another. In this volume, I focus on one of the actors in the world of film: directors. Therefore, the present study does not center on the movies per se but on those who produce films as a practice to come to terms with the new sociopolitical realities and come up with their subjectivities in Mao-era China (1949–1976). My research into film history in twentieth-century China will not stop here. I plan to turn my attention to other actors—projectionists, city administrators, political authorities, and moviegoers—in my next monograph about cinema in China in the long twentieth century.

Although I have written about film in the past decade, my effort was sporadic at best. It was not until 2018 that I began to take film history seriously. During the summer break that year, Professor Huang Wangli, the colleague of my longtime friend Zhou Wenji, invited me to teach a short course on film history in early twentieth-century China at the Shanghai Film Academy of Shanghai University. Although I was by no means a specialist back then, I accepted the offer. Therefore, I sincerely thank both Huang and Zhou for their invitation for me to enter the new world of film.

I came to know a great number of scholars and students at the Shanghai Film Academy in the summer of 2018 and beyond. Many of them have become my friends. I thank Chen Xihe, Wang Yanyun, Zhai Liying, Lu Jiajia, Wang Xinying, Wu Jun, and Chen Zhicheng for constantly sharing ideas. Lu Jiajia later invited me to give an online talk about opera films in China, which would eventually become a part of Chapter 4 of this book. Wang Xinying helped me conduct research at Shanghai Municipal Archives, also in the summer of 2018.

My special thanks to Wang Meng, who not only assisted me in doing research for this project over the years but also became my coauthor of two articles in relation to this project. I appreciate that she is willing to release the rights to the two articles to me. The topic of her doctoral thesis is highly relevant to my project. Therefore, we have also shared ideas about director Sun Yu and his movies. Tan Jie, also holding a PhD degree at Shanghai University, similarly helped me conduct archival research in the past couple of years. I am grateful to Li Zhen of the China Film Archive for his outstanding oral history project and his accompaniment when I gained special permission to watch unpublished and unreleased films in Beijing in 2019.

I am honored to have had quite a lot of opportunities to interact with Professor Po-Shek Fu when I was in Illinois. Professor Fu is widely known for his works on film history in both Shanghai and Hong Kong. It was Professor Fu who suggested that I submit this book manuscript to Hong Kong University Press. In Illinois, I also got assistance from my previous institution, Illinois State University. I spent my sabbatical semester in the spring of 2020 conducting research in Shanghai despite the outbreak of the COVID-19 pandemic. The School of Arts and Sciences and the Department of History at Illinois State University funded my research trips to China over the years. The International Office at Illinois invited me to give a talk on propaganda in socialist China in 2019. The topic was related to the present research. I thank Professors Kathryn Bernhardt and Zhuoyi Wang for having read my paper about Zhao Dan. Professor Jason McGrath deserves my special mention because he ushered me into the world of film studies when I was still a graduate student in Minnesota dozens of years ago.

In Hong Kong, I got help from my colleagues at Hong Kong Shue Yan University, so that I was able to finish writing the final portion of the book manuscript in the fall of 2021. I thank the two anonymous reviewers of my book manuscript for their recommendations and critical thoughts. The staff at Hong Kong University Press have been helpful throughout the process. Finally, I would like to thank my mother, Wang Zhonghua, and my wife, Chen Wenyu, for their wholehearted support. I could not have become what I am now without them.

Some of my articles include material that has entered two chapters in changed format here. Chapter 1 is based on "Wu Xun, Song Jingshi, and Lin Zexu: Cinema and Historiography in Mao's China (1949–1966)," *Asian Studies Review* 46, no. 2 (2022): 331–49. Chapter 2 is derived from "From Wu Xun to Lu Xun: Film, Stardom, and Subjectivity in Mao's China (1949–1976)," *Modern China* 48, no. 3 (2022): 650–75.

Introduction

In October 1980, Zhao Dan 趙丹 (1915–1980), a superstar film actor who had risen to fame in the mid-1930s and spent years in prison during the tumultuous Cultural Revolution (1966–1976), died of cancer. Shortly before his death, Zhao made some incisive comments on the relationship between the party-state and artists in China. In his deathbed essay, "There Is No Hope for Literature and the Arts If They Are Regulated Too Specifically" (*Guande taijuti, wenyi mei xiwang* 管得太具體，文藝沒希望), Zhao explicitly called on the Chinese Communist Party (CCP) to relinquish its control over culture and arts in post-Mao times.[1] This essay has long been interpreted as the final chapter of this film star's lifelong struggle with the CCP's intervention in filmmaking, inspiring Yingjin Zhang to hail Zhao as both a movie star and a "real-life martyr" in the history of Chinese film.[2] Zhao's putative martyrdom typifies a long-held assumption about the uneasy relationship between the interventionist party-state and the docile or recalcitrant artists/performers in the Mao Zedong era (1949–1976), and such an assumption has profoundly shaped the existing studies on the party's efforts to refashion Chinese culture in post-1949 China.

The present book, by comparison, calls into question the prevailing paradigm—a presumption that post-1949 artists and scholars were either cooperative with or resistant to the oppressive state—by examining the careers and day-to-day lives of five highly accomplished film directors based in Shanghai. I argue that the resistance/accommodation binary was oftentimes ex-post constructions and, therefore, differed markedly from those filmmakers' lived experiences during the early years of the People's Republic of China (PRC, 1949–present). Rather than offering another historical account of how the moviemakers willingly subscribed to the party's ideologies or mightily struggled with them, this study underscores how the changing political climates and unstable party policies in Mao's China enabled those

---

1. Zhao Dan, "Guande tai juti, wenyi mei xiwang" 管得太具體，文藝沒希望 [There is no hope for literature and the arts if they are regulated too specifically], *Renmin ribao* 人民日報 [People's Daily], October 10, 1980.
2. Yingjin Zhang, "Zhao Dan: Spectrality of Martyrdom and Stardom," in *Chinese Film Stars*, eds., Mary Farquhar and Yingjin Zhang (London: Routledge, 2010), 86–87.

filmmakers to create, maintain, and adjust their newfound subjectivities under this new sociopolitical system.

To this end, this book focuses on a pantheon of preeminent Shanghai-based filmmakers to investigate the making of the new citizenry in Mao-era China. The protagonists of the book represent a full spectrum of film directors: Zheng Junli 鄭君里 (1911–1969), Sun Yu 孫瑜 (1900–1990), and Wu Yonggang 吳永剛 (1907–1982), seasoned moviemakers who had earned considerable reputations before the founding of the PRC, Zhao Dan, a film superstar-turned-director whose fame peaked in the 1950s and 1960s, and Xie Jin 謝晉 (1923–2008), a rising star who came into prominence after 1949. Rather than presenting a hagiography of Shanghai-based film directors, the present book portrays them as ordinary people in the early years of the PRC who strove to survive the new sociopolitical system established by the CCP and were simultaneously eager to reap benefits from it. Their checkered careers and stressful personal experiences thus provide compelling case studies on how individuals' subjectivities took shape in a socialist regime.

Given film's unrivaled popularity across the country as a mass-consumed cultural product and its widespread use as an instrument of ideological indoctrination in post-1949 China, motion picture directors took on special significance as both a key component part of the PRC's propaganda machine—"the enunciator of revolutionary ideology"[3] or the constructor of "socialist subject"[4]—and the very target of the party's thought reform or ideological remodeling, a CCP-led campaign "to refashion mind-sets and instill new ways of thinking."[5] These directors were tasked with producing movies to reeducate the masses and thereby transform the latter into the Marxian "new man,"[6] who was expected to "make history and perpetuate revolution."[7] However, veteran directors, who had risen in esteem well before the founding of the PRC, could hardly win the party's favor because of their "very interesting" but "highly untidy" backgrounds.[8] It was thus vital that those filmmakers underwent rounds of "brainwashing," replacing their "old ideas with new ones,"[9] before they were allowed to produce films to disseminate communist ideologies. Film's cardinal importance as an instrument of state propaganda and

---

3. Yomi Braester, *Witness Against History: Literature, Film, and Public Discourse in Twentieth-Century China* (Stanford: Stanford University Press, 2004), 117.
4. Xiaoning Lu, *Moulding the Socialist Subject: Cinema and Chinese Modernity (1949–1966)* (Leiden: Brill, 2020), 4.
5. Aminda M. Smith, *Thought Reform and China's Dangerous Classes: Reeducation, Resistance, and the People* (Lanham, MD: Rowman & Littlefield, 2012), 4.
6. Maurice Meisner, *Mao Zedong: A Political and Intellectual Portrait* (Malden, MA: Polity, 2007), 147.
7. Yinghong Cheng, *Creating the "New Man": From Enlightenment Ideals to Socialist Realities* (Honolulu: University of Hawai'i Press, 2009), 1. Also, Yu Miin-ling (Yu Minling 余敏伶), *Xingsu "xinren": Zhonggong xuanchuan yu Sulian jingyan* 形塑"新人"：中共宣傳與蘇聯經驗 [Shaping the new man: CCP propaganda and Soviet experiences] (Taipei: Zhongyang yanjiu yuan jindaishi yanjiu suo, 2015), 2–11.
8. Paul G. Pickowicz, *China on Film: A Century of Exploration, Confrontation, and Controversy* (Lanham, MD: Rowman & Littlefield, 2012), 190.
9. Cheng, *Creating the "New Man"*, 3.

an indispensable pastime for the general population and the CCP's lack of complete confidence in film directors, as this book will show, led to a heavy irony. In most cases, opinions to reaffirm the directors' central role in making films were denounced as heretical. For the CCP authorities, such "director-centrism" (*daoyan zhongxin lun* 導演中心論) hinted at the film artists' rejection of the party's leadership in the film industry. However, directors were invariably singled out as the convenient scapegoats for ideologically questionable and politically incorrect filmic works in all political campaigns despite the CCP's avowed denial of "director-centrism."

The Relationship between the Party and Artists in Mao-Era China

The CCP authorities' intimate but strained relationship with moviemakers exemplified the party-state's general attitudes towards artists in China during the first three decades of the PRC. Recent scholarship has addressed the tension between the party's efforts to co-opt artists or cultural workers to advance its agenda to transform China, socially and culturally, and its eagerness to reeducate the latter and thereby refashion Chinese culture. The PRC government at various levels enlisted support from painters,[10] folklorists,[11] grassroots musicians,[12] dramatists,[13] and singing girls,[14] among others, to appropriate the existing art forms and to appeal to and edify the masses. While the PRC state kept alive the tradition of *jiaohua* 教化 (moral transformation) to effect changes to Chinese culture,[15] artists and performers also took the initiative to advance the CCP's agenda of reforming Chinese culture by proscribing "many conventions of previous art"[16] and censoring their own works.[17] The CCP's success in winning over the artists and entertainers did not necessarily result from mere coercion. In the world of filmmaking, Greg Lewis notes that "substantial members of Maoist film artists" were more cooperative with the CCP, at least before 1957, than conventional wisdom allows us to believe.[18] Paul

---

10. Julia F. Andrews, "Traditional Painting in New China: Guohua and the Anti-Rightist Campaign," *The Journal of Asian Studies* 49, no. 3 (August 1990): 559.
11. Marja Kaikonen, "*Quyi*: Will It Survive?" in *The Eternal Storyteller: Oral Literature in Modern China*, ed. Vibeke Børdahl (Richmond, Surrey: Curzon Press, 1999), 64; Chang-tai Hung, "Reeducating a Blind Storyteller: Han Qixiang and the Chinese Storytelling Campaign," *Modern China* 19, no. 4 (October 1993): 395.
12. Frederick Lau, "Forever Red: The Invention of Solo dizi Music in Post-1949," *British Journal of Ethnomusicology* 5 (1996): 127.
13. Brian James DeMare, *Mao's Cultural Army: Drama Troupes in China's Rural Revolution* (Cambridge: Cambridge University Press, 2015), 3.
14. Mi Zhao, "From Singing Girl to Revolutionary Artist: Female Entertainers Remembering China's Socialist Past (1949–The Present)," *Twentieth-Century China* 39, no. 2 (May 2014): 172.
15. Hsiao-t'i Li, *Opera, Society, and Politics in Modern China* (Cambridge, MA: Harvard University Press, 2019), 255.
16. Julia F. Andrews, *Painters and Politics in the People's Republic of China, 1949–1979* (Berkley: University of California Press, 1994), 2.
17. Jerome Silbergeld, *Contradictions: Artistic Life, the Socialist State, and the Chinese Painter Li Huasheng* (Seattle: University of Washington Press, 1993), 2.
18. Greg Lewis, "The History, Myth, and Memory of Maoist Chinese Cinema, 1949–1966," *Asian Cinema* 16, no. 1 (March 2005): 179.

Pickowicz reasons that the film circles in Shanghai wholeheartedly sided with the CCP in the early 1950s because of a heightened expectation that the new communist regime would implement strict measures to shield China-made films against the aggression of Hollywood movies.[19]

However, scholars have highlighted the CCP's establishment of its absolute authority and imposition of its will to bring about fundamental changes to Chinese culture, ideologically and artistically. Such changes were usually effected through disciplining, silencing, and even penalizing the artists or performers. Chang-tai Hung interprets the cooperation between the artists and the state as "a planned political maneuver directed from above," with which the CCP exerted "its authority by setting in no uncertain terms the limits of artistic expression."[20] Similarly, in her study on Yue opera (*Yueju* 越劇), an operatic form popular mainly in the Yangzi Delta, Jin Jiang posits that the PRC state "took responsibility for both the content of the production and the entertainers' livelihoods" since 1949.[21] Mark Bender also finds that the political authorities became the sole arbiter of folklorist arts and the driving force behind their artistic innovation in post-revolutionary China.[22]

As the CCP had long attached special significance to film, the party-state allegedly took "nearly monopolistic control" over the production, distribution, and criticism of movies.[23] To ensure that the party leadership became the sole "spectatorial position" of films in post-1949 China,[24] the world of Chinese cinema bore the brunt of state intervention. The nationwide campaign of criticizing *The Life of Wu Xun* (*Wu Xun zhuan* 武訓傳, 1951, dir. Sun Yu), a biographical movie centering on Wu Xun 武訓 (1838–1896), a peasant from modern-day Shandong who earned his reputation for raising funds for children's education as a beggar in the late eighteenth century, turned out to be the first political campaign against culture and arts in the PRC's history. It signaled the onset of the "absolute supremacy of politics over art in China"[25] and led to the demise of privately owned film studios in Shanghai and the nationalization of the film industry in China.[26] After that, Shanghai-based filmmakers came under the CCP's centralized management with the establishment of Shanghai United Film Studio (*Shanghai lianhe dianying zhipian chang* 上海聯合

---

19. Pickowicz, *China on Film*, 162.
20. Hung, "Reeducating a Blind Storyteller," 420.
21. Jin Jiang, *Women Playing Men: Yue Opera and Social Change in Twentieth-Century Shanghai* (Seattle: University of Washington Press, 2009), 184.
22. Mark Bender, *Plum and Bamboo: China's Suzhou Chantefable Tradition* (Urbana: University of Illinois Press, 2003), 16–18.
23. Pickowicz, *China on Film*, 209.
24. Stephanie Hemelryk Donald, *Public Secrets, Public Spaces: Cinema and Civility in China* (Lanham, MD: Rowman & Littlefield, 2000), 59.
25. Yingjin Zhang, *Chinese National Cinema* (London: Routledge, 2004), 195.
26. Zhang, *Chinese National Cinema*, 199; Qizhi 啓之, *Mao Zedong shidai de renmin dianying, 1949–1966 nian* 毛澤東時代的人民電影, 1949–1966年 [The people's cinema in the Mao Zedong era, 1949–1966] (Taipei: Xiuwei zixun keji gufen youxian gongsi, 2010), 115; Zhuoyi Wang, *Revolutionary Cycles in Chinese Cinema, 1951–1979* (London: Palgrave MacMillan, 2014), 8–9.

電影製片廠) in 1952 and then Shanghai Film Studio (*Shanghai dianying zhipian chang* 上海電影製片廠) in March 1953. In 1957, Shanghai Film Studio was split up, and three state-owned but relatively independent film companies—Shanghai Pegasus Film Studio (*Shanghai tianma dianying zhipian chang* 上海天馬電影製片廠), Shanghai Petrel Film Studio (*Shanghai haiyan dianying zhipian chang* 上海海燕電影製片廠), and Shanghai Jiangnan Film Studio (*Shanghai jiangnan dianying zhipian chang* 上海江南電影製片廠)—were established.

The nationalization of the film industry in the opening years of the PRC thus set an example of how the party-state disciplined and managed artists and entertainers in Mao's China. Structurally and organizationally, the state-owned Shanghai Film Studio bore a resemblance to a state-owned enterprise, whose "administrative structure [was] characterized by a hierarchy of positions filled with appointed officials, with graded ranks and corresponding emoluments."[27] Although some film veterans, such as Ying Yunwei 應雲衛 (1904–1967), Jin Yan 金焰 (1910–1983), and Chen Liting 陳鯉庭 (1910–2013), were given high-level administrative positions, as I will show later in this book, their appointments were not tantamount to their heightened political standings. On the contrary, their onerous administrative affairs could be an alternative way to deprive them of opportunities to direct their own films. In consequence, Ying produced mostly opera films (*xiqu dianying* 戲曲電影), while Jin and Chen never directed a single movie during Mao's years since their joining Shanghai Film Studio.

By comparison, "graded ranks and corresponding emoluments" were far more meaningful. In the early and mid-1950s, film stars and directors were usually ranked in accordance with their standings in the film industry in pre-1949 China. In the assessment report filed in 1956, for example, Zheng Junli, Sun Yu, Wu Yonggang, and Zhao Dan were all given a rank of level 2, reflecting the reputations in the world of the Chinese motion picture they earned before Liberation, whereas the inexperienced Xie Jin's rank was merely level 6.[28] Five years later, Zhao Dan moved one rank up to level 1, and Zheng Junli and Sun Yu stayed at level 2. Wu Yonggang, who had been denounced as a "Rightist" (*youpai* 右派) in 1957, was demoted to level 7. Xie Jin climbed to level 5 because of his promotion to directorship and a few highly successful films he directed in the second half of the 1950s.[29] It was clear that this ranking system was intimately tied to filmmakers' incomes, professional opportunities in film, and political careers.

Due to the state's total domination in the production of all films made in mainland China and a well-devised ranking system to organize and manage the filmmakers, it is tempting to presume that the film industry provided the most compelling case to study the party-state's accomplishment in building up a state culture

---

27. Morris L. Bian, *The Making of the State Enterprise System in Modern China: The Dynamics of Institutional Change* (Cambridge, MA: Harvard University Press, 2005), 1.
28. Shanghai Municipal Archives, B177-3-80, 2–3.
29. Shanghai Municipal Archives, B177-1-103, 6.

by coercing the artists into subscribing to communist ideologies and transforming them into the component parts of the state propaganda apparatus. Nevertheless, Matthew Johnson casts doubt on the success of such a "state-created official culture" by citing the "[u]nrealistic economic planning" and "organizational corruption" as the reasons behind its failure.[30] Likewise, Shan Windscript contends that the state-individual relationship in Mao-era China was more complex than most scholars have shown, and the CCP's propaganda apparatus could not erase individuals' "authentic self."[31] Although the state propaganda was not as effective as advertised, the CCP proved flexible. The PRC state has been well known for its adaptiveness and resilience in formulating and implementing economic, social, and cultural policies in response to differing environments, domestically and internationally.[32] During the seventeen years before the Cultural Revolution, the party's cultural policies swung between two extremes: the moderate and the radical.[33] In the realm of film, Zhuoyi Wang underscores the uncertainty and malleability of state policies, which resulted from "multiple agendas" pursued by different agents—filmmakers included—to adapt themselves to the ever-changing economic and political environments. In consequence, films produced in Mao's China "generated complex and contradictory meanings."[34]

Beyond the Resistance/Accommodation Paradigm

Zhuoyi Wang's observation thus calls into question a longstanding assumption about the party-state's success in transforming film into state propaganda and filmmakers' slavish submission to state domination. Indeed, the responses of artists, particularly filmmakers, to the PRC's unstable political environments and inconsistent party lines had been central to scholarly inquiries in understanding the CCP's sweeping efforts to reshape Chinese society in the early years of the PRC. Some historians tend to stress the artists' accommodation with the party authorities before they fell victim to the predatory state. Perry Link, for example, uses the metaphor of the African plover, known as the "crocodile bird," which feasts on parasites on the bodies of crocodiles but runs the risk of being devoured by the latter. In most cases, artists, filmmakers included, who had been willing to cooperate with the party-state

---

30. Matthew D. Johnson, "Beneath the Propaganda State: Official and Unofficial Cultural Landscapes in Shanghai, 1949–1965," in *Maoism at the Grassroots: Everyday Life in China's Era of High Socialism*, ed. Jeremy Brown and Matthew D. Johnson (Cambridge, MA: Harvard University Press, 2015), 199.
31. Shan Windscript, "How to Write a Diary in Mao's New China: Guidebooks in the Crafting of Socialist Subjectivities," *Modern China*, 47, no. 4 (2021): 432.
32. Sebastian Heilmann and Elizabeth J. Perry, "Embracing Uncertainty: Guerrilla Policy Style and Adaptive Governance in China," in *Mao's Invisible Hand: The Political Foundations of Adaptive Governance in China*, ed. Sebastian Heilmann and Elizabeth J. Perry (Cambridge, MA: Harvard University Press, 2011), 5.
33. Silbergeld, *Contradictions*, 9.
34. Wang, *Revolutionary Cycles in Chinese Cinema, 1951–1979*, 13–14.

and play their roles as the propagators of communist ideologies, could not escape the jaw of the authoritarian regime amid numerous political movements.[35]

In a similar fashion, Paul Pickowicz focuses his attention on the ups and downs of a few renowned filmmakers, such as Shi Hui 石揮 (1915–1957) and Zheng Junli, to investigate their relations with the new regime and emphasize their victimization despite their initial accommodations. In so doing, Pickowicz raises a series of questions:

> Who made accommodations with the Party? Who did not? To what extent were there degrees of accommodation? Why did artists choose to accommodate themselves to Party-state rule? Are accommodation and complicity the same thing?[36]

For Harry Kuoshu, the answer to Pickowicz's last question is simply "yes." Kuoshu argues that "films and plays do not act out their ideological role simply by coercion" but because of the "participation of the artists." In other words, film workers were "ideological subjects" in PRC times.[37] Likewise, Yomi Braester and Tina Mai Chen highlight the filmmakers' role in contributing to articulating socialism rather than "as a mirror to reflect political circumstances."[38]

Meanwhile, Pickowicz also attempts to explore the potential of the moviemakers' resistance to the oppressive PRC state: "Was resistance an option? Who resisted?" For Pickowicz, resistance was not necessarily a political action but could well become a tactic of survival "to make themselves, their families and their friends in the arts less vulnerable politically."[39] To respond to such questions, I have shown elsewhere that Chinese performers mounted their resistance to the interventionist state not by means of direct political confrontation but in "everyday forms."[40] In contrast, Laikwan Pang notes that even political agency could resist, if not consciously, state propaganda during the Cultural Revolution.[41] This accommodation/resistance paradigm, I argue, is highly problematic. It at once offers an oversimplified and distorted version of the sociopolitical realities and people's actual experiences in Mao's China and creates an artificial binary category that pits the "good" and "innocent" people against "bad" socialism. As Rubie Watson cogently points out, "[I]t is difficult to find a vocabulary that captures the elaborate and subtle forms of repression

---

35. Perry Link, "The Crocodile Bird: Xiangsheng in the Early 1950s," *Dilemmas of Victory: The Early Years of the People's Republic of China*, ed. Jeremy Brown and Paul G. Pickowicz (Cambridge, MA: Harvard University Press, 2007), 210.
36. Pickowicz, *China on Film*, 209–10.
37. Harry H. Kuoshu, *Lightness of Being in China: Adaptation and Discursive Figuration in Cinema and Theater* (New York: Peter Lang, 1999), 3.
38. Yomi Braester and Tina Mai Chen, "Film in the People's Republic of China, 1949–1979: The Missing Years?" *Journal of Chinese Cinemas* 5, no. 1 (2011): 9.
39. Pickowicz, *China on Film*, 210.
40. Qiliang He, "Between Accommodation and Resistance: Pingtan Storytelling in 1960s Shanghai," *Modern Asian Studies* 48, no. 3 (May 2014): 548.
41. Laikwan Pang, *The Art of Cloning: Creative Production during China's Cultural Revolution* (London: Verso, 2017), 15.

and subversion—of compliance and resistance" because they were defining features of state socialisms.[42]

All binaries invoked to describe the realities in socialist regimes, such as "oppression and resistance, repression and freedom, [and] the state and the people," according to Alexei Yurchak, are artificial and prove fruitless for both scholars and laypersons to arrive at a fuller understanding of individuals' lived experiences under socialism.[43] Beneath the binary between a hegemonic ideology and the subaltern people, according to Timothy Mitchell, lies a peculiar notion of "subjectivity or selfhood," which "pre-exists and is maintained against an objective, material world, and a corresponding conception of power as an objective force that must somehow penetrate this non-material subjectivity."[44] To rephrase Mitchell, the prevailing accommodation/resistance paradigm presupposes filmmakers' a priori subjectivities that remained impervious to China's seismic sociopolitical changes after 1949. Under such a scholarly assumption, hence, a filmmaker with this preexisting selfhood chose to resist the tyrannical PRC regime or make accommodations with it because of the latter's unmatched coercive power.

Filmmaking as a Subjectivizing Practice

The approach adopted in the present book deviates from the accommodation/resistance paradigm in that I call into question the filmmakers' stable and fixed selfhoods—or an "essential self" independent of the social and political contexts[45]—that existed prior to their encounters and interactions with the political authorities in the 1950s and 1960s. As Eddy U notes, individuals of diverse backgrounds were assigned classifications, such as "intellectuals" (*zhishi fenzi* 知識分子), in Mao's China. Such classifications and labels enabled those individuals to further negotiate with the authoritarian state. Those classifications were, nevertheless, constantly in flux.[46] Here, it is worth mentioning that the CCP government usually categorized filmmakers precisely as intellectuals or *zhishi fenzi*. Moreover, the political authorities' classifications of individuals only constituted a part of the story of these individuals' search for subjectivities in post-1949 China. Scholars specializing in Soviet history have emphasized the Soviet citizens' "self-fashioning" in the everyday context; that is, the individual's quest for an identity within the framework set up

---

42. Rubie S. Watson, "Memory, History, and Opposition under State Socialism: An Introduction," in *Memory, History, and Opposition under State Socialism*, ed. Rubie S. Watson (Santa Fe, NM: School of American Research Press, 1994), 2.
43. Alexei Yurchak, *Everything Was Forever, Until It Was No More: The Last Soviet Generation* (Princeton, NJ: Princeton University Press, 2005), 5–6.
44. Timothy Mitchell, "Everyday Metaphors of Power," *Theory & Society* 19, issue 5 (October 1990): 562.
45. Dorothy Holland, William Lachicotte Jr., Debra Skinner, and Carole Cain, *Identity and Agency in Cultural Worlds* (Cambridge, MA: Harvard University Press, 1998), 27.
46. Eddy U, *Creating the Intellectual: Chinese Communism and the Rise of a Classification* (Berkeley: University of California Press, 2019), 9–11.

by the Soviet regime.⁴⁷ Rather than investigating citizens' unchangeable subjectivities or the communist regimes' success in transforming them into *Homo Sovieticus* "completely devoid of individuality,"⁴⁸ those scholars underscore the making of subjectivities under the Soviet regime as a dynamic process, or a "becoming," that went through "a host of subjectivizing practices."⁴⁹

Not all scholars of post-1949 Chinese film take for granted the notion of a priori selfhoods and subscribe to the accommodation/resistance binary. Esther Yau, for example, questions the legitimacy of a scholarly assumption that viewers in China were "unanimously anti-Party or anti-communist from the start" in Mao's times.⁵⁰ While Yau's study focuses on filmgoers, the present study turns attention to highly reputed movie directors. Rather than investigating whether they were supportive of, complicit in, or resistant to the political authorities, I treat them as ordinary citizens keen on progressing their film careers under the new sociopolitical system. Sheila Fitzpatrick reminds us of the folly of asking "whether Soviet citizens did or did not accept the Soviet worldview" because people in the Soviet Union bore a resemblance to their counterparts living in medieval times who had to embrace the Christian worldview: "[T]here was simply no other available."⁵¹ Along a similar vein, the primary concerns of the filmmakers in the PRC, who did not have an alternative, were undoubtedly not their resistance to party policies. Properly working under the system devised and maintained by the party, without a doubt, helped to "build a career"⁵² or, as Paul Pickowicz has pointed out, at the least made "themselves, their families and their friends in the arts less vulnerable politically."⁵³

Here, I base my understanding of the filmmakers' careers and lives on the universality of human needs, such as earning political ranks, bringing in handsome incomes, garnering and securing job opportunities, and establishing excellent reputations. As György Enyedi notes, "the average citizen set his or her goals in basically the same way whether living in Eastern or Western Europe."⁵⁴ In reality, most of the directors at issue in this book had initially enjoyed outstanding ranks and guaranteed high pay. Many of them were also lent special political statuses, such as

---

47. Choi Chatterjee et al., "Introduction: The Genesis and Themes of Everyday Life in Russia Past and Present," in *Everyday Life in Russia Past and Present*, ed. Choi Chatterjee et al. (Bloomington: Indiana University Press, 2015), 4.
48. Krzysztof Tyszka, "'Homo Sovieticus' Two Decades Later," *Polish Sociological Review* 168 (2009): 508.
49. Jochen Hellbeck, *Revolution on My Mind: Writing a Diary Under Stalin* (Cambridge, MA: Harvard University Press, 2006), 187.
50. Ching-mei Esther Yau, "Filmic Discourse on Women in Chinese Cinema (1949–65): Art, Ideology and Social Relations" (PhD diss., University of California, Los Angeles, 1990), 125.
51. Sheila Fitzpatrick, *Everyday Stalinism: Ordinary Life in Extraordinary Times: Soviet Russia in the 1930s* (Oxford: Oxford University Press, 2000), 225.
52. Perry Link, *Evening Chats in Beijing: Probing China's Predicament* (New York: W. W. Norton & Company, 1992), 141.
53. Pickowicz, *China on Film*, 210.
54. György Enyedi, "Urbanization under Socialism," *Cities after Socialism: Urban and Regional Change and Conflict in Post-Socialist Societies*, ed. Gregory Andrusz, Michael Harloe, and Ivan Szeleny (Oxford: Blackwell, 1996), 105.

the "deputies to People's Congress" (*Renda daibiao* 人大代表) and the members of the National Committee of the Chinese People's Political Consultative Conference (*Zhengxie weiyuan* 政協委員) on different levels. However, they all faced pressing problems regarding how to win the CCP's favor, build up their own standings in the new society, and fathom annoyingly unstable party policies. They deployed different tactics, and the effectiveness of such tactics varied.

Zheng Junli, for example, internalized the CCP's historiography that highlighted the peasant warfare as the driving force of Chinese history and made a few historical/biographical movies in the 1950s. His reputation peaked in the late 1950s with the release of two films celebrating the PRC's tenth anniversary, *Nie Er* 聶耳 (1959) and *Lin Zexu* 林則徐 (1959). He thus refashioned himself into a specialist in historical films in post-1949 China. Zhao Dan managed to rebuild his stardom shortly after the debacle of *The Life of Wu Xun* by starring in a number of blockbuster films made in Shanghai. He accumulated enormous cultural and political capital in the world of the Chinese motion picture as a film superstar, a competent director, and a "model worker" (*laodong mofan* 勞動模範). His ability to return to superstardom before the outbreak of the Cultural Revolution resided in his connections with the upper-echelon leaders in Beijing. Sun Yu also recovered from the political campaign against *The Life of Wu Xun* in the mid-1950s, when he directed his only color film, *Brave the Wind and Waves* (*Chengfeng polang* 乘風破浪, 1957). In this movie, Sun revisited the topic of a young woman's maturation and displayed her healthy feminine body as he did in *Queen of Sports* (*Tiyu huanghou* 體育皇后, 1934), a commercially successful movie Sun directed in the mid-1930s.

Wu Yonggang fell victim to the political purge in the Anti-Rightist Movement but regained the opportunity to direct a few opera films in the early 1960s, when the political climate changed. Just like Sun Yu, Wu was able to find a niche in the movies to popularize his most cherished notions of class conciliation and interpersonal harmony, which he had attempted to instill in the audiences ever since the screening of his first film product, *The Goddess* (*Shennü* 神女, 1934). The full expression of Wu's humanism on the screen and artistic autonomy Wu was enjoying in the early 1960s was made possible because of a unique politico-cultural setting of the day: the Cold War in East Asia. To win the cultural war outside China during this period, Wu's works were shipped to the overseas market but were not intended to be shown domestically. Xie Jin, the youngest of the five protagonists, initially won the political authorities' confidence both thanks to his age and because of the CCP cadres' lack of trust in old-generation filmmakers. Xie thus stood out by producing a string of commercially, artistically, and ideologically successful films in the 1950s and 1960s. Xie's quick rise to prominence enabled him to build a status as a first-rate director who was entitled to challenge the party leadership in the film studio. Xie's constant interactions with the political authorities in both Beijing and Shanghai led to an unintended consequence: the making of his unique directorial style, known as the "Xie Jin mode of cinema" (*Xie Jin dianying moshi* 謝晉電影模式). In this sense, Xie conjured up his subjectivity as a first-class director because of his struggle against and compromise with the CCP cadres.

To varying degrees, all those filmmakers relished the opportunities to further their careers in film and benefited from the bureaucratized administrative structure in the state-owned film studios before they were finally dragged into the political turmoil during the Cultural Revolution. In all fairness, their success in reaching a much larger fan base and shooting to fame beyond Shanghai was principally due to the party-state's unremitting efforts to make film a mass-consumed cultural product. Due to the proliferation of cinemas in the cities and the assembling of itinerant film projection squads mainly in the countryside, the CCP authorities managed to enlarge the population of film viewers across China by one hundred times between 1949 and 1959.[55] Film's remarkable success was not just an outgrowth of the filmmakers' endeavors. More importantly, the CCP was capable of transforming ordinary people into filmgoers via the manipulation of their time and modes of entertainment. Shaoguang Wang notes that the state had "absorbed a great deal of the population's time and started to regulate how people conducted their leisure activities" since the 1950s.[56] Meanwhile, the political environment at the height of the Cold War led to what Poshek Fu calls the "cinematic Cold War" in Hong Kong and Southeast Asia,[57] paving the way for some films directed by Sun Yu, Wu Yonggang, and Xie Jin in this period to gain immense popularity outside mainland China.

It was thus clear that the filmmakers and Chinese film in the post-1949 era were mutually constitutive. The filmmakers' efforts and creativity steered China's film industry in a direction not entirely governed by the party, while the CCP's politico-cultural agendas and the domestic and international film markets the political authorities were opening up reoriented those moviemakers' careers and personal lives. The biographers and even researchers of those filmmakers, however, tend to tell one-sided stories without an awareness of such filmmaker-state reciprocity. Memoirs and biographies, predominantly published after the Cultural Revolution, the darkest age for the moviemakers, invariably contributed to publicizing the images of those directors as the staunch resisters to and/or the hapless victims of some intra-party cliques, if not the entire atrocious communist state. For example, Huang Chen 黃晨 (1914–1994), Zheng Junli's widow, in the commemorative essay she penned immediately after the Cultural Revolution,[58] both

---

55. Zhang, *Chinese National Cinema*, 192.
56. Shaoguang Wang, "The Politics of Private Time: Changing Leisure Patterns in Urban China," in *Urban Spaces in Contemporary China: The Potential for Autonomy and Community in Post-Mao China*, ed. Deborah Davis et al. (Cambridge: Cambridge University Press, 1995), 154.
57. Poshek Fu, "More than Just Entertaining: Cinematic Containment and Asia's Cold War in Hong Kong, 1949–1959," *Modern Chinese Literature and Culture* 30, no. 2 (Fall 2018): 43.
58. Huang Chen 黃晨, "Kongsu 'Siren bang' dui Zheng Junli tongzhi ji qita dianying gongzuozhe de canku pohai" 控訴"四人幫"對鄭君里通知及其他電影工作者的殘酷迫害 [Denouncing the "Gang of Four" for their cruel persecution of Comrade Zheng Junli and other film workers], in *"Siren bang" shi dianying shiye de sidi* "

angrily blamed the Gang of Four for having tortured and murdered her husband and looked back on Zheng's well-acclaimed film works produced after 1949 as if Zheng's considerable success in post-1949 years had nothing to do with the party-state. In a similar fashion, Chen Hong 陳虹 (b. 1948), the daughter of Chen Baichen 陳白塵 (1908–1994), a celebrated screenplay writer in Shanghai, proclaimed in her father's biography[59] that her father wrote nothing but "literature on demand" (*feng-ming wenxue* 奉命文學) after 1949 despite her father's status as a towering figure in scriptwriting in the film circles and an avid advocate of the CCP's new, peasant-centered historiography. Without a doubt, the most arresting example is the essay mentioned earlier written by Zhao Dan shortly before his death, "There Is No Hope for Literature and the Arts If They Are Regulated Too Specifically."

Practically all the memoirists and biographers pressed home their viewpoints about the victimhood of those directors based on their memories, if not hearsay. In other words, the binary between the rapacious state and the collaborative/resistant artists was, more often than not, a retrospective construction wrought up after the Cultural Revolution. The same thing happened in post-Soviet Russia, where "members of the intelligentsia" were eager to emphasize the use of their "own language" to struggle for "a free space" during the socialist era. The rhetoric, however, was merely a new creation in the late and post-perestroika years, and such a construction did injustice to history because those refreshed memories ran counter to those of the intellectuals' lived experiences in Soviet society.[60] Unfortunately, this mindset to reconstruct memories and tell one-sided stories that differed fundamentally from the individuals' day-to-day lives rang true in the writings about filmmakers in particular and the entire society in Mao-era China in general. Even worse, hopes are still high among present-day scholars that such retrospective constructions of "facts" could someday shed light on the conflicts between the "innocent" people and the oppressive state in socialist China. Bruce Gilley, for example, asserts that "[a] torrent of reinspections and revisions of history will flood out in the immediate years after dictatorship [of the PRC]."[61]

It is thus imperative to make a more nuanced interpretation of the relationship between citizens and the PRC state—as experienced by the individuals living in Mao's times but not as reconstructed memories offered by those biographers. First, is it possible to differentiate the sincere embracing of the CCP's ideologies from a surface allegiance? Indeed, learning to speak a specific political language introduced by the communist regime allowed the citizens both to pledge their loyalty to the party and to appropriate it to advance their own agendas and serve their own

---

四人幫" 是電影事業的死敵 ["The Gang of Four" are the archenemy of the film industry] (Beijing: Zhongguo dianying chubanshe, 1979), 203.

59. Chen Hong 陳虹, *Wutai yu jiangtai: Xiju jia Chen Baichen* 舞臺與講臺：戲劇家陳白塵 [The stage and the platform: Chen Baichen, the dramatist] (Nanjing: Nanjing daxue chubanshe, 2003), 15.

60. Yurchak, *Everything Was Forever, Until It Was No More*, 6.

61. Bruce Gilley, *China's Democratic Future: How It Will Happen and Where It Will Lead* (New York: Columbia University Press, 2004), 221.

interests. In consequence, it would be difficult to "distinguish genuine belief from widespread dissimulation" in a socialist society.[62] Second, does it matter to fathom an individual's mindset, either supportive or resistant to the communist state? As I have shown, human beings' decisions do not differ considerably in different societies. The goals pursued by the directors at issue in this book—monetary compensation, prestige, respect from the government, their fans, and their colleagues, and opportunities to make films—were essentially the same as those striven for by their counterparts in other parts of the world. What was unique to a socialist society was the possibility of resorting to the official rhetoric and displaying fidelity to the party to serve private interests.[63] In Timothy Johnston's words, most citizens in the Soviet Union "neither supported [nor] resisted Soviet power, they simply got by."[64] This universal "getting-by" mentality can, without a doubt, help to overcome a scholarly problem in understanding the individuals' everyday practices in the PRC when one clings to the collaboration/resistance paradigm.

Lastly, when an individual's a priori subjectivity as a "resister" to or a "collaborator" of the PRC state is in doubt, this book calls attention to viewing the directors' subjectivities or selfhoods not as preexisting, stable, or fixed but as changeable and malleable, constantly interacting with and responding to the changing political climates and their positions. Like the citizens in other socialist countries, they engaged in "self-fashioning" in the everyday context; that is, the individuals' quest for identities within the framework set up by the authoritarian regimes.[65] The "self-fashioning"—"a host of subjectivizing practices" in Jochen Hellbeck's words[66]—entailed decisions and actions that were consistent with, divergent from, or irrelevant to the party's principles and policies but were usually chosen to serve the individuals' best interests. To rephrase Stephen Kotkin, those filmmakers under scrutiny in the present book not only *worked under the system* formulated by the CCP but also "*work[ed] the system*" to maximally benefit from it or, at the least, to minimize the disadvantage brought about by the adverse working and living conditions and the hostile political environments.[67]

Film directors in Mao-era China provided the most compelling cases to study how the individuals in the early PRC years refashioned their subjectivities and managed to work the system. First, as I have stated, the directors bore the brunt of the CCP's various political campaigns. Therefore, they were generally more

---

62. Serhy Yekelchyk, *Stalin's Citizens: Everyday Politics in the Wake of Total War* (Oxford: Oxford University Press, 2014), 3.
63. Vladimir Shlapentokh, *Public and Private Life of the Soviet People: Changing Values in Post-Stalin Russia* (New York: Oxford University Press, 1989), 13–14.
64. Timothy Johnston, *Being Soviet: Identity, Rumour, and Everyday Life under Stalin, 1939–1953* (Oxford: Oxford University Press, 2011), xxxiii.
65. Chatterjee et al., "Introduction," 4.
66. Hellbeck, *Revolution on My Mind*, 187.
67. Stephen Kotkin, *Magnetic Mountain: Stalinism as a Civilization* (Berkeley: University of California Press, 1997), 237. My italics.

sensitive to the volatility of the PRC's political atmosphere. Moreover, they usually came under scathing criticism for producing politically incorrect movies although the party had given a flat refusal of their central role in filmmaking. Paul Clark posits that Chinese filmmaking has prioritized screenplay writing over the directing of the film ever since the 1930s, creating a deep-seated text-centered—instead of director-centered—mindset.[68] Leo Lee similarly finds that Chinese cinema tended to be "rich on plot and characterisation but rather sparing in what may be construed as montage sequences," making the film akin to the theater.[69] Indeed, the early PRC years witnessed the transfer of power from "Yan'an stalwarts" like Chen Bo'er 陳波兒 (1907–1951) and Yuan Muzhi 袁牧之 (1909–1978), who had actual work experience as directors and performers, to Xia Yan 夏衍 (1900–1995) and Chen Huangmei 陳荒煤 (1913–1996), who had mainly been scriptwriters and film critics.[70] However, although film directors were politically and artistically marginalized in filmmaking in Mao-era China, they cried for director-centeredness publicly or privately to confront or negotiate with the party authorities throughout the seventeen years before the Cultural Revolution.

Second, for those directors, filmmaking was one of the most significant subjectivizing practices, through which their selfhoods were reenacted, maintained, and played out. The new politico-cultural system had multifarious effects on filmmaking activities and the making of those directors' subjectivities: it considerably expanded the fan base of Chinese films, enabled the directors to obtain prestige both domestically and internationally, granted them such new categories as intellectuals and artists, afforded the opportunities to have their social and political standings elevated, allowed them to receive substantial revenues, proscribed certain topics and filmic techniques, stifled their artistic creativity, and, finally, penalized the majority of them during various political campaigns. It is true that film as a performing art lacked the flexibility of folklorist and theatrical arts,[71] for all screenplays needed to come under censors' inspection, and improvised performances were disallowed. As the entire book will show, however, the filmmakers still had much room for manipulation despite the CCP cadres' strict supervision in the whole process of film production. Along a similar vein, the filmmakers could manipulatively uphold the party-sanctioned political rhetoric and reap tangible benefits from it without having to embrace it wholeheartedly in their day-to-day life.

The filmmakers joining the state-owned film studios and mouthing of political slogans neither precluded them from exploring their own ways of making films

---

68. Paul Clark, *Chinese Cinema: Culture and Politics since 1949* (Cambridge: Cambridge University Press, 1987), 94–95.
69. Leo Ou-fan Lee, "The Tradition of Modern Chinese Cinema: Some Preliminary Explorations and Hypotheses," in *Perspectives on Chinese Cinema*, ed. Chris Berry (London: BFI Publishing, 1991), 13–14.
70. Matthew D. Johnson, "Propaganda and Censorship in Chinese Cinema," in *A Companion to Chinese Cinema*, ed. Yingjin Zhang (Malden, MA: Wiley-Blackwell, 2012), 168.
71. For improvised performances on the stage and their challenge to the CCP's censorship, see He, "Between Accommodation and Resistance," 532–33.

in order to serve their best interests nor guaranteed their safety amid political storms. Therefore, they were by no means "innocent" individuals facing the communist regime's oppression. Rather, they at times made fawning contributions to popularizing the state-sponsored ideologies and building a socialist society in China. Simply put, they were entangled with the party-state. Here, "entanglement" refers to a process of molding new citizenry in socialist regimes where individuals became "entangled" with the party-states as long as they had a grip on the narratives created by the communist regimes.[72] Therefore, it was unnecessary to differentiate their sincere acceptance of the communist ideologies from their parroting of the CCP's rhetoric: they could well do both. What mattered was that the filmmakers constantly adjusted their tactics, particularly in their filmmaking activities, to maximize the benefits and minimize the disadvantages. Rather than exploring their a priori subjectivities as resisters to or collaborators of the communist regime, the entire book underscores the process of making their subjectivities. Their checkered film careers revealed that they not only acclimated themselves to the ever-changing political atmosphere of Mao-era China but also sought to obtain benefits from it.

Chapter Design

Working the System centers on five film directors based in post-1949 Shanghai to explore their different ways of coming to terms with the novel politico-cultural system in Mao-era China. Chapter 1 centers on Zheng Junli, who was unfortunately drawn into the political maelstrom during the campaign of criticizing *The Life of Wu Xun* in the early 1950s. In the remainder of this decade, nevertheless, Zheng managed to redeem himself and win back his reputation as a first-rate director by directing a number of attention-grabbing historical/biographical films, such as *Song Jingshi* 宋景詩 (1955), *Nie Er*, and *Lin Zexu*. Given *Song Jingshi*'s status as the first Chinese movie centering on a peasant uprising leader and assessing the revolution of the peasant in a positive light, it was evident that Zheng deployed a tactic of fully subscribing to the CCP-endorsed historiography to reinterpret China's history in imperial times. This chapter argues that filmmakers like Zheng were not just enunciators of communist historiographical and ideological notions but their major contributors and propagators.

Chapter 2 highlights Zhao Dan's remarkable success as both a film star and a director in the 1950s and 1960s. Beginning in the mid-1930s, a host of highly successful films had catapulted Zhao into stardom. Despite this, he got off to a rocky start in the opening years of the PRC, when he endured heavy pressure because of the nationwide campaign against *The Life of Wu Xun*. Since the mid-1950s, however,

---

72. Stefan Arvidsson, Jakub Beneš, and Anja Kirsch, "Introduction: Socialist Imaginations," in *Socialist Imaginations: Utopias, Myths, and the Masses*, ed. Stefan Arvidsson, Jakub Beneš, and Anja Kirsch (London: Routledge, 2019), 7.

Zhao staged a glorious comeback by starring in several blockbuster movies, including the two anniversary films directed by Zheng Junli. He also began to chart new territory in filmmaking by directing several films during the Great Leap Forward (1958–1960) and beyond. Zhao's rise to superstardom under socialism resulted from his ability to mobilize all the resources accessible to him: his popularity ever since the 1930s, his intimate relationship with high-ranking officials in Beijing, including Zhou Enlai 周恩來 (1898–1976) and Jiang Qing 江青 (1914–1991), and his newly minted party membership. Meanwhile, his rise to fame as an exemplary artist or intellectual with the help of the political authorities and the CCP's endeavor to expand the national film market further allowed him to gain unprecedentedly wide recognition across the country. After 1949, the CCP established a national film distribution and projection network, including rural film projection teams that would travel the countryside, allowing movie stars to enjoy a much larger audience than they had before national liberation. Film attendance across China increased nearly one hundredfold between 1949 (47 million) and 1959 (4,170 million).[73] Therefore, the making of his stardom and a socialist model worker—or his new subjectivity in the PRC—was made possible because of both artistic and political reasons.

In comparison with the two relatively successful filmmakers examined in Chapters 1 and 2, the protagonists in Chapters 3 and 4 had to grapple with the problem of not losing the CCP's favor. The third chapter investigates Sun Yu's recourse to his familiar filmic technique— invoking the image of the female body to metaphorize China's nation-building efforts. *Braving the Wind and Waves*, the only color film in Sun's film career, depicts the growth and maturation of an energetic and passionate young woman who ended up becoming the PRC's first-generation female steamship captain. To popularize the PRC-sponsored notion of gender equality and women's emancipation, I argue, director Sun Yu brought back his interpretation of the connectedness between women and the Chinese nation in his 1934 film, *Queen of Sports*. However, Sun's strategy of "putting new wine into old bottles" could hardly convince the political authorities and fell short of helping him reestablish his status as a star filmmaker. In other words, this subjectivizing practice proved futile, and Sun was thereafter marginalized professionally and politically.

The protagonist of Chapter 4, Wu Yonggang, took the most dramatic plunge in professional standing of the filmmakers discussed in this book. He earned one of the highest ranks among filmmakers shortly after Liberation but was singled out as the black sheep during the Anti-Rightist Movement in 1957. The relatively relaxing political climate in the early 1960s enabled Wu to regain his status as a director, if only for opera films. Despite this, Wu's *The Jade Hairpin* (*Biyu zan* 碧玉簪, 1962), a coproduced opera film between a Shanghai-based film studio and a Hong Kong left-wing motion picture company, notched up phenomenal market success in Hong Kong. More importantly, Wu capitalized on this opportunity and took advantage

---

73. Zhang, *Chinese National Cinema*, 192.

of the unique cinematic Cold War environment to unleash his pent-up resentment and articulate his desire to conciliate with the party, that is, his victimizer. In other words, while the CCP authorities weaponized opera films to wage a cultural war in the Hong Kong and overseas markets, those movies endowed Wu with an otherwise inaccessible means to express himself and attain a certain degree of artistic autonomy.

Chapter 5 highlights Xie Jin, the youngest director of the five in this book. Xie benefited from the CCP leadership's unspoken agenda to push aside old-generation directors, such as Sun Yu and Wu Yonggang, and make way for the younger ones. Despite his uneasy relationship with the CCP cadres in the Shanghai-based film studio, he managed to produce a series of high-profile, award-winning films that commanded enormous viewership nationwide and across the globe. Notwithstanding such marked success, the friction between strong-willed Xie and the nosy supervisors, inspectors, and censors proved demoralizing but unintentionally led to the "co-authorship" or "multilayered authorship" of practically all his films.[74] Hence, it is fair to argue that the party policies and the political authorities' interventionism were at once enabling, empowering, and restraining factors behind the lionization of Xie as a rising star in the film firmament and the creation of his peculiar directorial style known as the "Xie Jin mode of cinema," that is, associating "the grand narrative of the nation" to "the vicissitudes of individual lives"—especially those of women—and using the mode of family melodrama to interpret the PRC's sociopolitical order.[75]

---

74. Xiao Liu, "*Red Detachment of Women*: Revolutionary Melodrama and Alternative Socialist Imaginations," *Differences: A Journal of Feminist Cultural Studies* 26, no. 3 (2015): 119.
75. Lu, *Moulding the Socialist Subject*, 59.

1
Wu Xun, Song Jingshi, and Lin Zexu
Cinema and Historiography in Mao's China (1949–1966)

In the past decade, scholars have investigated the vital role of post-1949 film in participating in the articulation of socialism rather than "as a mirror to reflect political circumstances."[1] In other words, cinema in the PRC constituted a "site of knowledge production" for Chinese citizens.[2] This chapter focuses on Director Zheng Junli's efforts to make historical/biographical films in the 1950s to explore Chinese filmmakers' engagement in the production and dissemination of a specific type of episteme in relation to the cinema in Mao's China: historiography. Zheng, who had been under the influence of Marxist historiography as early as the 1930s,[3] was afforded new opportunities throughout the 1950s to make films set in pre-1949 China, such as *Song Jingshi* and *Lin Zexu*, centering on historical figures in imperial times. Zheng thus earned a reputation as a specialist in historical/biographical movies.

During the PRC's first decade, when movies about the CCP's revolution and post-1949 accomplishments were indisputably the mainstream, Zheng Junli's historical films took on special significance. They assumed a unique role in not only popularizing the CCP-endorsed historical perceptions but also reconciling the tension between two historiographical tendencies, the class view (*jieji guandian* 階級觀點)—an assertion that the peasant class provided the impetus for the progress of history—and historicism (*lishi zhuyi* 歷史主義)—an approach to analyzing historical events and figures based on their historically specific conditions. Hence, as a seasoned film director, Zheng acquired his new identity as not just a disseminator of historiographical knowledge but an active participant in and a significant contributor to reconceptualizing and restructuring historiography in Mao-era China. Unfortunately, the tension between the two historiographical approaches escalated into an ideological and factional war and finally led to the purge of historians, writers,

---

1. Braester and Chen, "Film in the People's Republic of China, 1949–1979," 9.
2. Lu, *Moulding the Socialist Subject*, 3.
3. Cheng Mo 程沫, "Makesi zhuyi shiguan xia de dianying lisih yanjiu—jiyu dui *Xiandai Zhongguo dianying shilue* de fenxi" 馬克思主義史觀下的電影歷史研究—基於對《現代中國電影史略》的分析 [Historical studies on film under the Marxist conception of history—An analysis of *Brief History of Contemporary China*], *Shiting* 視聽 [Seeing and Hearing], no. 4 (2019): 232.

dramatists, and filmmakers in the mid-1960s. During the Cultural Revolution, the incarcerated, tortured, and persecuted Zheng fell victim to his own success in the preceding decade.

Historiography and film were thus intertwined in Mao's China. Back in the years in the immediate wake of the PRC's founding, the restructuring of historiographical approaches and knowledge did not start within the circles of historians but was triggered by the new republic's first major cultural movement; that is, the nationwide campaign in 1951 against *The Life of Wu Xun*. This campaign signaled the CCP's commitment to disciplining Chinese artists and reshaping Chinese culture as soon as the PRC was established.[4] The existing scholarship has primarily focused on its impact on China's film industry: the end of private ownership in China's film industry[5] and the CCP's enforcement of film censorship.[6] This chapter departs from all the previous research by underscoring a largely ignored aspect of this movement, its contribution to the recalibration of historical studies in Mao's China.[7] It argues that the campaign against *The Life of Wu Xun* not only brought about a sea change in China's film industry but also led to the "disciplinization" of Chinese historiography. "Disciplinization" in the 1950s and 1960s China, according to Huaiyin Li, refers to "the efforts to turn the revolutionary narrative developed by CCP historians into a standard representation of China's past."[8]

The most dominant revolutionary narrative ushered in by the party was the vital role of the laboring people, especially peasants, as the driving force of historical development. Given the nature of Mao Zedong's revolution as a peasant movement, it came as no surprise that studies on peasant uprisings in imperial China were of special importance among historians in the first three decades of the PRC.[9] In

---

4. Wang, *Revolutionary Cycles in Chinese Cinema*, 33.
5. Shen Yun 沈芸, *Zhongguo dianying chanye shi* 中國電影產業史 [History of the Chinese Film Industry] (Beijing: Zhongguo dianying chubanshe, 2005), 149–50; Ding Yaping 丁亞平, *Zhongguo dianying tongshi 1* 中國電影通識1 [The common knowledge about Chinese cinema 1] (Beijing: Zhongguo dianying chubanshe, 2016). 401–2.
6. Zhang Shuoguo 張碩果, "1950 niandai zaoqi Shanghai de dianying wenhua lunzheng yu gaizao—cong 'wenyi ke bukeyi wei xiao zichan jieji fuwu' taolun dao 'wenyi zhengfeng xuexi yundong'" 1950年代早期上海的電影文化論爭與改造—從"文藝可不可以為小資產階級服務"討論到"文藝整風學習運動" [Debates and reform of film culture in early 1950s Shanghai—From "whether literature and arts can serve the petty bourgeoisie" to "the movement of reform and studies of literature and arts"], in *Zhizao "guomin": 1950–1970 niandai de richang shenghuo yu wenyi shijian* 製造"國民": 1950–1970年代的日常生活與文藝實踐 [Creating the "national citizenry": The day-to-day life and practice of literature and arts, the 1950s–1970s], ed. Luo Xiaoming 羅小茗 (Shanghai: Shanghai shudian chubanshe, 2011), 284–85.
7. Susanne Pepper's observation about the role of the campaign against *The Life of Wu Xun* in refashioning China's education system in post-1949 China is highly relevant to my research. However, this chapter focuses on a specific discipline: Chinese history. See Suzanne Pepper, *Radicalism and Education Reform in 20th-Century China: The Search for an Ideal Development Model* (Cambridge: Cambridge University Press, 2010), 167.
8. Huaiyin Li, *Reinventing Modern China: Imagination and Authenticity in Chinese Historical Writing* (Honolulu: University of Hawai'i Press, 2013), 19.
9. Wang Qingjia 王晴佳 (Q. Edward Wang), *Renxie de lishi bixu shi rende lishi ma* 人寫的歷史必須是人的歷史嗎 [Does history written by humans has to be history about humans] (Shanghai: Shanghai renmin chubanshe, 2020), 337.

line with this new historiographical turn, the embattled Shanghai-based filmmakers immediately decided to rectify their "mistake" in having made *The Life of Wu Xun* and thereby redeem themselves by producing a movie centering on Song Jingshi 宋景詩 (1842–?), one of Wu Xun's contemporaries and fellow villagers, an obscure peasant revolutionist, and a byproduct "rediscovered" during the nationwide campaign of criticizing Wu Xun.

The making of *Song Jingshi* in 1955 exemplified the entanglement of historians and non-historians who provided mutual support to articulate and popularize both the CCP-sanctioned historical views and their own interpretations of history. I use the term "entanglement" in two ways. First, it illustrates a blurred line between historians and laypersons. As Timothy Cheek indicates, the complete "professionalization of intellectual work" would not materialize until post-Mao times.[10] Contrary to the existing scholarship on historiography in Mao's China that places a premium on historians' monopolistic role in the production and circulation of historical knowledge, the present study argues that it had never been historians' exclusive province but was a joint venture undertaken by both academics and non-historians. Second, entanglement refers to a process of molding new citizenry in socialist regimes where people—regardless of their true convictions—became "entangled" with the party-state, as long as they came to know and were able to "co-narrate" the narratives created in this political climate.[11] I further add that the realm of such narratives could well be the participants' own creation under the guidance of the prevailing ideologies. Here, the production of *Song Jingshi* was testimony to the filmmakers' and historians' foray into such a narrative where the peasant's central role in Maoist historiography was confirmed, articulated, and visually represented.

Although *Song Jingshi* was far from a success, artistically or ideologically,[12] its cinematic narrative concretized two threads of historical views: the class view (peasants as the creator of history) and historicism—the recognition of "the importance of context and empathy in historical interpretations," "the complexity of historical reality," and "objectivity and balance in judging that reality."[13] The moviemakers were anxious not to upset the equilibrium between the two by simultaneously portraying Song as a dauntless peasant leader and dismissing him as a flawed historical figure who once surrendered to the Qing government. Contrary to a scholarly assumption of the class viewpoint's ultimate triumph over the historicist approach and its complete domination in historical writings during the PRC's first decade,[14]

---

10. Timothy Cheek, "Historians as Public Intellectuals in Contemporary China," in *Chinese Intellectuals between State and Market*, ed. Edward Gu and Merle Goldman (London: Routledge, 2004), 205.
11. Arvidsson, Beneš, and Kirsch, "Introduction," 7.
12. Wang, *Revolutionary Cycles in Chinese Cinema*, 28.
13. Clifford Edmunds, "The Politics of Historiography: Jian Bozan's Historicism," in *China's Intellectuals and the State: In Search for New Relationship*, ed. Merle Goldman, Timothy Cheek, and Carol Lee Marmin (Cambridge, MA: Harvard University Press), 75.
14. Harold Kahn and Albert Feuerwerker, "The Ideology of Scholarship: China's New Historiography," *The China Quarterly* 22 (April–June 1965): 2.

Song Jingshi, along with many historical works published in the same decade, testifies to a high degree of integration between the two.

Entering into the 1960s, the relatively peaceful coexistence between historicism and the class view gave way to a bitter controversy in both academia and popular culture,[15] leading to the purge of intellectuals who advocated and practiced historicist theories on the eve of the Cultural Revolution.[16] This fateful debate had resulted from a vogue for reevaluating "hitherto malefic persons" in China's feudal past among historians, dramatists, writers, and filmmakers.[17] The movement in academia of reevaluating historical figures coincided with the proliferation of historical dramas and historical/biographical films—such as *Lin Zexu*—across the country. Here, Zheng Junli, the director of both *Song Jingshi* and *Lin Zexu* and the subject of this Chapter, provides an apt case for studying the intersection between Marxist historians and moviemakers. Zheng's *A Brief History of Contemporary Chinese Film* (*Xiandai Zhongguo dianying shilue* 現代中國電影史略), authored in the 1930s, has gained widespread recognition as the first historical work on China's film industry under the heavy influence of Marxist historiography, and its publication was cited as the evidence of the triumph of Marxist historical views in China long before the founding of the PRC.[18] Hence, this chapter highlights the reciprocity and complementarity between historians and non-historians—particularly filmmakers—and further argues that the (re)interpretation of history provided a common language and allowed for the making of a public space for professional historians and laypersons alike to make sense of the present by looking back at the past and thereby communicate with one another.

The rise of such a history-centered public space of communication in the late 1950s and early 1960s was comparable to the boom of public culture in Stalin's Soviet Union when the public sphere, as described by Jürgen Habermas, had vanished.[19] Likewise, the late 1950s witnessed the crackdown on outspoken critics of the PRC during the Anti-Rightist Movement and the silencing of intellectuals and professionals across China. There was, in Perry Link's words, "no free speaking any more."[20] Although Yomi Braester posits that the Anti-Rightist Movement effectively

---

15. Kahn and Feuerwerker, "The Ideology of Scholarship," 1–2; Susanne Weigelin-Schwiedrzik, "Back to the Past: Chinese Intellectuals in Search of Historical Legitimacy (1957–1965)," *Berliner China-Hefte/Chinese History and Society* 31 (2006): 4.
16. Merle Goldman, *China's Intellectuals: Advise and Dissent* (Cambridge, MA: Harvard University Press, 1981), 19.
17. Kahn and Feuerwerker, "The Ideology of Scholarship," 2.
18. Zheng Rui 鄭睿, "Makesi zhuyi shiguan guanzhao xia de Zhongguo zaoqi dianying shi xiezuo—Xiandai Zhongguo dianying shilue de lishi yanjiu fangfa" 馬克思主義史觀觀照下的中國早期電影史學寫作—《現代中國電影史略》的歷史研究方法 [The historical writing of early Chinese film history inspired by Marxist historiography—The methodology of historical studies in *Brief History of Contemporary China*], *Dangdai dianying* 當代電影 [Contemporary Cinema], no. 2 (2016): 144.
19. James Von Geldern, "Conclusion: Epic Revisionism and the Crafting of a Soviet Public," in *Epic Revisionism: Russian History and Literature as Stalinist Propaganda*, ed. Kevin M. F. Platt and David Brandenberger (Madison: The University of Wisconsin Press, 2006), 326.
20. Link, *Evening Chats in Beijing*, 130.

"shut down" any criticisms of the CCP's political control,[21] the catastrophic famine during the Great Leap Forward necessitated the revival of "a time-honored form of remonstrance" as a way for intellectuals, no matter whether they were affiliated with the party or not, to proffer their advice to the political authorities. History, which "has always served in China as a depository of precedents in the light of which the present was discussed," became one of the few viable means of communication at a time when dissenting voices were disallowed.[22] In some cases, talking history was weaponized to launch veiled attacks on Mao and his policies.[23]

As soon as Maoist dogmatists and radicals joined this history-centered public space, as manifested in the bitter controversy between the class viewpoint and historicism in the early 1960s, historians, filmmakers, novelists, and dramatists became intensely vulnerable. It thus came as no surprise that the Cultural Revolution was triggered by Yao Wenyuan's 姚文元 (1931–2005) infamous attack on *Hai Rui Dismissed from Office* (*Hai Rui baguan* 海瑞罷官), a historical play written by historian Wu Han 吳晗 (1909–1969). In a sense, the outbreak of the Cultural Revolution signaled the radicals' final domination in this history-oriented space, and its initial participants—historians and non-historians alike—became the victims of their own making. For those familiar with the CCP's mode of political struggle, the history-qua-political discussion and polemic that prompted the Cultural Revolution can be traced to the campaign against *The Life of Wu Xun* in 1951.[24]

The Wu Xun Film and New Historiography in the PRC

On May 20, 1951, Mao Zedong personally penned an editorial in *The People's Daily* (*Renmin ribao* 人民日報), titled, "[We] Must Emphasize the Discussion of the Film *The Life of Wu Xun*" (*Yingdang zhongshi dianying* Wu Xun zhuan *de taolun* 應當重視電影武訓傳的討論), accusing the movie of prioritizing gradualist social reformism over full-scale revolution.[25] In response, two heavyweight scholar-officials, Guo Moruo 郭沫若 (1892–1978) and Zhou Yang 周揚 (1908–1989), had their essays published three months later. They both anticipated the lasting impact of the Wu Xun case on historians in China. In his essay published in *The People's Daily* on August 4, 1951, Guo acclaimed the ongoing movement against *The Life of Wu Xun* and the production of the investigation report on Wu Xun for "adding a glorious

---

21. Yomi Braester, "A Genealogy of Cinephilia in the Maoist Period," in *The Oxford Handbook of Chinese Cinema*, ed. Carlos Rojas and Eileen Cheng-yin Chow (Oxford: Oxford University Press, 2013), 105–9.
22. Rudolf Wagner, *The Contemporary Chinese Historical Drama: Four Studies* (Berkeley: University of California Press, 1990), xi.
23. Goldman, *China's Intellectuals*, 36.
24. Tan Qiuwen 檀秋文, *Zhongguo dianying ren koushu lishi yinhai chenfu lu Luo Yijun koushu lishi* 中國電影人口述歷史 銀海沉浮錄 羅藝軍口述歷史 [Oral history of Chinese filmmakers, the record of ups and downs, Luo Yijun's oral history] (Beijing: Zhongguo dianying chubanshe, 2015), 106.
25. "Yingdang zhongshi dianying *Wu Xun* zhuan de taolun" 應該重視電影《武訓傳》的討論 [(We) must emphasize the discussion of the film *The Life of Wu Xun*], *Renmin ribao* 人民日報 [People's Daily], May 20, 1951.

chapter to the people's historiography in China."[26] Four days later, Zhou Yang reconfirmed this investigation report's role in remolding historians in China. He noted, "[The report] has set a model for historical research, social surveys, and literary criticism." He further called for making historical or biographical movies under the guidance of "a correct view of history"; that is, "The creator of human society and history must be the laboring people, for they generate material wealth." Bourgeois historians failed to fully embrace this class viewpoint, Zhou continued, because they lacked "a good judgment based on Marxist-Leninist standpoints." Similarly, film artists were responsible for "[representing] the reality and unearthing the historical [truth]" because the motion picture was art that "faithfully reflects the reality."[27]

The Class Viewpoint and Marxist Historiography

The Investigation Report of the History of Wu Xun (*Wu Xun lishi diaocha ji* 武訓歷史調查記) that both Guo Moruo and Zhou Yang profusely praised had been published in installments in *The People's Daily* between July 23 and 28, 1951. It was an outcome of Mao's editorial in May 1951 that called for *The Life of Wu Xun* to be denounced. Led by Jiang Qing, or Madam Mao, the investigation team of thirteen members spent over twenty days in June 1951 interviewing more than 160 local villagers in Pingyuan 平原[28] and Hebei provinces.[29] Upon returning to Beijing, Jiang Qing and her two colleagues drafted a report on their findings before Mao personally revised it and made the changes that he considered necessary.[30] Throughout the process of research and writing, Jiang Qing insisted, she and her coworkers had been the "practitioners of rigorous empiricism [in line with] Chairman Mao's directives on scientific investigation."[31]

This "scientific investigation" approach resonated well with historians across the country. Professor Huang Yuanqi 黃元起 (1900–1990) posited that this investigation report, a role model for future historical studies, reminded his fellow historians to pay rapt attention to the "class nature" of source materials, given that the "reactionary ruling classes had long distorted and concocted" historical facts. With all

---

26. Guo Moruo 郭沫若, "Du *Wu Xun lishi diaocha ji*" 讀《武訓歷史調查記》 [On the *Investigation report of the history of Wu Xun*], *Renmin ribao* 人民日報 [People's Daily], August 4, 1951.
27. Zhou Yang 周揚, "Fan renmin, Fan lishi de sixiang he fan xianshi zhuyi de yishu dianying *Wu Xun zhuan* pipan" 反人民、反歷史的思想和反現實主義的藝術電影《武訓傳》批判 [(A work) against the people, against historicist thoughts, and against realist art: A criticism of the film *The Life of Wu Xun*], *Renmin ribao* 人民日報 [People's Daily], August 8, 1951.
28. Pingyuan province was established in 1949. When it was abolished in 1952, its component territories were given to Henan and Shandong provinces.
29. In her interview with Roxanne Witke in the mid-1970s, Jiang Qing stated that ten members of two investigation groups "suddenly appeared" when she and her two colleagues from Beijing were conducting an investigation, and she "was unsure who commissioned" them. See Roxanne Witke, *Comrade Chiang Ch'ing* (Boston, MA: Little, Brown and Company, 1977), 241.
30. Dai Zhixian 戴知賢, *Wentan san gong'an* 文壇三公案 [Three complicated cases in the literary circles] (Zhengzhou: Henan renmin chubanshe, 1994), 11–12.
31. Witke, *Comrade Chiang Ch'ing*, 241.

its methodological and conceptual mistakes, the traditional historiography usually committed "anti-history and anti-people" fallacies.³² In comparison, Zhao Qizhi 趙 憨之, a rank-and-file history teacher, made a more explicit connection between the investigation report and the "new people's history" (*xin de renmin shi* 新的人民 史). Zhao maintained that the "discovery" of Song Jingshi during the investigation of Wu Xun shed light on the possibility of recovering authentic "people's historical materials" as long as historians abided by the principles of Marxism and listened to Mao's instructions. He felt confident that the "new people's history" would help uncover more nameless peasant heroes like Song Jingshi and correct distorted and erroneous narratives of peasant leaders.³³

Such essays that capitalized on the Wu Xun campaign to preach the class viewpoint revealed the intellectuals' willingness to adopt a new, Marxian epistemology; that is, a "position that took class division as the most important datum in the interpretation of the past and regarded the struggle of the oppressed against their oppressors as the motive force of history."³⁴ For historians who began to be co-opted in this new socialist regime, the class-based Marxist historiography afforded a new analytical and interpretive device to understand the progress of human societies and their positions in this process. Therefore, their embracing of the class viewpoint was a testimony to their commitment to siding with the oppressed class and seeing themselves as worthy participants in the drama of history. In Huaiyin Li's words, historians in the early 1950s were more concerned with the "manifestation of [their] political identity rather than revealing the truth of the past."³⁵

Historicism and the Reevaluation of Historical Figures

The prevailing assumption that "everything [in the] new [society] must be good" and the unreserved endorsement of the class viewpoint among post-1949 historians³⁶ did not necessarily preclude them from continuing to advocate historicist principles. Although Harold Kahn and Albert Feuerwerker contend that historical writings in the first decade of the PRC were "heavily weighted towards the 'class viewpoint,'"³⁷ it is worth mentioning that historicism had never lost ground in the

---

32. Huang Yuanqi 黃元起, "*Wu Xun lishi diaocha ji* suo tishi de zhishi fangfa" 《武訓歷史調查記》所提示的治史方法 [The approach of historical studies as proposed by *The Investigation Report of the History of Wu Xun*], *Xin shixue tongxun* 新史學通訊 [Newsletter of New Historical Studies] 1, no. 6 (September 15, 1951): 1.
33. Zhao Qizhi 趙憨之, "*Wu Xun lishi diaocha ji* yu xin shixue" 武訓歷史調查記與新史學 [*The investigation report of the history of Wu Xun* and new historiography], *Lishi jiaoxue* 歷史教學 [History Teaching], no. 4 (October 1951): 115–16.
34. Arif Dirlik, "The Problem of Class Viewpoint versus Historicism in Chinese Historiography," *Modern China* 3, no. 4 (October 1977): 467.
35. Li, *Reinventing Modern China*, 4.
36. *Lishi jiaoxue* bianji bu 《歷史教學》編輯部 [The editorial office of History Teaching], "1951 nian de *Lishi jiaoxue*" 1951年的《歷史教學》 [*History Teaching* in 1951], *Lishi jiaoxue* 歷史教學 [History Teaching], no. 1 (2011): 71.
37. Kahn and Feuerwerker, "The Ideology of Scholarship," 2.

opening years of the PRC. On the contrary, the mainstream view among historians before 1957 was to properly apply historicism to make fair and balanced assessments of figures in China's feudal past.[38] For example, *The People's Daily* printed an editorial about two weeks before Mao's fateful article against *The Life of Wu Xun* was published, to caution against a prevailing tendency among dramatists to make "ancient people think and act in the same ways as people of today."[39] Indeed, the campaign against Wu Xun afforded historians a chance to not only openly uphold the class view but also reemphasize historicism as a fundamental approach to passing judgments on heroes and villains in history.

In this context, the editors of *Newsletter of New Historical Studies* (*Xin shixue tongxun* 新史學通訊), an academic journal based in Henan, felt compelled to "broaden the [scope of movement of] denouncing [*The Life of*] *Wu Xun* to the analyses and critiques of historical figures."[40] To this end, the journal released a special issue in October 1951, by assembling four academic papers with regard to the reevaluation of figures in imperial China. Among the four, the article authored by Ji Wenfu 嵇文甫 (1895–1963), then-president of Henan University (*Henan daxue* 河南大學) and future vice-chair of Henan province, received the editors' special recommendation. Ji's article bluntly disavowed a rigid class-view criterion that portrayed all ruling class members as villainous in history. Instead, Ji classified them into nine categories. Those in the first three were deemed "progressive," "enlightened," or "just." Wu Xun was placed in category seven, that is, "sordid, despicable, angling for undeserved fame, and willing to be the tools of the reactionary rulers."[41]

In the same year, Professor Wu Ze 吳澤 (1913–2005) of East China Normal University (*Huadong shifan daxue* 華東師範大學) similarly sought to consolidate historicist theories and practices by joining the choir of criticizing *The Life of Wu Xun*. In his book-length work, Wu acknowledged that Wu Xun did not belong to "the class of agricultural proletariats" but had been "the enemy of the people."[42] But he also cautioned that all historical figures could be deemed villainous if his fellow historians judged them through present-day criteria. He emphatically pointed out, "[We] must position historical figures in [the historical contexts] of social

---

38. Zhou Yiping 周一平, *20 shiji houbanqi Zhongguo shixue shi shang* 20世紀後半期中國史學史上 [The history of Chinese historiography in the second half of the twentieth century, part one] (Shanghai: Shanghai shudian chubanshe, 2017), 170.
39. "Zhongshi xiqu gaige gongzuo" 重視戲曲改革工作 [Emphasize the reform of the (traditional) opera], *Renmin ribao* 人民日報 [People's Daily], May 7, 1951.
40. "Bianzhe de hua" 編者的話 [The editors' remarks], *Xin shixue tongxun* 新史學通訊 [Newsletter of New Historical Studies] 1, no. 5 (1951): 2.
41. Ji Wenfu 嵇文甫, "Fengjian renwu jiudeng lun—cong *Wuxun zhuan* shilun suo yinqi de lishi renwu pingjia wenti" 封建人物九等論—從武訓傳時論所引起的歷史人物評價問題 [On nine ranks of people in feudal (society)—The issue of appraising historical figures stemming from the current discussions of *The Life of Wu Xun*], *Xin shixue tongxun* 新史學通訊 [Newsletter of New Historical Studies] 1, no. 5 (1951): 2.
42. Wu Ze 吳澤, *Lishi renwu de pingpan wenti—wei kaizhan Wu Xun pipan er shilun* 歷史人物的評判問題—為展開武訓批判而試論 [The issue of evaluating historical figures—A tentative treatise for unfolding (the movement) of criticizing Wu Xun] (Shanghai: Tangdi chubanshe, 1951), 8.

development to judge them; [We] don't want to evaluate ancient people with today's standards so as to commit [an error of] a-historicist negativism."[43] Based on the writings of Ji Wenfu, Wu Ze, and likeminded historians, it is thus fair to argue that Chinese historians of this generation attached more weight to historicism despite their overt support of the class view.

Song Jingshi: The Integration of the Class View and Historicism

Just like Guo Moruo and Zhou Yang, whose censures of *The Life of Wu Xun* served as a reminder of the need to usher in new, Marxist historiography in the early years of the PRC, Wu Ze called filmmakers and dramatists to employ both the class view and historicist theories as "the basic weaponry" of "understanding and analyzing [historical] issues."[44] In response, Shanghai-based filmmakers—the scriptwriters, the directors, and actors alike—endeavored to make *Song Jingshi* a biographical movie in full compliance with the historical practices (onsite investigation and interviews) and theories (the class view and historicism) as popularized in the media and academic works.

Beginning in March 1952, in preparation for the film and dramatic scripts about Song Jingshi's peasant revolution, nine writers and dramatists—including Chen Baichen and Jia Ji 賈霽 (1917–1985), the author of the very first critical essay against *The Life of Wu Xun* that wound up unfolding the anti-Wu Xun campaign—followed in the footsteps of Jiang Qing and her company to conduct an investigation and glean information about this peasant leader in Pingyuan and Hebei provinces. This investigative squad traveled to "eight counties and 163 villages to interview 719 elderly villagers and produce a 180,000-character long draft investigation report."[45]

Five years later, Chen Baichen submitted some portions of the draft for publication under the title *The Investigation Report on the History of Song Jingshi* (*Song Jingshi lishi diaocha ji* 宋景詩歷史調查記). In its preface, Chen extolled the peasants he and his colleagues had interviewed as "the protectors of the peasant's history and also the peasants' own historians" (*nongmin lishi de baohuazhe, yeshi nongaming ziji de lishijia* 農民歷史的保護者，也是農民自己的歷史家), for their remarks "corrected many errors in government-sponsored history books and made a complement to histories that had been covered up or neutered [by the dynastic governments]."[46] As late as 1982, Chen still adhered to his class-view rhetoric, stating that the peasant class was the possessors and defenders of historical truth.

---

43. Wu, *Lishi renwu de pingpan wenti*, 26, 44.
44. Wu, *Lishi renwu de pingpan wenti*, 3.
45. Chen Baichen 陳白塵, "Nongmin geming yingxiong Song Jingshi ji Heiqi jun—'Song Jingshi lishi diaocha baogao' tiyao," 農民革命英雄宋景詩及其黑旗軍—"宋景詩歷史調查報告提要" [The peasant revolutionary hero Song Jingshi and the Black Flag Army—Abstract of "the investigation report on the history of Song Jingshi"], *Renmin ribao* 人民日報 [People's Daily], November 11, 1952.
46. Chen Baichen 陳白塵, *Song Jingshi lishi diaocha ji* 宋景詩歷史調查記 [The investigation report on the history of Song Jingshi] (Beijing: Renmin Chubanshe, 1957), 5.

Thus, he kept wondering why his investigation report had failed to gain Chinese historians' recognition in the past three decades.[47]

Chinese historians' scorn for Chen Baichen's investigation report has been best illustrated in Joseph Esherick's book on the Boxer Uprising (1899–1900). Esherick finds that Chinese historians often cite Chen's report as the prime example of "the abuse to which oral history material can be put."[48] In reality, Chen was not totally unaware of the possibility that his interviewees might have tweaked the information they provided to cater to the needs of the interviewers:

> In their mouths, Song Jingshi's character (*renge* 人格) practically attained perfection, and [Song thus] became a matchless paragon in history and a saint-like man. In their mouths, the relationship between the Black Flag Army (*Heiqi jun* 黑旗軍) and the people was too intimate to be true. [I sometimes] suspected that [they might] have confused the deeds [of the Black Flag Army with those] of the People's Liberation Army of China.

Under mounting political pressures, however, Chen elected to believe those villagers because they were able to cite "hundreds of irrefutable examples" to substantiate their stories.[49]

Indeed, this report's precedent, the report on Wu Xun penned by Jiang Qing and her colleagues, had set an example of abusing the practice of oral history. According to Roxanne Witke, Jiang Qing's interviewer and biographer, while other members failed to obtain any evidence to prove Wu Xun's connections with the landlord class during the 1951 investigation, disgruntled Madam Mao coerced and intimidated the local cadres by lecturing them about "the evil potential of 'the spirit of Wu Hsun (Wu Xun).'"[50] At the end of the Cultural Revolution, more evidence surfaced:

> Materials that initially told the truth but did not suit Jiang Qing's needs were all thrown away. Later, the grassroots cadres learned to fathom what the investigation team wanted and then began to provide 'new' historical materials. Despite this, Mao Zedong still felt unsatisfied with the investigation report. So, he took up his brush to add some more 'historical facts.'[51]

No matter how he misinterpreted and mishandled the source materials, Chen Baichen chose not to concoct the storylines out of thin air when working on the film script, as many writers or dramatists of the day did. First, considering that Wu Xun was still a juvenile when the Song Jingshi rebellion was in full swing, Chen stood his ground firmly that Wu would not show up in a film about Song, hence

---

47. Chen Baichen 陳白塵, "Chen Baichen dianying ju xuan" 陳白塵電影劇選 [Selected film and dramatic scripts of Chen Baichen], *Dushu* 讀書 [Reading], no. 7 (1982): 102.
48. Joseph W. Esherick, *The Origins of the Boxer Uprising* (Berkeley: University of California Press, 1987), 359n50.
49. Chen Baichen 陳白塵, "Ganxie yu zhufu—wei *Song Jingshi* shangying zuo" 感謝與祝福—為宋景詩上映作 (Gratitude and best wishes—for the exhibition of *Song Jingshi*), *Tianjin ribao* 天津日報 [Tianjin Daily], June 23, 1957.
50. Witke, *Comrade Chiang Ch'ing*, 242.
51. *Lishi jiaoxue* bianji bu, "1951 nian de *Lishi jiaoxue*," 71

contradicting Jiang Qing's suggestion that Zhao Dan should portray Wu Xun again in this new film.[52] To Madam Mao's disappointment, in consequence, the film fell short of becoming a production that served the exclusive purpose of battling *The Life of Wu Xun*.[53] By comparison, some dramatists were more enthusiastic about letting the personae of Wu Xun and Song Jingshi share the same stage. Fan Cuiting 樊粹庭 (1905–1966), known as the founding father of modern Yu opera (*Yuju* 豫劇),[54] crafted an episode about the connection between Song Jingshi and a young Wu Xun in his Yu opera play, *Song Jingshi and Wu Xun* (*Song Jingshi yu Wu Xun* 宋景詩與武訓) despite his testimony that he had been unable to discover any "records about the relationship between Song Jingshi and Wu Xun."[55]

Second, Chen Baichen retained the plot about Song Jingshi's surrender to the Qing army in all the editions of the script despite a strong ideological urge to build Song's image as a perfect peasant revolutionary leader. Chen Baichen's daughter later admitted that her father was emboldened to retain such a storyline because of strong backing from Beijing. Both political authorities (including Madam Mao) and prestigious historians (such as Fan Wenlan 范文瀾 [1893–1969]) gave him a nod.[56] Later, the Film Bureau (*Dianying ju* 電影局) in Beijing expressly wrote to reconfirm the need to keep the portions about the surrender.[57] Despite this, Song Jingshi's surrender would remain a major pitfall in the process of making this historical/biographical movie.

To reach the goal of gaining access to "historical truth," the Shanghai Film Studio hired Rong Mengyuan 榮孟源 (1913–1985), a historian affiliated with the Institute of Modern History, the Chinese Academy of Science (*Zhongguo kexue yuan jindai shi yanjiu suo* 中國科學院近代史研究所) in March 1954.[58] In the same year, Rong published *The Issues of Evaluating Historical Figures* (*Lishi renwu pingjia wenti* 歷史人物的評價問題) to clarify his historicist stance:

> We must not use today's standards to measure the ancient people . . . but need to make case-by-case analyses in line with the specific historical conditions of the day. Historical figures must be assessed based on their impacts on history. The same person [could] well play different roles under different historical conditions.[59]

---

52. Shen Ji 沈寂, *Huashuo dianying* 話說電影 [The story about motion pictures] (Shanghai: Shanghai sanlian shudian, 2008), 130.
53. Song Song 宋嵩, "Song Jingshi jiqi yansheng wenben de chuangzuo"《宋景詩》及其衍生文本的創作 [Song Jingshi and the creation of its derivative texts], *Wenyi bao* 文藝報 [Literature and Arts Paper], June 24, 2016.
54. Yu opera is a local operatic art mainly in Henan province.
55. Fan Cuiting 樊粹庭, *Fan Cuiting wenji jumu chuangzuo xia* 樊粹庭文集·劇目創作下 [Fan Cuiting's anthology—Playwriting part 2] (Zhengzhou: Henan daxue chubanshe, 2012), 134.
56. Chen Hong 陳虹, *Chen Baichen pingzhuan* 陳白塵評傳 [Critical biography of Chen Baichen] (Chongqing: Chongqing chubanshe, 1998), 237.
57. Li Zhen 李鎮, *Zheng Junli quanji di 6 juan* 鄭君里全集 第6卷 [Zheng Junli's anthology, vol. 6] (Shanghai: Shanghai wenhua chubanshe, 2016), 100.
58. Shanghai Municipal Archives, B177-3-69, 7.
59. Rong Mengyuan 榮孟源, *Lishi renwu pingjia wenti* 歷史人物的評價問題 [Issues of evaluating historical figures] (Shanghai: Huadong renmin chubanshe, 1954), 41.

What Professor Rong underscored was precisely the thorny issue that the filmmakers considered to be most intractable. In 1957, Zheng Junli pointed out, "During the entire process of making [the film], the most nerve-wracking issue was the proper evaluation of the historical figure Song Jingshi." The director felt deeply concerned that "the legitimacy of the film would be in doubt if Song Jingshi did betray the people."[60] Zheng's son also sensed his father's inward struggle: "Song Jingshi did end up capitulating to the Qing court, but, out of political necessity, [my father] was compelled to construct [his image] as an adamant revolutionist."[61]

In fact, Song Jingshi's surrender has been a subject of a lengthy discussion in academia and the media ever since the publication of *The Investigation Report of the History of Wu Xun* in 1951. One of the earliest essays published in *The People's Daily* exclusively on Song Jingshi's rebellion asserted that the peasant leader merely feigned surrender, and the peasant combatants kept attacking the Qing troops after that.[62] However, the circulation of the theory of Song's false surrender failed to convince everyone. During the preview of *Song Jingshi* in March 1956, a high-ranking officer of the People's Liberation Army voiced his opposition to the movie on the grounds of Song's surrender. Such a controversy resulted in an extra year of revision and remaking of the film.[63]

Despite this setback, Zheng Junli brimmed with confidence that all knotty problems would be solved as long as he and his coworkers were to "apply the viewpoints of historical materialism to reflect the historical realities in a given time period." Hence, the entire crew was required to diligently study history to "arm [their] minds [with right historical views]."[64] To achieve this goal, as the archival record shows, perusing historical materials about Song Jingshi was mandatory for anyone involved in making the film. The film studio also invited "history experts"—including Professor Rong Mengyuan—as well as "the leftovers of the former Qing dynasty" (*qian Qing yilao* 前清遺老) for conversations and lectures.[65]

Despite such sustained efforts, Song Jingshi's betrayal of the peasant revolution consistently plagued Zheng Junli. In the year between the film's preview and its final release in 1957, the main task was to reshoot some of the footage to rationalize

---

60. Zheng Junli 鄭君里, "Women zai tansuo qianjin—guanyu 'Song Jingshi' de xiugai" 我們在探索前進—關於 "宋景詩" 的修改 [We're exploring and making progress—on the revision of Song Jingshi], *Zhongguo dianying* 中國電影 [China Cinema], no. 3 (1957): 13.
61. Li Jing 李菁, *Wangshi bu jimo Koushu jingxuan ji—2006–2008* 往事不寂寞《口述》精選集—2006–2008 [The past is not lonesome: The best of *Oral Accounts*—2006–2008] (Beijing: Shenghuo dushu sanlian shudian, 2009), 398.
62. Wang Zhulou 王竹樓, "Youguan Song Jingshi de ziliao" 有關於宋景詩的資料 [Materials concerning Song Jingshi], *Renmin ribao* 人民日報 [People's Daily], September 17, 1951.
63. Wu Couchun 吳湊春, *Dangdai Zhongguo zhuanji pian chuangzuo xianxiang piping* 當代中國傳記片創作現象批評 [Criticism of the phenomena of making biographical films in contemporary China] (Guangzhou: Jinan daxue chubanshe, 2013), 180.
64. Zheng Junli 鄭君里, *Huawai yin* 畫外音 [Offscreen Voice] (Beijing: Zhognguo dianying chubanshe, 1979), 40.
65. Shanghai Municipal Archives, B177-3-69, 5.

Figure 1.1: *Song Jingshi* has been known for providing images with historical accuracies, particularly the attires of the Qing imperial family and officials. Screenshot from *Song Jingshi*.

Figure 1.2: Upon consulting with historians, the filmmakers of *Song Jingshi* presented the audience with various cavalry, infantry, and firearm formations similar to those in real-life battlegrounds in late-Qing times. Screenshot from *Song Jingshi*.

Song's capitulation. In the process, Zheng Junli was caught in a quandary that the film "should avoid disgracing this revolutionary peasant leader but, meantime, lay bare the limits of the time and [the peasant] class."[66] In other words, the class view (the necessity of making Song a superhero) and historicism (the depiction of Song's surrender to expose the peasant class's weakness and to provide the explanation of its failure to overcome feudalism) constituted the two horns of the dilemma. When the film was finally released in 1957, Zheng was convinced that he had struck the right balance between the two and fully addressed the complexity of history:

> In order to tackle the issue of [Song Jingshi's] surrender, we, on the one hand, must analyze the historical conditions of the day on a case-by-case basis. [The surrender] should not undermine Song Jingshi's accomplishments in his life. . . . On the other hand, we can't . . . unduly [defend] his intentions and actions during the 'surrender' and downplay the damage his 'surrender' had inflicted on the revolution.[67]

Nevertheless, the audience did not feel the impulse of a complex history as the filmmakers boasted. What film viewers saw was nothing but another heavy-handed work of propaganda that peddled a one-dimensional truth about the class view centering on an "idealized" and "simplified" peasant leader capable of "overcoming all the limitations of the time and class." As a consequence, Song Jingshi was shown as "an idealized 'immortal'" or an emotionless "revolutionary machine" (*gemin jiqi* 革命機器) rather than "a living man of flesh and blood."[68] Under the pressure of multifarious and sometimes contradictory opinions voiced by high-ranking CCP officials, the playwright Chen Baichen had done nothing but find excuses for Song Jingshi's surrender in his final version of the screenplay, filling it with "awkward slogan-like expressions" and "deep preachy tones."[69] Film reviewers in later generations accused Zheng Junli of lavishing a large segment of the movie on portraying the surrender and "rationalizing" Song's action at the cost of a detailed and in-depth characterization of the protagonist.[70]

Such comments were not baseless. Throughout the movie, the audience was given the impression that the artists sought to depict Song Jingshi as a "superior revolutionary elite" and "an educator enlightening the other peasants of the correct revolutionary goals and strategies." From time to time, Song's remarks in the film parroted the dominant party discourse on class and peasant revolution.[71] The film was far from the success anticipated by Jiang Qing and Shanghai-based artists: It

---

66. Song, "Song Jingshi jiqi yansheng wenben de chuangzuo."
67. Zheng Junli 鄭君里, "Tantan Song Jingshi—shidai beijing he lishi pingjia" 談談宋景詩—時代背景和歷史評價 [On Song Jingshi—The historical background and (his) evaluation in history], *Zhongguo qingnian bao* 中國青年報 [China Youth Daily], May 31, 1957.
68. Qiuyun 秋耘, "Chongkan *Song Jingshi*" 重看《宋景詩》 [Watching *Song Jingshi* for the second time], *Renmin ribao* 人民日報 [People's Daily], June 13, 1957.
69. Song, "Song Jingshi jiqi yansheng wenben de chuangzuo."
70. Wu, *Dangdai Zhongguo zhuanji pian chuangzuo xianxiang piping*, 81.
71. Wang, *Revolutionary Cycles in Chinese Cinema, 1951–1979*, 38–39.

collapsed under the weight of the contradiction between the class view for the sake of eulogizing the peasant leader and the historicist demand to faithfully represent the historical realities and display the complexity of history. In consequence, as Zhuoyi Wang posits, the movies proved a failure for every party involved:

> [T]he CCP authorities failed to use the film for any effective propagandistic purpose, critics against *The Life of Wu Xun* failed to use it to gain critical authority, and the Shanghai artists failed to use it to adjust and defend their private studio filmmaking legacy.⁷²

Shi Hui, who portrayed the Mongol prince Sengge Rinchen 僧格林沁 (1811–1865) in the film, had similarly complained that making such a film was a thankless task: it was intended to please everyone—particularly the critics and political authorities—but wound up becoming a bowl of "shaved noodles" (*daoxiao mian* 刀削麵, that is, acting in a Procrustean way).⁷³ By comparison, a film reviewer in 1957 fully understood the artists' "eclecticism and compromise" in this political climate although he was similarly disturbed to find that the lengthy footage on Song's surrender "idealized and oversimplified the character" and thereby "diluted the tragic atmosphere of the movie." Rather than pointing the finger at the filmmakers, however, he voiced strident criticism of "dogmatists" (*jiaotiao zhuyi zhe* 教條主義者) for their total ignorance of the complexity of history.⁷⁴

The Disputes between Dogmatists and Historicists: The 1960s

The Debates

The clash between "dogmatists" who mechanically applied the class view and historians upholding historicism finally intensified in 1963 and 1964.⁷⁵ Throughout the 1950s, as mentioned, most historians placed a premium on historicism despite the growing popularity of the class view.⁷⁶ It is under this circumstance that Zheng Junli and his colleagues, despite onerous political shackles and doctrinaire constraints, made a herculean effort to maintain a subtle balance between the two although such an effort later proved a failure in all respects. As Zheng proudly summarized in 1957, he and his fellow filmmakers "had grasped historicist [principles] to vanquish a-historicist and dogmatic [mis]understandings" in the entire filmmaking process.⁷⁷

---

72. Wang, *Revolutionary Cycles in Chinese Cinema, 1951–1979*, 28.
73. Shi Hui 石揮, *Shi Hui tanyi lu wuhai yehang* 石揮談藝錄 霧海夜航 [Shi Hui on arts—Navigating at night on a foggy ocean] (Beijing: Beijing lianhe chuban gongsi, 2017), 171.
74. Qiuyun, "Chongkan *Song Jingshi*."
75. Kahn and Feuerwerker, "The Ideology of Scholarship," 1; Dirlik, "The Problem of Class Viewpoint versus Historicism in Chinese Historiography," 465.
76. Zhou, *20 shiji houbanqi Zhongguo shixue shi shang*, 170.
77. Zheng, "Women zai tansuo qianjin," 17.

Into the 1960s, virtually all renowned historians in China, such as Jian Bozan 翦伯贊 (1898–1968) and Wu Han, were embroiled in a bitter dispute with dogmatists who clung to the class-view shibboleth. Wu Han, for example, came up with the slogan "let interpretation emerge from facts" (*Lun cong shi chu* 論從史出) to counter the dogmatists' efforts to pass judgment on historical figures and events purely on the basis of the participants' class backgrounds.[78] Jian Bozan went a step further to diminish the significance of "class" by focusing on "national struggle" rather than "class struggle" because of his presumption that "the Chinese people as a whole [constituted] the oppressed class." In this way, Jian managed to reconcile Marxism and nationalism.[79] Susanne Weigelin-Schwiedrzik similarly argues that those well-established historians' insistence on historicism stemmed from their eagerness to "[look] for roots reaching beyond the victory of the [Chinese] revolution" and search the continuity between past and present at a time of "growing nationalism."[80]

The Revaluation of Historical Figures and Lin Zexu

The search for historical continuity entailed a new, more positive assessment of historical figures. Arif Dirlik finds that the disagreements on the settling of "all the question of the interpretive and evaluative criteria appropriate to the Marxist analysis of Chinese history" among historians in the late 1950s and early 1960s resulted in the debates between the class view and historicism.[81] In an essay published in *The People's Daily*, Wu Han, for example, blamed most historical textbooks and readings published in the past decade for having deliberately left out figures from the ruling classes in ancient China, such as Qin Shihuang 秦始皇 (259–210 BCE), Emperor Wu of Han (*Han wudi* 漢武帝) (141–87 BCE), Cao Cao 曹操 (155–220 CE), and Wu Zetian 武則天 (624–705 CE), and claimed that they were all bland and "hollow." Wu further pointed out that the same problem haunted the dramatists, too.[82] Wu Han, who would famously author *Hai Rui Dismissed from Office*, had long been involved in producing and reviewing dramatic plays. In 1959, Wu took advantage of his commentary essay on the new historical play, *Emperor Zetian* (*Zetian huangdi* 則天皇帝), to reiterate this historicist viewpoint:

> In order to evaluate a historical figure, [we] need to see what a role he [*sic*] was playing in his own time. Who supported him, and who opposed him? What did he

---

78. Weigelin-Schwiedrzik, "Back to the Past," 3–4.
79. Edmunds, "The Politics of Historiography," 67.
80. Weigelin-Schwiedrzik, "Back to the Past," 4–9.
81. Dirlik, "The Problem of Class Viewpoint versus Historicism in Chinese Historiography," 465–66.
82. Wu Han 吳晗, "Lun lishi renwu pingjia" 論歷史人物評價 [On the evaluation of historical figures], *Renmin ribao* 人民日報 [People's Daily], March 23, 1962.

support, and what did he oppose? Did what [he] had done benefit most people or just a small group of people?[83]

This new historiographical trend coincided with Chinese filmmakers' redoubled efforts to shoot biographical movies (*zhuanji pian* 傳記片). In a meeting in June 1959, Chen Huangmei, vice-director of the Film Bureau, called for offering "hundreds of millions of Chinese viewers" more entertaining movies, such as thrillers and biographical films.[84] Between 1956 and 1964, as Paul Clark finds, Chinese moviemakers endeavored to highlight "patriotic figures" in "the more distant past" in their film works.[85] As a result, film studios nationwide released or planned to make a vast number of films featuring prominent historical figures, such as *Li Shizhen* 李時珍 (1956, dir. Shen Fu 沈浮 [1905–1994]), *Lin Zexu, Nie Er, Naval Battle of 1894* (*Jiawu fengyun* 甲午風雲, 1962, dir. Lin Nong 林農 [1910–2002]), and the stillborn blockbuster film, *The Life of Lu Xun* (*Lu Xun zhuan* 魯迅傳). Zhao Dan, who starred in *Lin Zexu* and *Nie'er*, entertained the idea of playing more ancient greats, including Li Bai 李白 (701–762 CE) and Qu Yuan 屈原 (343?–278 BCE?).[86] Many of those films featured upper-class members as their protagonists and usually gave them positive appraisals. Among them, *Naval Battle of 1894* offers an arresting example of this moviemaking trend, as it was produced by the Changchun Film Studio (*Changchun dianying zhipian chang* 長春電影製片廠), a film company better known for its films about the CCP's revolutions and wars. To portray Captain Deng Shichang (鄧世昌, 1849–1894) of the Qing dynasty's navy as a patriot and a born anti-imperialist in the movie, the filmmakers purposely downplayed his upper-class family background but accentuated the anti-foreign political climate in Guangzhou during his childhood.[87]

The growing trend in the film circles renders problematic Paul Pickowicz's observation that, considering Chinese filmmakers "had generally avoided sensitive imperial-era historical topics," choosing Lin Zexu as the film's protagonist to celebrate the PRC's tenth anniversary was "strange."[88] Those aware of the contemporary vogue for appraising historical figures among historians, dramatists, and filmmakers in this period should not feel shocked by Zheng Junli's choice of a high-ranking Qing official but not another Song Jingshi-type peasant revolutionist in the late 1950s. After the release of *Lin Zexu*, Zheng resorted to the typical historicist rhetoric of highlighting a historical figure's contribution to the progress of his or her own time by proclaiming that he harbored an intention to make Lin Zexu an exemplar

---

83. Wu Han 吳晗, "Lishi de zhenshi yu yishu de zhenshi" 歷史的真實與藝術的真實 [The historical reality and the artistic realness], *Xiju bao* 戲劇報 [The Drama Journal], no. 20 (1959): 6.
84. Shanghai Municipal Archives, B177-1-21, 13.
85. Clark, *Chinese Cinema*, 114.
86. Shanghai Municipal Archives, B177-3-553, 3.
87. Li Moran 李默然, "Deng Shichang xingxiang de chuangzao" 鄧世昌形象的創造 [The creation of the image of Deng Shichang], *Dianying yishu* 電影藝術 [Cinematic Arts], no. 3 (1962): 54.
88. Pickowicz, *China on Film*, 197.

of "the people's heroes and progressive figures in [Chinese] history."[89] Meanwhile, Zheng applied Jian Bozan's historicist approach of prioritizing "national struggle" over class struggle to his filmmaking. In hindsight, Zheng admitted that he and his company self-consciously downplayed the feud between Manchu officials and Han Chinese citizens since both were, after all, Chinese nationals and had stressed the unresolvable conflicts between the Chinese and the British when revising the script.[90] Zheng's approach to handling history earned him wide acclaim. Chen Huangmei, for example, emphatically praised *Lin Zexu*'s "ideological" (*sixiang xing* 思想性) sophistication.[91]

The filmmakers' historicist stance in making *Lin Zexu* would come under severe criticism in 1965, when Zheng Junli and Zhao Dan were pressed to make public confessions to denounce themselves. Zhao, for example, admitted his mistake in having deviated from "[the approach] of class analysis" (*jieji fenxi* 階級分析) by displaying Lin Zexu's noble morality as if such feudal morality "transcended class boundaries" (*chao jieji* 超階級).[92] Zhao's recognition of the class view's triumph over historicism coincided with the purge of intellectuals holding historicist viewpoints, including Wu Han and Jian Bozan.[93] The debacle of Wu Han, Jian Bozan, and likeminded historians (and non-historians) stemmed, first, from their emphasis on ruling class members' contributions, which essentially ran counter to the CCP-endorsed theory that viewed class struggle—culminating in peasant wars—as the central concern of historical studies. Without a large-scale bourgeois revolution or labor movement in China's long history, peasants' revolts had usually been viewed as "the direct forerunners of the communist revolution."[94]

In all fairness, the filmmakers did not turn a blind eye to the ordinary people's contributions to this anti-imperialist struggle despite their eagerness to highlight Lin Zexu as a patriotic hero. Zheng Junli later recalled that he and his colleagues complied with Zhou Enlai's directive and finally made a decision to end the film with an empathic representation of the anti-British uprising led by the people's militia in Sanyuanli 三元里, reconfirming the role of the people, rather than the feudal lords, as the leaders in China's anti-imperialist causes.[95] The author of the film's first draft, Ye Yuan 葉元, explained that the juxtaposition of crestfallen Lin Zexu in exile and the ongoing massive anti-imperialist movement revealed the truth in history—the pioneering role of the laboring class in the Chinese revolution.[96]

---

89. Li, *Zheng Junli quanji di 6 juan*, 345.
90. Li, *Zheng Junli quanji di 6 juan*, 346–47.
91. Shanghai Municipal Archives, B177-1-21, 6.
92. Shanghai Municipal Archives, B177-3-553, 6–7.
93. Goldman, *China's Intellectuals*, 119.
94. James P. Harrison, *The Communists and Chinese Peasant Rebellions: A Study in the Rewriting of Chinese History* (New York: Atheneum, 1969), 5.
95. Zheng, *Huawai yin*, 69–70.
96. Ye Yuan 葉元, "Luetan lishi ju de xugou" 略談歷史劇的虛構 [Briefly on the fictionalization of historical films], *Dianying yishu* 電影藝術 [Cinematic Arts], no. 2 (1979): 46–47.

Figure 1.3: *Lin Zexu* ends with the mobilization of the ordinary people in Guangzhou to resist British invaders and Commissioner Lin Zexu's watchful gaze upon the victory of the people. Screenshot from *Lin Zexu*.

The film's abrupt turn to displaying the people's political activism bemused Jay Leyda, who complained about its incoherence: "As a historical reconstruction *Lin Tse-hsu* (*Lin Zexu*) is remarkably rich ... but suddenly, halfway through, you can see its collapse into shoddiness and hasty solutions." Leyda further noticed that Zhao Dan's characterization of the protagonist accordingly "changed from careful to hasty well before the film."⁹⁷ In this sense, Zheng Junli's feeble attempt to strike a balance between the class view and historicism and his failure to please neither film critics nor dogmatic Maoists was reminiscent of the fate of *Song Jingshi*.

Second, historicists collapsed under the weight of the contradiction between a commitment to developing an objective narrative of historical events or figures and citing examples in the past to perpetuate present-day sociopolitical struggles. Given the class view's self-evident connectedness to the CCP's revolution and rule in China, most such studies in Mao's times were somehow guilty of "uncritically idealizing rebels" and "inappropriately employing historical source materials."⁹⁸ In contrast, historicists pledged to pursue the historical truth and attempted to confine their discussions to academia. The depoliticization of their interpretations of history was thus purported to keep them away from political maelstroms. Wu Han stated in 1959 that he, Fan Wenlan, and many other left-leaning historians had deployed a tactic of "reviling the locust tree while pointing to the mulberry" (*zhisang mahuai* 指桑罵槐), lodging oblique accusations against the ruling Nationalist Party, before 1949. In post-1949 China, nevertheless, such a tactic should be relinquished since the target of criticism had long disappeared.⁹⁹

Wu Han's disclaimer was hardly convincing. He contradicted his avowed undertaking of interpreting history "in its own rather than present terms" by writing an operatic play about Hai Rui 海瑞 (1514–1587) for the purpose of "comment[ing] upon the present."¹⁰⁰ As Susanne Weigelin-Schwiedrzik cogently puts it, historicists' efforts to reevaluate historical figures had been driven by a conviction of helping the new republic search for "a historical legitimation that would go farther than the victory in the Chinese revolution."¹⁰¹ Moreover, in the post-Leap years defined by nationwide economic woes, intellectuals intended to revive a time-honored "censorial tradition" as a form of remonstrance with the top leadership.¹⁰² Under this circumstance, historicists' "objective" readings of China's past merely functioned as an "academic umbrella" for "subtle attacks on Mao and the party through the

---

97. Jay Leyda, *Dianying: An Account of Films and the Film Audience in China* (Cambridge, MA: The MIT Press, 1972), 258.
98. Yu Huanqing 余煥卿, "Guanyu jianguo hou nongzhan shi yanjiu de pinglun wenti—yu Huang Minlan tongzhi shangque" 關於建國後農戰史研究的評價問題—與黃敏蘭同志商榷 [On the issue of how to evaluate the research about the peasant war after the establishment of the PRC—A discussion with comrade Huang Minlan], *Shixue lilun* 史學理論 [Historical Theories], no. 2 (1996): 15.
99. Wu, "Lishi de zhenshi yu yishu de zhenshi," 6.
100. Edmunds, "The Politics of Historiography," 65.
101. Weigelin-Schwiedrzik, "Back to the Past," 4.
102. Wagner, *The Contemporary Chinese Historical Drama*, xi.

allegorical media of historical essay and plays."¹⁰³ In this sense, the historicist stance with a pretense of decoupling the academic and the political by emphasizing an unbiased way of reconstructing the past could hardly justify the "objectiveness" of their research and thereby become vulnerable to attacks from dogmatists who unambiguously linked the present to the past. Consequently, historians such as Jian Bozan and Wu Han came under scathing criticism in the mid-1960s for their use of history to unleash attacks on Mao.

History as a Public Realm of Communication

As is widely known, Wu Han was finally drawn into the political maelstrom on the eve of the Cultural Revolution, not because of his historical scholarship but the Beijing opera play he penned. Writing historical drama, Rudolf Wagner posits, constituted one of the forms of remonstrance for Chinese intellectuals in the late 1950s and early 1960s.¹⁰⁴ While Wu Han transformed himself into a playwright, more historians played a role as professional advisers to dramatists, such as Tian Han 田漢 (1898–1968), to produce scripts and thereby engage in "implied bitter polemics" at a time of economic crisis and political instability.¹⁰⁵ Wu Han's close friend and coauthor, Deng Tuo 鄧拓 (1912–1966), further extended the remonstrance tradition to *zawen* 雜文 (historical or miscellaneous newspaper essays) and more explicitly resorted to history to pass comments to the present. For Deng, the past was a "storehouse of human experience not fundamentally different from contemporary experience: it [was] the valuable condensation of extensive examples of previous scholar-administrators facing similar administrative and political issues."¹⁰⁶

Zawen, historical scholarship, historical drama, and motion pictures on China's history and the CCP's revolutionary cause, according to Rudolf Wagner, were lumped together and weaponized during the years between the Great Leap Forward and the outbreak of the Cultural Revolution, to implicitly criticize Mao and the party leadership.¹⁰⁷ All four forms had one thing in common: the centrality of history, essentially a common language for competing factions.¹⁰⁸ Although Wagner focuses on Mao's times, it is worth mentioning that history has consistently been at the center of Chinese culture. In Andrew Plaks's words, history for millennia enjoyed "quasi-religious pre-eminence."¹⁰⁹ In a similar fashion, in post-1949 China, where "the [P]arty was coming to dominate the public sphere," historical narratives in whatever form proved an effective way of speaking more freely in the "public

---

103. Edmunds, "The Politics of Historiography," 72.
104. Wagner, *The Contemporary Chinese Historical Drama*, 16.
105. Wagner, *The Contemporary Chinese Historical Drama*, 138.
106. Cheek, "Historians as Public Intellectuals in Contemporary China," 209.
107. Wagner, *The Contemporary Chinese Historical Drama*, xi–xiii.
108. Wagner, *The Contemporary Chinese Historical Drama*, 236.
109. Andrew H. Plaks, "Towards a Critical Theory of Chinese Narrative," in *Chinese Narrative: Critical and Theoretical Essays*, ed. Andrew H. Plaks (Princeton, NJ: Princeton University Press, 1977), 312.

political space."[110] The historical drama, for example, became "a hotly contested battleground," where "different factions and groupings" were afforded "a chance to voice their feelings openly and publicly in the very face of their opponents."[111]

In the context of the complementarity and reciprocity between historians and non-historian writers/artists in the pre–Cultural Revolution years, the motion picture provided a more widely utilized space that revolved around the discussion of China's past and present, given its enormous viewership across the country. *Lin Zexu*, for example, appealed to over 18.5 million viewers in the year after its release in 1959.[112] Hence, this film, whose script was initially authored by amateur writers and whose production received the assistance of various historians, exemplified a concerted effort by grassroots writers, professional filmmakers, historical researchers, and, finally, the filmgoers to resort to history as a means of communication. While semi-literate audiences were more attracted to the killing of British "devils" (*guizi* 鬼子) as a way of eliciting national pride,[113] more sophisticated viewers appreciated the filmmakers' endeavor to recast the Opium War (1840–1842) vividly. During a symposium on *Lin Zexu* in October 1959, for example, the participating historians, philosophers, writers, and dramatists lauded the film for its accurate portrayal of the historical background and highlighting peasants' role in the anti-imperialist cause.[114]

On a separate occasion, historian Zhang Kaiyuan 章開沅 (1926–2021) proclaimed that the making of *Lin Zexu* revealed the filmmakers' ability to understand highly controversial and notoriously elusive topics in modern Chinese history as well as, if not better than, his fellow historians, because they were capable of "drawing a correct historical conclusion" in an artistic way.[115] Zhang later confirmed that his praise so galvanized Zheng Junli that the Shanghai-based film studio kept communicating with the historian, inviting him to write a script for another historical film and consult about historical facts.[116] Meanwhile, dramatist Tian Han's film review made an explicit connection between the history of the Opium War and the present-day world politics: the anti-imperialist spirit shown on the screen would undoubtedly boost the Chinese people's confidence and encourage the revolutionary masses in the Third World.[117]

---

110. Mary G. Mazur, *Wu Han: Historian: Son of China's Times* (Lanham, MD: Lexington Books, 2011), 415.
111. Wagner, *The Contemporary Chinese Historical Drama*, 236–44.
112. Shanghai Municipal Archives, B177-1-262, 51.
113. Shuicao 水草, "Nongmin qunzhong relie huanying guochan yingpian" 農民群眾熱烈歡迎國產影片 (Rural viewers warmly greet domestically produced films), *Dianying yishu* 電影藝術 [Cinematic Arts], no. 6 (1960): 47.
114. Yang Futian 楊福田, "*Dianying yishu* dui guoqing xianli yingpian de pingjie" 《電影藝術》對國慶獻禮影片的評介 [Film art's evaluation of and review of films to celebrate the national day], *Dushu* 讀書 [Reading], no. 19 (1959): 40.
115. Zhang Kaiyuan 章開沅, *Xinhai gemin yu jindai shehui* 辛亥革命與近代社會 [The 1911 revolution and the modern society] (Wuhan: Huazhong shifan daxue chubanshe, 2011), 334.
116. Zhang, *Xinhai gemin yu jindai shehui*, 341.
117. Tian Han 田漢, "Suzao yingxiong renwu de chubu chengjiu—kan jibu yingpian de ganxiang" 塑造英雄

As mentioned, many of Tian Han's plays could be interpreted as an oblique criticism of Mao's China. Generally speaking, *Lin Zexu* had been immune to the allegation that it resorted to China's past to chastise Mao and his policies. When the tide of radicalism was on the rise in 1965, the film's lead actor, Zhao Dan, testified in public that focusing on a ruling class member rather than the revolutionary masses in *Lin Zexu* was a testimony of the filmmakers' defection to "the bourgeois views of literature and arts" (*zichan jieji wenyi sixiang* 資產階級文藝思想) upheld by Xia Yan and Chen Huangmei.[118] Similarly, Zheng Junli criticized the film for being an embodiment of the "Xia Yan-Chen Huangmei Line" (*Xiachen jituan* 夏陳路線), an embattled "anti-Maoist" political clique.[119] Evidently, *Lin Zexu* was found guilty of factionalism but not of an indirect assault upon Maoism at this point. It was another Zheng Junli project, tentatively entitled *Li Bai and Du Fu* (*Li Bai yu Du Fu* 李白與杜甫), that was blasted for purportedly launching a blistering attack on Mao's political agendas. During the Cultural Revolution, the incarcerated Zheng parroted his critics' rhetoric to accuse himself of viciously planning this unmade film as a *roman à clef* work to rail against the party's purge of intellectuals and the widespread famine during the Great Leap Forward.[120]

Conclusion

Zheng Junli's confession attests to the predicament all historians and cultural workers were facing during Mao's times. In Roxanne Witke's words, all re-creations and representations of the past had "been read proverbially ... as *romans à clef*" in Mao's China.[121] In this sense, historians of any camps could not justifiably claim their scholarship as unbiased, freestanding, and apolitical. In comparison, the political and ideological implications of the reconstructed Chinese history by dramatists, filmmakers, and writers were even more evident. They all subscribed to the time-honored "history as a mirror" concept and adopted the "utilitarian approach of early modern Chinese historiography" to manipulate history to serve political ends.[122]

The centrality of history manifested itself in the political authorities' campaign against *The Life of Wu Xun*, through which the party created a peculiar political culture and a new temporality that the present was shifted into the past. This history-centered culture could be traced to Stalinist Soviet Union, where "withdrawal

---

人物的初步成就——看幾部影片的感想 [Preliminary accomplishments in creating historical characters—Thoughts on viewing a number of films], *Dianying yishu* 電影藝術 [Cinematic Arts], no. 7 (1960): 14.
118. Shanghai Municipal Archives, B177-3-553, 3.
119. Shanghai Municipal Archives, B177-3-553, 72.
120. Li Zhen 李鎮, *Zheng Junli quanji di 7 juan* 鄭君里全集 第7卷 [Zheng Junli's anthology, vol. 7] (Shanghai: Shanghai wenhua chubanshe, 2016), 459–60.
121. Witke, *Comrade Chiang Ch'ing*, 233.
122. Edmunds, "The Politics of Historiography," 85.

into history" paved the way for the "entrance into the present."¹²³ Anyhow, history afforded everyone—historians or dramatists, filmmakers or filmgoers, historicists or dogmatists—a sense-making arena for engaging in meaningful communication by harking back to the past to understand and interpret the present-day sociopolitical realities. By participating in such a space, Zheng Junli salvaged his career and elevated his standing within the film circles. Back in 1951, Zheng's *Between a Married Couple* (*Niwo fufu zhijian* 你我夫婦之間, 1951) was accused of catering to "the vulgar, petit-bourgeois tastes of unreformed Shanghai audiences."¹²⁴ The making of *Song Jingshi* allowed Zheng to return to prominence after four years in obscurity.¹²⁵

It merits mentioning that Zheng had earned his reputation as a competent filmmaker because of his filmic works on social realities in pre-1949 China, such as *The Spring River Flowers East* (*Yijiang chunshui xiangdong liu* 一江春水向東流, dir. Cai Chusheng 蔡楚生 [1906–1968] and Zheng Junli, 1947) and *Crows and Sparrows* (*Wuya yu maque* 烏鴉與麻雀, dir. Zheng Junli, 1949), and had never been known for making any historical/biographical movies before he accepted the project of shooting *Song Jingshi*. In this sense, the newly fashioned historiographic knowledge and approaches to historical studies equipped Zheng Junli with a strategy to survive and gain a new identity: a major player in this history-centered public space in the late 1950s and early 1960s. In this sense, making historical/biographical movies functioned as Zheng's subjectivizing practice to help him secure a new subjectivity in post-1949 China. However, as a beneficiary of this public space, Zheng was unavoidably drawn into the bitter disputes between historicists and dogmatists in the 1960s. This debate would be construed as a war of ideology between revolutionary and counterrevolutionary historians on the eve of the Cultural Revolution. It is thus safe to argue that the martyrs of the Cultural Revolution—historians, dramatists, and filmmakers (Zheng Junli included)—fell prey to their own efforts to weave such a web of communication.

---

123. Evgeny Dobrenko, *Stalinist Cinema and the Production of History: Museum of the Revolution*, trans. Sarah Young (Edinburgh: Edinburgh University Press, 2008), 6–22.
124. Clark, *Chinese Cinema*, 51.
125. Leyda, *Dianying*, 352.

2
From Wu Xun to Lu Xun

Film, Stardom, and Subjectivity in Mao's China

This chapter focuses on Zhao Dan's career in film—mostly as a film star and as a director—after 1949, to investigate his subjectivizing practice to develop with a new subjectivity; that is, Zhao's success in (re-)rising to stardom. The specific type of stardom Zhao enjoyed was unique to Mao Zedong-era China. Recent scholarship on film in post-1949 China has questioned the legitimacy of the term "film star" (*dianying mingxing* 電影明星) in the context of PRC society. Xiaoning Lu, for example, posits that this word was often linked with "corrupted lifestyles, loftiness, individualism and liberalism" and, therefore, "fell out of fashion in everyday speech" in the first seventeen years of the PRC.[1] Hence, star appeal was "no longer viable."[2] Both Krista Van Fleit Hang[3] and Sabrina Qiong Yu[4] assert that the film star in Mao's China had been transformed into a "film worker" (*dianying gongzuo zhe* 電影工作者). Nonetheless, the best-known of these "film workers" did achieve a form of stardom in Mao-era China. "Socialist red stars" like Zhang Ruifang 張瑞芳 (1918–2012) became "iconic figures at the stage of socialist modernization" and "constituted mass culture in the Mao era."[5] Yet, unlike many socialist red stars, whose stardom was tied to the rise of the CCP, Zhao Dan was already a well-established star actor in China, his popularity first having soared in the 1930s, when he joined their ranks after 1949.[6]

By examining Zhao Dan's checkered career between the 1950s and 1970s, this chapter argues that the PRC's politico-cultural circumstances created a peculiar star system closely imbricated with the party-state's political environment. In the first two decades of the PRC, Zhao Dan initially fell prey to the CCP regime's very first

---

1. Xiaoning Lu, "Zhang Ruifang: Modelling the Socialist Red Star," in *Chinese Film Stars*, ed. Mary Farquhar and Yingjin Zhang (London: Routledge, 2010), 97.
2. Esther Ching-mei Yau, "Compromised Liberation: The Politics of Class in Chinese Cinema of the Early 1950s," in *The Hidden Foundation: Cinema and the Question of Class*, ed. David E. James and Rick Berg (Minneapolis: University of Minnesota Press, 1996), 142.
3. Krista Van Fleit Hang, "Zhong Xinghuo: Communist Film Worker," in *Chinese Film Stars*, ed. Mary Farquhar and Yingjin Zhang (London: Routledge, 2010), 108.
4. Sabrina Qiong Yu, "Vulnerable Chinese Stars: From *Xizi* to Film Worker," in *A Companion to Chinese Cinema*, ed. Yingjin Zhang (Malden, MA: Wiley-Blackwell, 2012), 225.
5. Lu, "Zhang Ruifang," 97.
6. Yingjin Zhang and Zhiwei Xiao, *Encyclopedia of Chinese Film* (London: Routledge, 1998), 392.

major cultural movement, the campaign against *The Life of Wu Xun*, but swiftly rose back to stardom by 1960. In contrast to existing scholarship that plays down star power in the early years of the PRC, I contend that by the 1960s, Zhao's stardom was similar to what has conventionally defined film stardom in China—"the sky-high salaries stars receive," their "ability to attract investment and audiences, and their control over scripts, casting, or even direction and production"[7]—but with an added political dimension: his acquisition of high political standing in the preceding decade.

Yingjin Zhang notes that Zhao's self-constructed image of martyrdom—"having [his] self-sacrifice and suffering 'witnessed' in public"—on and off the screen predicated the establishment of his stardom in the Mao era.[8] Zhang's notion of martyrdom qua stardom, however, testifies to the tenacity of an analytical mode of the victimizer and the victimized in assaying the relationship between the PRC and the artist. Both Perry Link[9] and Paul Pickowicz[10] have delineated the ups and downs that artists experienced in Mao's China: their initial collaboration with the political authorities and their subsequent victimization because of changing political climates. Pickowicz further raises a question about the possibility of resisting the oppressive state or maneuvering to survive.[11] Although recent studies on the state–artist relationship have been fruitful, most scholars remain within the paradigm of accommodation and resistance between the tyrannical state and subordinated artists. This paradigm is problematic because it presupposes "a subjectivity or selfhood that pre-exists and is maintained" against intrusive hegemonic ideologies.[12] As I have stated in the introductory chapter, citizens in socialist regimes did not possess fixed and stable identities but consistently engaged in the self-fashioning of their subjectivities through "a host of subjectivizing practices."[13] Following this line of thought, this chapter seeks to illustrate the making of Zhao Dan's subjectivity—and his stardom—in post-1949 China. Too often, Zhao has been portrayed as an artist with a conscience who relentlessly pursued artistic autonomy and as a martyr-like victim under an authoritarian regime. To borrow Mary Mazur's words,[14] the selective memory regarding Zhao has "mythologized" him.

This mythologized narrative originates in *The Life of Wu Xun*, in which he starred and which bore the brunt of the PRC's early political campaigns against the arts, signaling the arrival of "absolute supremacy of politics over art in China."[15] This narrativization of Zhao Dan as a dauntless dissident defying the party's political

---

7. Yu, "Vulnerable Chinese Stars," 222.
8. Zhang, "Zhao Dan," 86–87.
9. Link, "The Crocodile Bird," 207–31.
10. Pickowicz, *China on Film*, 210.
11. Pickowicz, *China on Film*, 210.
12. Mitchell, "Everyday Metaphors of Power," 562.
13. Hellbeck, *Revolution on My Mind*, 187.
14. Mazur, *Wu Han*, 5.
15. Zhang, *Chinese National Cinema*, 195.

intervention in the arts and culture in China culminates with the publication of his deathbed essay, "There Is No Hope for Literature and the Arts If They Are Regulated Too Specifically," in which he asserted that great artists and writers could excel without party leadership.[16] This widely circulated essay, which really resonated with writers and artists who had recently survived the Cultural Revolution, was cited as evidence of the PRC's failure to preserve and develop China's arts and literature, especially by the media outside China, and, therefore, instantly provoked an anti–Zhao Dan and anti-liberal backlash among hard-line party cadres.[17]

It is in light of those circumstances that Yingjin Zhang portrays Zhao Dan as a "real-life martyr" suffering from "criticism, deprivation, betrayal and incarceration" in Mao's China.[18] What this account of Zhao's identity as victim/martyr/dissident leaves out, however, is his meteoric rise to stardom under the same politico-cultural system that at other times victimized him. It is not an overstatement that Zhao earned more tremendous popularity than before because of an expanded national film market, a massive project engineered by the PRC government. Meanwhile, his faithful service to various political campaigns and affairs in Mao's China proved rewarding: he was admitted into the party, elected as a deputy to the People's Congress, and ranked as a level 1 artist within the newly created hierarchy for the circles of artists. In other words, the management of the Chinese film industry and the broader cultural policies enacted after 1949, for all their fickleness, allowed for Zhao's self-refashioning and acquisition of a new identity as a star in the PRC.

Zhao Dan's reputation reached its peak in the early 1960s, when he starred in two commemorative anniversary films and was preparing to portray the iconic writer Lu Xun 魯迅 (1881–1936) in *The Life of Lu Xun*, which was expected to be one of the most significant film releases of the era. *The Life of Lu Xun* would, unfortunately, remain unreleased after three long years in preproduction. Although many of Zhao's biographers cite the incident as further evidence of the political persecution that Zhao experienced,[19] it is worth mentioning that the selection of Zhao to play Lu Xun, whom Mao had personally canonized since the mid-1930s and who had gained an unrivaled status second only to Mao after 1949,[20] itself evidenced

---

16. Zhao, "Guande tai juti, wenyi mei xiwang."
17. Shen Pengnian 沈鵬年, *Xingyun liushui jiwang erji (xia)* 行雲流水記往二集（下）[Remembering the past (like) floating clouds and flowing water, vol. 2, bk. 2] (Shanghai: Shanghai sanlian shudian, 2011), 533; Huang Zongying 黃宗英, *Huang Zongying wenji di 1 juan: cun zhi tianxia* 黃宗英文集第1卷：存之天下 [The collected writings of Huang Zongying, vol. 1: Conserve (Zhao Dan's paintings) in the world] (Shenzhen: Haitian chubanshe, 2017), 9.
18. Zhang, "Zhao Dan," 87.
19. For example, Zhao Dan's daughter believes that the project of making *The Life of Lu Xun* was terminated because of an ongoing campaign launched by the Shanghai-based party authorities to promote literary and artistic works on post-1949 China. See Zhao Qing 趙青, *Wode diedie Zhao Dan* 我的爹爹趙丹 [My father Zhao Dan] (Beijing: Zhongguo dianying chubanshe, 2005), 187.
20. Jin Taipin 金肽頻, *Anqing xin wenhua biannian 1915-2015: pinglun juan* 安慶新文化編年1915-2015: 評論卷 [The one-hundredth anniversary of Anqing new culture, 1915–2015: Commentaries] (Hefei: Anhui wenyi chubanshe, 2016), 244.

the special political privilege that Zhao was enjoying. Indeed, Zhao not only took pride in accepting this assignment by making conscientious preparations over the course of several years but also felt honored and excited by Mao's reception and praise of his efforts.[21] Despite this, the project of shooting this highly anticipated film was eventually aborted. Although both Pickowicz[22] and Yingjin Zhang[23] are correct in pointing out that factionalism within the CCP and other political factors led to this epic failure, this chapter shows that Zhao's rumbling personal tensions with Chen Liting, the film's appointed director, wound up being a significant contributory factor in its eventual collapse. Zhao's somewhat overbearing attitude—an outgrowth of both his loathing for Chen since the 1940s and his newly acquired stardom—certainly did not help the project.

While Zhao Dan thrived in the late 1950s and early 1960s, he was forced to revert to the role of a survivor between the mid-1960s and the end of the Cultural Revolution. In this tumultuous decade, the harassed, tortured, and incarcerated Zhao was compelled to author a blizzard of "confessions" (*jiancha* 檢查 or *jiantao* 檢討), self-criticizing and even self-degrading statements widely used in all political struggles in the PRC. Writing confessions was such a common practice in Mao's China that the confession became not only a means of regulating, indoctrinating, and punishing intellectuals and artists[24] but also a uniquely ritualized literary genre in which authors mimicked their victimizers' rhetoric and vocabulary to castigate themselves.[25] Robert Jay Lifton viewed such confessions as a peculiar psychological technique that impelled the "culprit" to make up "not [necessarily] true, but believable" stories.[26] Although Aminda Smith deems confessions as accounts that came "through mediators," she does not discount their value. In her words, those accounts were still official sources that "tell us how they shaped and changed" history.[27] Building on existing scholarship on the confession, this chapter argues that Zhao's confessions—in which he variously demanded leniency, swore allegiance to the party, and sought death—were not only a survival tactic but also a "subjectivizing practice" that finally contributed to the consolidation of Zhao's subjectivity of martyrdom qua stardom.

Zhao's career during Mao's time could be best summarized as a cycle of surviving (during the campaign against *The Life of Wu Xun*), thriving (in the 1950s

---

21. Zhao, *Wode diedie Zhao Dan*, 187.
22. Pickowicz, *China on Film*, 206.
23. Zhang, *Chinese National Cinema*, 93.
24. Wang Wei 王維, *Zhongguo wenxue jie "jiantao" yanjiu (1949–1955)* 中國文學界"檢討"研究 (1949–1955) [A study on the "confession" in the literary circles in China (1949–1955)] (Beijing: Qunyan chubanshe, 2015), 9–10.
25. Guo Xiaohui 郭曉惠, *Jiantao shu: shiren Guo Xiaochuan zai zhengzhi yundong Zhong de linglei wenzi* 檢討書：詩人郭小川在政治運動中的另類文字 [The confession: The poet Guo Xiaochuan's alternative literature during political movements] (Beijing: Zhongguo gongren chubanshe, 2001), 347.
26. Robert Jay Lifton, *Thought Reform and the Psychology of Totalism: A Study of "Brainwashing" in China* (Chapel Hill: The University of North Carolina Press, 1989), 41.
27. Smith, *Thought Reform and China's Dangerous Classes*, 6–7.

and early 1960s), and then surviving again (during the Cultural Revolution). This cycle does not completely accord with what Zhuoyi Wang calls "revolutionary cycles": constant oscillations of party policies that contributed to a gnawing sense of insecurity among "elite artists, critics, and bureaucrats in the film industry."[28] This chapter, nevertheless, indicates that Zhao not only acclimated to this ever-changing political atmosphere but also sought to benefit from it. In other words, rather than showing how such cycles confirm that China's film culture was "self-negating and self-destructive" and how artists were poised to "get kicked in the teeth" by the looming party authorities, to borrow Perry Link's phrase,[29] this chapter highlights Zhao Dan's tactics of surviving, thriving, and, ultimately, making his own subjectivity: he worked to his minimal disadvantage when the tide turned against him but sought the maximal benefit—artistically, financially, and politically—when he was riding high. It is not my intention to depict him as self-interested, but his subjectivities—as a star and a martyr—were fashioned and refashioned in response to the very politico-cultural conditions in Mao's China. In other words, when working under the PRC system, Zhao Dan was actually "work[ing] the system."[30]

To Survive: Zhao Dan and *The Life of Wu Xun*

Zhao Dan began to earn his reputation as a stellar film actor in the mid-1930s, when he starred in films such as *Crossroads* 十字街頭 (1937, dir. Shen Xiling 沈西苓 [1904–1940]) and *Street Angel* 馬路天使 (1937, dir. Yuan Muzhi 袁牧之 [1909–1978]). In the late 1930s, Zhao migrated to Xinjiang to pursue a new career but was soon detained by the local warlord. Pronounced a communist, Zhao was imprisoned in Xinjiang between 1939 and 1942. Returning to Shanghai after 1945, Zhao resumed his cinematic career and starred in several films before the CCP seized power in 1949. *The Life of Wu Xun* was in production both before and after the founding of the PRC.

The massive campaign of criticizing *The Life of Wu Xun*, initiated by Mao in May 1951, led to the demise of privately owned film studios in Shanghai and the nationalization of the film industry in China.[31] Zhuoyi Wang has argued that this "ideological campaign" served the goal of "economically transform[ing] the film industry."[32] If the motive behind launching the movement against *The Life of Wu Xun* was as much economic as political/ideological, it comes as no surprise that it differed fundamentally from other political campaigns in the same period, such as the movement to condemn the "Hu Feng Anti-Party Clique" (*Hu Feng fandang jituan* 胡風反黨集團). Over ninety intellectuals were arrested for their connections

---

28. Wang, *Revolutionary Cycles in Chinese Cinema*, 33.
29. Link, "The Crocodile Bird," 210.
30. Kotkin, *Magnetic Mountain: Stalinism as a Civilization*, 237.
31. Zhang, *Chinese National Cinema*, 199; Qizhi, *Mao Zedong shidai de renmin dianying, 1949–1966 nian*, 115.
32. Wang, *Revolutionary Cycles in Chinese Cinema*, 8–9.

with Hu Feng 胡風 (1902–1985) in the 1950s. In contrast, the campaign against *The Life of Wu Xun* inflicted minimal damage upon the filmmakers responsible for its production, including Zhao Dan and the writer-director, Sun Yu.

While Sun Yu and Zheng Junli were compelled to perform public self-criticism for their directing of *The Life of Wu Xun* and *Between A Married Couple*, respectively,[33] Zhao Dan was not even asked to submit a report to criticize himself, partly because of his status as a public figure "outside the Party" (*dangwai* 黨外).[34] At the height of the Cultural Revolution, Yao Wenyuan blamed Zhou Yang, vice-chairman of the Propaganda Department of the CCP Central Committee in the early 1950s, and his "henchman," Yu Ling 于伶 (1907–1997), director of the Shanghai Culture Bureau (*Shanghai wenhua ju* 上海文化局), for protecting "a motley crew of ghosts and monsters"—Zhao Dan included—in the midst of the nationwide movement against *The Life of Wu Xun*. In his infamous 1967 booklet, *On the Counter-Revolutionary Double-Dealer Chou Yang*, Yao Wenyuan quoted a letter written by Zhou Yang, in which Zhou demanded that Yu Ling "use caution and care in handling specific problems" and avoid "crude methods and impatience," shortly after criticisms of *The Life of Wu Xun* emerged.[35] Although Zhou Yang and his colleagues were eager to provide Zhao Dan with protection, Zhao appeared more than willing to repent for his "mistake" in public by parroting the rhetoric and phrases used by his critics and consistently calling himself "a performer in the counterrevolutionary film [*The Life of*] *Wu Xun*."[36] As the final portion of this chapter will show, Zhao would resort to the same tactic to survive his imprisonment during the Cultural Revolution.

To Thrive

Rebuilding Zhao Dan's Stardom in Mao's China

Following the debacle of *The Life of Wu Xun*, the embattled Zhao Dan briefly slipped into obscurity. During the Cultural Revolution, Zhao admitted that he once considered leaving Shanghai and working for the army, but his request gained no support from the CCP authorities in Shanghai.[37] Instead, he was dispatched to war-torn Korea to gain first-hand experience of the war and "improve [his] ideological understanding."[38] In the second half of the 1950s, however, Zhao staged a glorious

---

33. Wang, *Revolutionary Cycles in Chinese Cinema*, 35.
34. Zhao Changju 趙長聚 and Tong Zi'an, "Zhao Dan yu Wu Xun" 趙丹與武訓 [Zhao Dan and Wu Xun], *Chun Qiu* 春秋 [Spring and Autumn], no. 3 (1995): 38.
35. Yao Wen-yuan (Yao Wenyuan 姚文元), *On the Counter-Revolutionary Double-Dealer Chou Yang* (Beijing: Foreign Languages Press, 1967), 6–7.
36. Shen Ji 沈寂, "Yinhai yizhu" 銀海遺珠 [The unrecognized treasure in the silver ocean], in *Xu Changlin wenji: yige dianying gongzuozhe de shouji* 徐昌霖文集：一個電影工作者的手記 [The collected writings of Xu Changlin: Notes of a film worker], ed. Xu Changlin 徐昌霖 (Shanghai: Wenhui chubanshe, 2010), 3.
37. Li Hui 李輝, *Zhao Dan zishu* 趙丹自述 [Zhao Dan in his own words] (Zhengzhou: Daxiang chubanshe, 2003), 136.
38. Shanghai Municipal Archives, B177-3-553, 34.

comeback. Between 1955 and 1959, he managed to star in five high-profile films and directed another two, arousing pervasive envy in the world of filmmaking in China.[39] Meanwhile, Zhao was awarded the rank of level 1 in the literary and art circles. Only five individuals were given such a high rank among all Shanghai filmmakers.[40] In the hierarchy of state-employed cadres, Zhao thus stood above Chen Liting and Ying Yunwei, two of the three heads of the film studios in Shanghai.[41] This ranking system was translated into the discriminatory treatment of the lower-ranking staff. Director Yang Xiaozhong 楊小仲 (1899–1969) recalled that actors and actresses of higher ranks exercised the privilege of taking "soft seats" (*ruanzuo* 軟座). In contrast, Yang could only take a "hard seat" (*yingzuo* 硬座) on the same train heading to Hainan for a business trip in the mid-1950s.[42]

As soon as he acquired status as a privileged artist in this hierarchical system, Zhao had his political standing enhanced by securing his party membership. In 1957, he was officially inducted into the CCP. When looking back at the process of joining the party, Zhao testified in 1965 that he felt that it would have been a shame on the CCP organization had it failed to award him a membership, considering his long-standing service. Therefore, the CCP was under an obligation to give him a new, glorious "political life" (*zhengzhi shengming* 政治生命).[43] Later, Zhao confirmed that joining the party was a testimony to his desire to accumulate "political capital" (*zhengzhi ziben* 政治資本).[44] What Zhao seemed to have forgotten was not just the incident of *The Life of Wu Xun* that had deeply frustrated him six years before but the ongoing Anti-Rightist Movement, during which many of his colleagues were pronounced the foes of the people. Zhao barely extricated himself from this political storm, as he had coauthored with some of his colleagues and friends, such as Zheng Junli and Liu Qiong 劉瓊 (1912–2002), an essay questioning the justification for the party's intervention in filmmaking in December 1956. In the essay, entitled "Night Talks beside the Hearth" (*Lubian yehua* 爐邊夜話), Zhao and his coauthors, all of whom were film directors, reiterated the necessity of reestablishing a director's absolute authority in making a film.[45]

---

39. Liu Shu 劉澍, "Dang yinhai zaoyu bingshan—Wu Xun zhuan de xiaoshi yu Lu Xun zhuan de yaowang" 當銀海遭遇冰山—《武訓傳》的消失與《魯迅傳》的夭亡 [When the silver sea meets the iceberg: The disappearance of *The Life of Wu Xun* and the demise of *The Life of Lu Xun*], *Tongzhou gongjin* 同舟共進 [Advancing in the Same Boat], no. 7 (2009): 65. The five films Zhao starred in between 1955 and 1959 are *Li Shizhen* 李時珍 (1956, dir. Shen Fu 沈浮 [1905–1994]), *For Peace* (*Weile heping* 為了和平, 1957, dir. Huang Zuolin 黃佐臨 [1906–1994]), *Soul of the Sea* (*Haihun*, 海魂 1957, dir. Xu Tao 徐韜 [1910–1966]), *Lin Zexu* (1959), and *Nie Er* (1959).
40. Shanghai Municipal Archives, B177-1-103, 6.
41. Xia Yu 夏瑜, *Yaoyuan de ai—Chen Liting zhuan* 遙遠的愛—陳鯉庭傳 [Remote love: The biography of Chen Liting] (Beijing: Zhongguo dianying chubanshe, 2008), 107.
42. Shanghai Municipal Archives, B177-1-268, 44.
43. Shanghai Municipal Archives, A31-2-30, 36.
44. Li, *Zhao Dan zishu*, 173.
45. Li Zhen 李鎮, *Zheng Junli quanji di 3 juan* 鄭君里全集 第3卷 [Zheng Junli's anthology, vol. 3] (Shanghai: Shanghai wenhua chubanshe, 2016), 223.

While many who expressed similar opinions challenging the party's leadership in filmmaking would be branded "rightists," Zhao suffered no such assault. Zhao later recalled that he was able to evade further punishment during this political campaign because of his acute awareness of the need to distance himself from some of the CCP's most outspoken critics, such as Chen Renbing 陳仁炳 (1909–1990). More importantly, he was put under the protection of upper-echelon officials in Beijing.[46] A memoir authored by Huang Chen, Zheng Junli's wife, recalled that on the eve of the Anti-Rightist Movement, Madam Mao unexpectedly summoned both Zhao Dan and Zheng Junli to Hangzhou and arranged a meeting with her for a reunion. Although Jiang Qing kept her mouth shut about the ongoing political storm, an unintended (or intended) consequence of this unheralded encounter was pulling the unprepared Zhao and Zheng out of a fateful meeting that would end up persecuting quite a few of their fellow filmmakers.[47] To save his filmic and political careers, Zhao reversed his position one year later to bring a scathing indictment against Shi Hui, the black sheep of the film world, by coauthoring an essay accusing Shi of being an opportunist and a representative of the "declining classes" (*moluo jieji* 沒落階級), that often denigrated communist heroes on the screen.[48] As such, Zhao not merely weathered this political campaign but also benefited from it.

After the Anti-Rightist Movement, Zhao's newly minted party membership further contributed to rebuilding his stardom. In April 1960, Shanghai Pegasus Film Studio nominated Zhao an "outstanding worker" (*xianjin gongzuo zhe* 先進工作者). The studio's statement to publicize Zhao's "meritorious deeds" (*xianjin shiji* 先進事蹟) shows that Zhao had overcome his bourgeois artistic thoughts—that is, art for art's sake—and fostered a full understanding of the party's leading role in arts. As the director of *The Evergreen Tree* (*Changqing shu* 常青樹, 1958), a short movie about steelworkers in Shanghai during the Great Leap Forward, Zhao had reportedly implemented the guiding principle of the Great Leap in order to quickly complete the shooting of the film and thereby lower the costs. To this end, Zhao broke a record by filming one hundred takes per day.[49] This portrayal of Zhao as a Stakhanovite drew a parallel between his heroic image on the screen and his commitment to the Great Leap Forward off the screen. The construction of the meaning of a star, according to Jackie Stacey, entails the audience's identification with the actor/actress both in "the cinematic context" and "beyond the cinema itself."[50]

---

46. Li, *Zhao Dan zishu*, 192.
47. Huang Chen 黃晨 and Zheng Dali 鄭大里, *Wo he Junli* 我和君里 [Junli and I] (Shanghai: Shanghai wenhua chubanshe, 2013), 88–89.
48. Zhao Dan 趙丹 and Qu Baiyin 瞿白音 "Shi Hui 'gun' de yishu he tade 'caineng'" 石揮 "滾" 的藝術和他的 "才能" ["Shi Hui's arts of 'rolling-out' and his 'talents'"], in *Hanwei dang dui dianying shiye de lingdao xubian* 捍衛黨對電影事業的領導續編 [Defending the party's leadership in the film industry, supplementary volumes] (Beijing: Zhongguo dianying chubanshe, 1958), 33–39.
49. Shanghai Municipal Archives, A31-2-30, 76.
50. Jackie Stacey, "Feminine Fascinations: Forms of Identification in Star/Audience Relations," in *Stardom: Industry of Desire*, ed. Christine Gledhill (London: Routledge, 1991), 149.

In this sense, Zhao's personae in those films and his real-life contributions to the CCP-led Great Leap Forward jointly augmented his political and artistic prestige.

In the post-Leap years, the practice of filming one hundred takes per day that had helped Zhao Dan build up enormous political capital came under criticism, for it embodied the irrational fanaticism peculiar to the Great Leap Forward.[51] It was, nevertheless, crystal clear that Zhao Dan not only made a fawning contribution to popularizing the Great Leap mentality but also reaped profit from it in the late 1950s. On the eve of the Cultural Revolution, Zhao grew more proficient in the CCP's political language. In a 1963 meeting, for example, he took the initiative to contrast bitterness in the "old society" and happiness in post-1949 China to put forth his viewpoint that the party had made his star status.[52] As a film star, a party member, and an "outstanding worker," Zhao Dan was unofficially crowned in 1961 as one of the twenty-two film stars in the country, along with the red star Zhang Ruifang, and had his portrait hung in theaters in China.[53] At the height of the Cultural Revolution, the practice of hanging giant pictures of "star performers" and "star directors" inside theaters nationwide was convicted as the revival of the "capitalist star system" (*ziben zhuyi de mingxing zhidu* 資本主義的明星制度).[54]

This "star system" afforded Zhao Dan not only political capital but also monetary gain. Statistics from the early 1960s show that the highest monthly pay for a film actor/actress in Shanghai reached 351 yuan, as opposed to the minimum salary of forty-one yuan for the lowest-ranking performers.[55] Hence, it was not an exaggeration for Red Guards during the Cultural Revolution to charge actors like Zhao Dan with the misdeed of having received pay seven times higher than that of an ordinary worker in the purportedly egalitarian Chinese society. Such a gulf between stars and average performers in film studios in Shanghai, according to radical Maoist propagandists, exemplified the "Three Principles of Famous" (*sanming zhuyi* 三名主義), "famous screenwriters, famous directors, and famous actors/actresses," and the "Policy of the Three Highs" (*sangao zhengce* 三高政策):

---

51. Shanghai Municipal Archives, B177-3-533, 4–5.
52. Shanghai Municipal Archives, B177-1-23, 98.
53. Liu Shu 劉澍, "Liuguang yicai de 22 da mingxing" 流光溢彩的22大明星 [The shimmering twenty-two great stars], *Dazhong dianying* 大眾電影 [Mass Film], no. 12 (2005): 31–32.
54. Shanghai hongqi dianying zhipianchang hongqi geming zaofan bingtuan xuanchuan zu 上海紅旗電影製片廠紅旗革命造反兵團宣傳組 [The propaganda team of the revolutionary and rebellious corps at the Shanghai Red Flag Film Studio], "Gaoju Mao Zedong sixiang weida hongqi, chedi zalan fangemin xiuzheng zhuyi wenyi heixian" 高舉毛澤東思想偉大紅旗 徹底砸爛反革命修正主義文藝黑線 [Hoist the great red banner of Maoist thought to completely smash the reactionary and revisionist black line of arts and literature], in *Gaoju Mao Zedong sixiang weida hongqi, chedi zalan fangemin xiuzheng zhuyi wenyi heixian* 高舉毛澤東思想偉大紅旗 徹底砸爛反革命修正主義文藝黑線 [Hoist the great red banner of Maoist thought to completely smash the reactionary and revisionist black line of arts and literature], ed. Shanghai hongqi dianying zhipianchang hongqi gemin zaofan bingtuan Shanghai haiguan xuanchuan zu 上海市紅旗電影製片廠紅旗革命造反兵團上海海關宣傳組 [The customs propaganda team of the revolutionary and rebellious corps at the Shanghai Red Flag Film Studio] (n.p., 1967), 5.
55. Shanghai Municipal Archives, B177-1-324, 31.

"high remuneration, high salaries, and high bonuses."[56] As a gentle parody of the well-known "Three Principles of the People" (*sanmim zhuyi* 三民主義) enacted by Sun Yat-sen (1866–1925), the "Three Principles of Famous" was said to be proposed by Xia Yan and his political patron, Premier Zhou Enlai. For remuneration, an essay published in 1967 claimed that the screenwriter of a "long" feature film was entitled to receive several thousand yuan for an "excellent script" in the late 1950s and early 1960s.[57] The charge was not entirely unfounded. The archival records show that scripts for "long dramas" were ranked as categories 1, 2, and 3, and were paid 3,000–4,000 yuan, 2,000–3,000 yuan, and 1,000–2,000 yuan, respectively, in the early 1960s.[58]

Indeed, it was Premier Zhou Enlai who openly advocated such a hierarchical system among artists. In a meeting in May 1959, Zhou called for giving celebrated film stars special treatment, both politically and financially. To justify his statement, Zhou reasoned that higher pay for those individuals signaled the CCP's commitment to respecting and protecting artists' labor and services.[59] In Zhao Dan's case, it is certain that he, as the director-scriptwriter of *Love in the Green Mountains* (*Qingshan lian* 青山戀, 1964), a film about the displaced life of urban youths in the mountains of Fujian, must have received remuneration of over 1,000 yuan, given that the author of the novel from which the movie was adapted was awarded 800 yuan.[60] A written rule in the Shanghai-based film studios was that a screenplay writer was paid twice as much as the original author of an adapted novel.[61] Furthermore, rumor had it that Zhao received about 3,000 yuan for making two films in the mid-1950s,[62] including *Li Shizhen*, a less popular movie, particularly in the countryside.[63]

To sum up, beginning in the mid-1950s, Zhao Dan enjoyed a slew of privileges, including a significant income and high status. It is thus safe to argue that not only his pre-1949 fame but also his connections with various political figures in both Beijing and Shanghai contributed to his remaking as a star for several years in the

---

56. Shanghai hongqi dianying zhipianchang hongqi geming zaofan bingtuan xuanchuan zu, "Gaoju Mao Zedong sixiang weida hongqi," 3–5.
57. Hongqi geming zaofan bingtuan 404 zongdui 紅旗革命造反兵團404縱隊 [The 404 column of the red flag revolutionary and rebellious corps], "Zalan 'gao xingchou' zhidu" 砸爛"高薪酬"制度 [Smash the system of "high renumeration"], in *Gaoju Mao Zedong sixiang weida hongqi, chedi zalan fangemin xiuzheng zhuyi wenyi heixian* 高舉毛澤東思想偉大紅旗，徹底砸爛反革命修正主義文藝黑線 [Hoist the great red banner of Maoist thought to completely smash the reactionary and revisionist black line of art and literature], ed. Shanghai hongqi dianying zhipianchang hongqi gemin zaofan bingtuan Shanghai haiguan xuanchuan zu 上海紅旗電影製片廠紅旗革命造反兵團上海海關宣傳組 [The customs propaganda team of the revolutionary and rebellious corps at the Shanghai Red Flag Film Studio] (n.p., 1967), 20.
58. Shanghai Municipal Archives, B177-1-324, 31.
59. Shanghai Municipal Archives, A22-1-439, 84.
60. Shanghai Municipal Archives, B177-1-281, 14.
61. Shanghai Municipal Archives, B177-3-363, 23–27.
62. Shanghai hongqi dianying zhipianchang hongqi geming zaofan bingtuan xuanchuan zu, "Gaoju Mao Zedong sixiang weida hongqi," 5.
63. Paul Clark, "Closely Watched Viewers: A Taxonomy of Chinese Film Audiences from 1949 to the Cultural Revolution Seen from Hunan," *Journal of Chinese Cinemas* 5, no. 1 (2011): 81.

Mao era. For the cadres in charge of the film studios in Shanghai and who were, in theory, Zhao's superiors, his intimate relations with the leadership in Beijing seemed both mysterious and intimidating, as Zhao personally admitted in 1965. Zhao's ability to minimize the damage inflicted by the campaign against *The Life of Wu Xun* in the early 1950s upon his filmmaking career and enhance his political standing despite his authoring of an essay that called for undermining the party's leading role in China's film industry during the Anti-Rightist Movement was, to his contemporaries, testimony to the fact that he had powerful backers in Beijing.[64] In this sense, Yao Wenyuan's infamous 1967 essay against Zhou Yang merely articulated what had been pervasively believed. Zhou Yang was quoted as saying in 1961 that the significance of Zhao Dan and other stars in the film industry was comparable to that of a leading cadre in a political party.[65]

Zhao Dan's political standing was further raised because of his interactions with the PRC's supreme leaders, Mao Zedong and Premier Zhou Enlai. Mao reportedly met with Zhao numerous times. Their private conversation in May 1961 was long cited as Mao's endorsement of Zhao's political and artistic accomplishments.[66] Meanwhile, Zhao was widely known to have maintained good relations with Premier Zhou. During a meeting in 1961, Zhao not only openly debated with Zhou but also demanded a "plaque absolving him of prosecution" (*miandou pai* 免鬥牌), in order to facilitate his escape from future political troubles.[67] When the project of making *The Life of Lu Xun* came to an abrupt end in 1963, Zhou, who had failed to meet with Zhao in Shanghai, personally called Zhao's colleague, asking for Zhao's whereabouts.[68] Given Zhao's unique connections with various leaders, he was often assigned a role as an ambassador of Chinese film and culture. In 1960, for example, Zhao's extremely tight schedule included thirty days abroad and another thirty-two days receiving foreign delegations in China.[69]

Most intriguingly, Zhao's relationship with "Madam Mao," Jiang Qing (aka Lan Ping 藍蘋), in the 1930s and 1940s was widely known but remains a mystery. Not only did Jiang Qing and Zhao marry their respective spouses at a joint ceremony in the spring of 1936, but Jiang had also written a letter to Zhao in person in 1946, encouraging her longtime friend to find a new partner and get on the right track of his filmmaking career after years in prison in Xinjiang. Ye Zhou 葉周, son of Ye Yiqun 葉以群 (1911–1966), one of the core members of the team making *The Life of Lu Xun* in the early 1960s, cites this letter as evidence of Jiang Qing's enduring love

---

64. Shanghai Municipal Archives, B177-3-553, 43.
65. *"Hunshi mowing"—Zhao Dan* "混世魔王" 一趙丹 [Zhao Dan, "a fiend in human shape"], unpublished, 3.
66. Zhao, *Wode diedie Zhao Dan*, 187.
67. Chen Huangmei 陳荒煤, *Chen Huangmei weji di 3 juan: sanwen (xia)* 陳荒煤文集第3卷：散文（下）[The collected writings of Chen Huangmei, vol. 3: Essays, bk. 2] (Beijing: Zhongguo dianying chubanshe, 2013), 79–80.
68. Zhao, *Wode diedie Zhao Dan*, 188.
69. Shanghai Municipal Archives, B177-1-231, 22.

for Zhao.⁷⁰ Zhao's widely known intimate relationship with Madam Mao could have spelled more catastrophic trouble during the Cultural Revolution. Zhao, however, wisely remained silent on Jiang Qing in all the written confessions he authored in jail, avoiding harsher political persecution and private revenge.⁷¹ Unfortunately, the well-kept, but still commonly known, secret of his connection with Madam Mao continued to haunt him in the wake of the Cultural Revolution: he was stripped of the opportunity to portray the late Zhou Enlai, a political figure whom he admired and had been friends with for years, in a film in the late 1970s, in light of his alleged relationship with this leader of the Gang of Four.⁷²

Nevertheless, in the late 1950s and 1960s, Zhao's perceived connection with the upper echelon of the authorities in Beijing affected his perception and treatment by party cadres in Shanghai and his colleagues in the film studios. A testimony penned by Zhao in 1965 indicated that local CCP cadres were worried that the "experts" (*zhuanjia* 專家) like him were difficult to deal with, for they had "a path to the sky" (*tongtian* 通天), meaning direct access to the highest authorities.⁷³ In the same testimony, Zhao equated "experts" with "intellectuals," a novel identity all film actors and actresses were assigned after 1949. In Suzanne Ogden's equation, intellectuals in post-1949 China, albeit a vaguely defined concept, were usually called "experts," as opposed to "those who were red."⁷⁴ Zhao, nonetheless, was in a uniquely advantageous position as both an "expert" and a Stakhanovite, who was "red" enough for the time being. Furthermore, as Zhao confessed, he was able to manipulate his dual status as both a party member and an intellectual/artist for a long while. Party cadres regarded him as an "expert" and the object of the "united front" (*tongzhan* 統戰)—the political necessity of compromising with nonparty specialists and professionals. However, the general public looked up to him as a towering figure, a combination of a "special" party member and a well-established artist.⁷⁵

Zhao's reputation as both a CCP member and an expert reached its peak with the release of two high-profile films he would star in, *Lin Zexu* and *Nie Er*, to celebrate the PRC's tenth anniversary.⁷⁶ The two films were both critically and financially successful. Statistics from 1962 showed that *Lin Zexu* attracted 18.5 million viewers, while *Nie Er*'s audiences reached 18.53 million. By comparison, another

---

70. Ye Zhou 葉周, "Yidai ren de Lu Xun meng" 一代人的魯迅夢 [A generation's dream of Lu Xun], in *Wenmai chuancheng de jianxing zhe: Ye Yiqun bainian danchen jinian wenji* 文脈傳承的踐行者：葉以群百年誕辰紀念文集 [The practitioner of inheriting the literary heritage: An anthology (to commemorate) Ye Yiqun's one-hundredth birthday], ed. Ye Zhou 葉周 (Shanghai: Shanghai sanlian shudian, 2011), 11.
71. Li, *Zhao Dan zishu*, 100.
72. Ye, "Yidai ren de Lu Xun meng," 210.
73. Shanghai Municipal Archives, B177-3-553, 43.
74. Suzanne Ogden, "From Patronage to Profits: The Changing Relationship of Chinese Intellectuals with the Party-state," in *Chinese Intellectuals between State and Market*, ed. Edward Gu and Merle Goldman (London: Routledge, 2004), 111.
75. Shanghai Municipal Archives, B177-3-553, 35.
76. In Jay Leyda's words, star performers such as Zhao and the director Zheng Junli "[leaped] from one anniversary film to another" in several months at this time. See Leyda, *Dianying*, 308.

anniversary film from that year, *The Lin Family Shop* (*Linjia puzi* 林家鋪子, 1959, dir. Shui Hua 水華 [1916–1995]), was a market failure, finding an audience of only 7.42 million. The box office success of Zhao's two anniversary films triggered a fundamental change in film distribution in the PRC. Before 1962, film studios across the country sold all films at a flat price, but after mid-1962, movies would be priced based on their box office revenues.[77]

Zhao Dan's stardom in the late 1950s and early 1960s differed from that in pre-1949 China in that the latter stemmed largely from the market success of his films, whereas the former was the outgrowth of the marriage between his impressive performance skills and unmatched political capital. These two factors reinforced one another in the politico-cultural setting of Mao's China, lending Zhao unrivaled political privileges and economic benefits. Following the debacle of the making of *The Life of Lu Xun*, a crestfallen Zhao was assigned to shoot *Love in the Green Mountains*. Although Zhao's daughter has repeatedly underscored her father's reluctance to produce a film that eulogized the ongoing movement of sending young urbanites down to the countryside,[78] Zhao and his companions enjoyed material comfort in a time of widespread economic difficulty. Later, during the Cultural Revolution, Red Guards charged Zhao and his company for leading a decadent life during the shooting of *Love in the Green Mountains* in Fujian, by staying in luxury hotel rooms, eating delicacies, and regularly playing poker and billiards. More importantly, Zhao was able to capitalize on his political status as a deputy to the People's Congress to demand that local authorities provide a military escort when the film crew made an excursion to some heavily fortified islands on the frontier of the Taiwan Strait.[79]

In all fairness, Zhao Dan worked quite hard to make *Love in the Green Mountains* in Fujian. The making of the film helped Zhao complete his transition from a film star to a director although he had already directed two shorter films during the Great Leap Forward. More importantly, the production of this movie contributed to making Zhao a well-round filmmaker by deepening his understanding of the motion picture. Zhao, originally a spoken-drama actor, had long presumed that film was nothing but a derivative of drama. Deep in the mountains in Fujian, Zhao was facing the space in the woods so different from that of the stage and began to contemplate the artistic specificity of the motion picture: he was pondering the use of a wider space in nature. Hence, the movie exemplifies a filmic work that was not its filmmakers' top priority but still deserved their maximal efforts in Mao-era China.[80] Despite Zhao's endeavor, his critics during the Cultural Revolution

---

77. Shanghai Municipal Archives, B177-1-262, 51.
78. Zhao, *Wode diedie Zhao Dan*, 188–98.
79. "Hunshi mowing"—Zhao Dan, 6.
80. Zhu Anping 朱安平, "*Qingshan lian*: 'jiadang' zhong qiusuo" 《青山戀》："夾檔" 中求索 [*Love in the Green Mountains*: Exploration between two opinions], *Dazhong dianying* 大眾電影 [Mass Film], no. 22 (2013): 38–39.

severely censured him for the limelight he grabbed in making *Love in the Green Mountains*.

In the Red Guards' words, Zhao's name showed up on the screen multiple times, as the screenwriter, the film star, and the director of the film, testifying to a concerted effort to build up Zhao's stardom.[81] Nevertheless, *Love in the Green Mountains* was by no means the earliest film that Zhao directed. For a while, Zhao boasted of his dual identity as both a performer and a director. The previously mentioned controversial article, "Night Talks beside the Hearth," which Zhao and his colleagues coauthored in 1956, unequivocally expounded the necessity of reaffirming the director's leading role in film production.[82] Zhao's standpoint, however, kept shifting in accordance with his own positions in making films. In 1965, he publicly acknowledged that he subscribed to the theory of "director-centeredness" when he worked as a director, adding that he could smoothly switch to "actor-centeredness" (*yanyuan zhongxin lun* 演員中心論) when he starred in other films. In his own words, he was the "most special among special artists" (*teshu zhong de teshu yishujia* 特殊中的特殊藝術家), adept at shifting ground to serve his best interests on different occasions.[83] "Director-centeredness," a notion Zhao intermittently advocated, had been initially put forth by a number of seasoned film directors, such as Sun Yu and Chen Liting. In his article published on November 23, 1956, Chen Liting complained that administrators (CCP cadres), not directors, dominated film production in China. He thus called for full recognition of the director as the centerpiece of filmmaking.[84] Chen's biographer posits that Chen's insistence on the director's central role in filmmaking stemmed from his experiences as a director of both film and theater and his tireless inquiry into film theory over many decades. Therefore, Chen arrived at an understanding that all film stars must act within the framework determined by the director.[85] Before 1949, Chen's stance ran counter to Zhao Dan's penchant for overacting and improvisation in front of the camera. Their disagreement occurred when shooting *Rhapsody of Happiness* (*Xingfu kuangxiang qu* 幸福狂想曲, 1947). Zhao Dan reportedly blamed Chen Liting for adhering to dogmatic

---

81. Shanghai hongqi dianying zhipian chang hongqi geming zaofan bingtuan 217 zongdui 上海紅旗電影製片廠紅旗革命造反兵團217縱隊 [The 217 column of the Red Flag Film Studio revolutionary and rebellious corps], "Dadao xiuzheng zhuyi de 'sanming zhuyi' he 'sangao zhengce'" 打倒修正主義的 "三名主義" 和 "三高政策" [Down with the revisionist "three principles of famous" and "policy of three highs"], in *Gaoju Mao Zedong sixiang weida hongqi, chedi zalan fangemin xiuzheng zhuyi wenyi heixian* 高舉毛澤東思想偉大紅旗，徹底砸爛反革命修正主義文藝黑線 [Hoist the great red banner of Maoist thought to completely smash the reactionary and revisionist black line of art and literature], ed. Shanghai hongqi dianying zhipianchang hongqi gemin zaofan bingtuan Shanghai haiguan xuanchuan zu 上海紅旗電影製片廠紅旗革命造反兵團上海海關宣傳組 [The customs propaganda team of the revolutionary and rebellious corps at the Shanghai Red Flag Film Studio] (n.p., 1967), 19.
82. Zheng, *Zheng Junli quanji di 3 juan*, 223.
83. Shanghai Municipal Archives, B177-3-553, 37.
84. Chen Liting 陳鯉庭, "Daoyan yinggai shi shengchan de zhongxin huanjie" 導演應該是生產的中心環節 [The director should take the center stage in film production], *Wenhui bao* 文匯報 [Wenhui Daily], November 23, 1956.
85. Xia, *Yaoyuan de ai*, 73.

filmmaking theories while lacking filmmaking experience.[86] Their repeated quarrels led Chen Liting to swear, "I wouldn't be a human if I invited you for my next film." The indignant Zhao Dan shot back, "I wouldn't be a human if I starred in your next film."[87] Another source indicated that the infuriated Zhao cursed, "[I would be] a son of bitch if I worked with you anymore."[88]

The Debacle of The Life of Lu Xun

An opportunity to reunite this disgruntled duo befell them in the mid-1950s, when the Shanghai Film Studio was making preparations for producing *Li Shizhen*, a movie about a renowned Ming dynasty (1368–1644) physician and pharmacologist. Zhao Dan starred in this film, while Chen Liting was initially appointed the director. The Zhao-Chen clash surfaced at the preproduction stage. To better understand Li Shizhen's career, Chen spent two years taking notes from Li's herbology book, *The Compendium of Materia Medica* (*Bencao gangmu* 本草綱目), and producing a large number of flashcards. The piqued Zhao Dan yelled, "We are not running a research institute in traditional Chinese medical science. What's the use of those flashcards?" Zhao Dan finally enlisted help from the film studio's party committee to oust Chen Liting from the film crew,[89] costing Chen the chance to direct his first film since 1952. Indeed, Chen, who had enjoyed high sociocultural status but was purposely excluded from meaningful filmmaking activities, exemplified a generation of artists' failure to win the party's favor after 1949, because of their "very interesting" but "highly untidy" backgrounds.[90] His "untidy" past included adhering to the "cinematic line of the petty bourgeoisie" (*xiao zichan jieji dianying luxian* 小資產階級電影路線), the main target of criticism during a political campaign in 1952.[91] Chen had been marginalized to such a degree that an internal file created in 1962 witheringly listed him as one of the only two directors affiliated with two Shanghai-based film studios who had failed to produce a single feature film between 1950 and 1962.[92]

By the early 1960s, Chen Liting grasped his final chance to direct a film of his own. Beginning in the opening months of 1960, the preparatory work for *The Life of Lu Xun* was set in motion. The decision to make this film attests to a nationwide trend in filmmaking deriving from the remarkable success achieved by *Lin Zexu* in 1959: an eagerness to produce movies with "significant themes" (*zhongda ticai* 重大

---

86. Shen, *Xingyun liushui jiwang erji (xia)*, 370.
87. Laolaoxia 老老夏, "Huanxi yuanjia Chen Liting he Zhao Dan" 歡喜冤家陳鯉庭和趙丹 [Chen Liting and Zhao Dan: A quarrelsome and loving duo], *Shanghai caifeng* 上海采風 [Folk Art Collection in Shanghai], no. 5 (2010): 28.
88. Shen, *Xingyun liushui jiwang erji (xia)*, 370.
89. Shen, *Xingyun liushui jiwang erji (xia)*, 370.
90. Pickowicz, *China on Film*, 190.
91. Qizhi, *Mao Zedong shidai de renmin dianying*, 152.
92. Shanghai Municipal Archives, B177-1-232, 53.

題材).⁹³ Under these circumstances, a star-studded team was assembled in Shanghai in 1960, that consisted of film stars from Shanghai and Beijing, and the duo of Chen Liting (as the director) and Zhao Dan, who volunteered to portray Lu Xun. Zhao was willing to recant his previous words and cooperate with Chen Liting, in no small part because of his lasting admiration for Lu Xun. Zhao later testified that he was reluctant to read the works of any Chinese writer but Lu Xun.⁹⁴ In the following three years, Zhao was obsessed with the Lu Xun role: he wore a Lu Xun–style mustache and rearranged the furniture in his house to make the living room resemble Lu Xun's study.⁹⁵

Despite Zhao Dan's extraordinary enthusiasm, the making of *The Life of Lu Xun* was predestined to be tortuously difficult. The film's advisory team, for example, gathered together multiple heavyweight writers, scholars, and CCP officials: Mao Dun 茅盾 (1896–1981), the celebrated left-wing novelist and the sitting Minister of Culture; Zhou Jianren 周建人 (1888–1984), Lu Xun's brother and the governor of Zhejiang province; Xu Guangping 許廣平 (1898–1968), Lu Xun's widow; Xia Yan; and Yu Ling.⁹⁶ The aforementioned Zhou Yang, by then the deputy Minister of Culture, was also to join the group.⁹⁷ The roster appeared dazzling, but the aggregation of so many authoritative figures was poised to create more problems than it resolved. In hindsight, Jay Leyda summarizes the film's failure quite cogently:

> There were more people who knew Lu Hsun's [Lu Xun's] difficult actuality, and more who would dare to object to a conveniently neat film frame fitted around him.... There were ironies (and extra problems) in showing Lu Hsun in a Chinese communist film as a revolutionary hero: revolutionist and hero he certainly was— and wonderful artist, too—but his running war with the Shanghai dogmatists of the Chinese Communist Party was too well known to be wiped out.⁹⁸

Lu Xun's "running war" refers to his ideological clash with the chief officers of the China League of Left-Wing Writers (*Zhongguo zuoyi zuojia lianmeng* 中國左翼作家聯盟) in the 1930s, including Zhou Yang himself, as well as Tian Han and Xia Yan, and his subsequent personal grudge against them.⁹⁹ In fact, Zhou Yang, Lu Xun's main foe three decades before, would assume a dominant role in drafting the film script. The process of writing numerous drafts of the screenplay

---

93. Shanghai Municipal Archives, B177-1-233, 33–54.
94. Shanghai Municipal Archives, B177-3-553, 12.
95. Chen Qingquan 陳清泉, *Yuebai fengqing: Shanghai yingtan wangshi ji qita* 月白風清：上海影壇往事及其他 [The moon is bright and the air serene: The past in the film circles in Shanghai and other matters]. (Shanghai: Shanghai wenyi chubanshe, 2015), 169.
96. Shanghai Municipal Archives, A22-2-875, 30.
97. Tian Yiye 田一野, "Choupai lishi jupian *Lu Xun zhuan* shimo" 籌拍歷史巨片《魯迅傳》始末 [The whole story of planning and preparing for the epic film *The Life of Lu Xun*], *Dazhong dianying* 大眾電影 [Mass Film], no. 8 (1985): 10.
98. Leyda, *Dianying*, 308.
99. Fang Xiangdong 房向東, "*Hengzhan*": *Lu Xun yu zuoyi wenren* "橫站"：魯迅與左翼文人 ["Standing horizontally": Lu Xun and left-wing writers] (Shanghai: Shanghai sanlian shudian, 2014), 203–12.

was unendurably long and tormenting. Chen Baichen was assigned as the primary screenwriter. In the following three years, he had to listen to various—oftentimes mutually contradictory—opinions and comments from different parties. Chen's daughter later looked back at her father's career after 1949, stating that Chen did nothing but produce "literature on demand." Most of Chen's works in the 1950s, including the much-criticized script of the film *Song Jingshi*, were ill-fated.[100] When the opportunity arose to coauthor the screenplay of *The Life of Lu Xun*, Chen Baichen could not afford to pass up the chance. After many years of producing works "tasting like chewing wax [i.e., like cardboard]" (*weitong juela* 味同嚼蠟), Chen could not resist the temptation of writing a masterpiece about a literary giant whom he deeply admired.[101] The script of *The Life of Lu Xun*, nevertheless, proved to be yet another, albeit far more wearisome and troublesome, "on-demand" assignment. Chen's daughter observed that many authoritative figures from Shanghai and Beijing pulled strings behind the scenes. Consequently, Chen and his coworkers had to limp along very slowly, enduring frantic script revisions between 1960 and 1963. In three years, Chen and his colleagues produced six drafts but still fell short of depicting Lu Xun as a flesh-and-blood human.[102]

When *The Life of Lu Xun* came to a disappointing end in 1963, Chen Baichen and his colleagues decided to publish one of the screenplay drafts; it became an instant bestseller, attesting to a veritable avalanche of enthusiasm among film fans.[103] In the afterword, the heartbroken Chen Baichen lamented that it was beyond his ability to meet the expectations and requirements of everyone, hinting at how suffocating the commentary on his drafts had been.[104] Indeed, the Ministry of Culture had already grown fed up with the endless revisions and rewritings of the script one year before and demanded prompt action to start shooting the film.[105] Various sources indicated that different individuals were responsible for the excessive revisions. Chen Baichen's daughter, for example, pointed the finger at Zhou Yang for mercilessly vetoing Chen's second draft, some parts of which were published in *People's Literature* (*Remin wenxue* 人民文學) in 1961, receiving positive reviews.[106] Zhao Dan, by contrast, blamed Chen Liting for disapproving of the two versions.[107]

The stalemate indeed fueled the renewed feud between Zhao Dan and Chen Liting. What infuriated Zhao most was Chen's insistence on accumulating more information about Lu Xun's life, even in 1962, when the Ministry of Culture was

---

100. Chen Hong 陳虹, "Fuqin de gushi" 父親的故事 [(My) father's story], in *Wutai yu jiangtai: xiju jia Chen Baichen* 舞臺與講臺：戲劇家陳白塵 [The stage and the podium: The dramatist Chen Baichen], ed. Chen Hong 陳虹 (Nanjing: Nanjing daxue chubanshe, 2003), 15–16.
101. Chen Hong, *Chen Baichen pingzhuan*, 261.
102. Chen, "Fuqin de gushi," 16.
103. Shen, *Xingyun liushui jiwang erji (xia)*, 376.
104. Chen Baichen et al., Dianying wenxue juben *Lu Xun* (shangji) 電影文學劇本魯迅（上集）[The script of (*The Life of*) *Lu Xun*, part 1] (Shanghai: Shanghai wenyi chubanshe, 1963), 163–64.
105. Shanghai Municipal Archives, A22-2-1055, 42–44.
106. Chen, *Chen Baichen pingzhuan*, 262.
107. Shen, *Xingyun liushui jiwang erji (xia)*, 370.

already pressing for expedited production of the film. Just as in the case of preparing for *Li Shizhen*, Chen once again sent his assistants to Shaoxing and Hangzhou in search of source materials and to make flashcards, further slowing down preparatory work. The conflict between the impatient Zhao and the overly conscientious Chen finally broke out when the latter moved to discuss the classification of the characters based on their class backgrounds. After browsing a file handed out by Chen for each character's class categorization, Zhao voiced his opposition and stated that such investigations were neither correct nor necessary for making a film. Finally, Zhao publicly proclaimed that he refused to speak with Chen, until the director was able to write a script that was ready for production.[108]

Shen Pengnian 沈鵬年, who had been working as an assistant to Chen Liting in the team, traced the constant friction between Chen and Zhao to the pre-1949 years but pointed out that the key issue at this time lay in their swapped positions before and after national liberation. In the late 1940s, when Zhao Dan worked under Chen Liting, he was on a lower rung of the filmmaking crew.[109] After a one-decade hiatus between Zhao's departure from Shanghai (to Chongqing and then to Xinjiang) in 1937 and his return after the Second Sino-Japanese War (1937–1945), his status as a film star was in doubt. Wu Yin 吳茵 (1909–1991), Zhao Dan's friend and colleague, for example, felt unconvinced by Zhao's acting in the late 1940s. Before making *Crows and Sparrows*, Wu was unsure as to whether Zhao, who tended to show off "foreign" (nontraditional and exaggerated) acting techniques in his previous movies, could succeed in portraying a petty urbanite in Shanghai.[110] By the early 1960s, however, Chen Liting, who had passed a fruitless decade, paled in comparison with Zhao's newly acquired stardom and political status. In the hierarchy of artists stipulated by the party, Zhao was one rank higher than Chen. Despite his disadvantaged position, Chen chose not to compromise. Later, the film studio's CCP leaders tried to intervene, asking Zhao to tolerate Chen. Zhao Dan, however, continued to accuse Chen of being "fastidious but incompetent," "dogmatic," and "bureaucratic." As Zhao pointed a finger, Chen dragged his feet by taking himself to the hospital, waiting for the contracts of stars loaned from Beijing to run out.[111]

The program of making *The Life of Lu Xun* reached its breaking point by September 1962, when Xia Yan realized, with some amazement, that making the film was not a part of the studio's plan for 1963–1964. However, the hospitalized Chen Liting stubbornly vetoed all plans to accelerate the production schedule. After three long years, the film studio was carrying an unbearable financial burden: half a million yuan had been expended to cover the lodging and transportation expenses in Shanghai, Beijing, Hangzhou, and Shaoxing and pay actors from Beijing. This

---

108. Shen, *Xingyun liushui jiwang erji (xia)*, 362.
109. Shen, *Xingyun liushui jiwang erji (xia)*, 362–69.
110. Wu Yin 吳茵, *Huishou hua dangnian* 回首話當年 [Looking back at the past] (Beijing: Zhongguo dianying chubanshe, 1993), 94.
111. Shen, *Xingyun liushui jiwang erji (xia)*, 370–71.

excessive expenditure in three years far exceeded the cost of most movies produced in the Mao era.[112] In 1963, the group finally disbanded upon the approval of the Propaganda Department of the CCP Central Committee.[113]

To Survive: Zhao Dan's Confessions as a Survival Tactic

The time-consuming, expensive, but ultimately futile project of making *The Life of Lu Xun* was demoralizing; it was also scandalizing. In 1964, Zhang Chunqiao 張春橋 (1917–2005), director of the Propaganda Department of the CCP Shanghai Committee, expressly pursued an investigation into the aborted production of *The Life of Lu Xun*. Some discontented staff members of the film studio reported to Zhang that half a million yuan had been spent on nothing but some star filmmakers' trips across the country and their luxury hotel rooms in various cities. The waste of resources was egregious, particularly in the severe economic hardship in the post-Leap era. Zhang, who had intended to utilize this debacle to attack Xia Yan, lambasted the filmmaking team of *The Life of Lu Xun* for being a "rotten" organization and compared it with the Petofi Circle—an intellectual movement in the mid-1950s that triggered the 1956 Hungarian Revolution—thereby equating the filmmakers with seditionist elements.[114]

Zhang's action against the team of *The Life of Lu Xun* constituted a vital part of a nationwide campaign to re-radicalize culture. In Zhuoyi Wang's analysis, with the assertion that the entire cultural bureaucracy had not followed party policies, Mao and dogmatic Maoists mounted a renewed attack on writers, filmmakers, and officials, paving the way for "a new revolutionary cycle, the Cultural Revolution."[115] In the film world, Xia Yan became the main target of a new round of political persecution. The re-radicalization of culture in the mid-1960s was a testimony to the intensification of the struggle between what Timothy Cheek calls "faith Maoism" and "bureaucratic Maoism" in the 1960s.[116] The campaign led by Zhang Chunqiao—an exemplary "faithful," or radical, Maoist—and his allies against Xia Yan, a bureaucratic Maoist, signaled the former's triumph over the latter, ultimately leading to the Cultural Revolution across the nation.

After Xia Yan, who had rewarded Zhao Dan with the full panoply of his patronage, fell out of the CCP's favor in 1964, Zhao's career began to spiral downward. In the following decade, Zhao was compelled to write a great number of confessions

---

112. Shen, *Xingyun liushui jiwang erji (xia)*, 371–74.
113. Wu Yigong 吳貽弓, *Shanghai dianying zhi* 上海電影志 [Chronicle of Shanghai film] (Shanghai: Shanghai shehui kexue chubanshe, 1999), 68.
114. Chen Shuyu 陳漱渝, "*Dazhong dianying* kandeng de yipian bushi zhi wen" 《大眾電影》刊登的一篇不實之文 [A misleading article published in *Mass Film*], *Lu Xun yanjiu dongtai* 魯迅研究動態 [The Trend of Studies on Lu Xun], no. 3 (1986): 8.
115. Wang, *Revolutionary Cycles in Chinese Cinema*, 150–51.
116. Timothy Cheek, *Propaganda and Culture in Mao's China: Deng Tuo and the Intelligentsia* (Oxford: Clarendon Press, 1997), 2.

on different occasions. Zhao made his first lengthy public confession on April 20, 1965. This confession was penned for the principal purpose of condemning his connection with Xia Yan since the 1930s. In so doing, Zhao deployed a tactic of self-denial and self-abnegation. First, he blamed Xia for selecting him to star in both *Lin Zexu* and *Nie Er*, two sensational anniversary movies that finally established Zhao's stardom in post-1949 China. Playing "ancient people" (*guren* 古人) and "dead people" (*siren* 死人) was at odds with Mao's call to represent the realities in the PRC, Zhao confessed. Second, he admitted that the trumpeting of his film accomplishments in the 1930s helped to serve Xia Yan's broader agenda of asserting the achievements of prerevolutionary Chinese filmmakers in contributing to the communist culture of the PRC, essentially negating the importance of cultural works produced in Yan'an. Third, Xia Yan's patronage had contributed to boosting Zhao's political status and reputation as an artist, further feeding his outsized ego. Zhao thus blamed himself for advocating absolute individualism and leading a corrupt way of life.[117]

Zhao Dan's self-criticism featured two crucial elements of a confession in the PRC: "the exposure and renunciation of past and present 'evil'" and the "re-education [and] the remaking of a man in the Communist image."[118] Like many who wrote confessions in Mao's China, Zhao Dan crafted his own by "guess[ing] what they really want[ed]."[119] In this case, "they"—the radical Maoists—wanted overwhelming evidence of Xia Yan's anti-party schemes. At this stage, Zhao Dan clearly harbored an intention to satisfy the party authorities and thereby extricate himself from the ongoing political maelstrom. Therefore, he drew up a strategy to "expose" the facts selectively. He ascribed all his "mistakes" to Xia Yan and unequivocally expressed his desire to sever ties with his former patron completely. Zhao also refrained from mentioning the Mao-initiated campaign against *The Life of Wu Xun*, his unerasable political stigma in post-1949 China, and kept silent on his imprisonment in Xinjiang in the early 1940s.[120] In this sense, he did not necessarily make a "false confession," as Robert Jay Lifton has observed, but merely made some real things "bigger" and simultaneously played down some others.[121]

For all his well-devised survival tactics in the mid-1960s, Zhao failed to weather this political firestorm. He was thrown into prison shortly after the Cultural Revolution broke out. Beginning in late 1967, Zhao was imprisoned for five years, during which time he was physically abused, mentally tortured, and, of course, forced to produce more confessions. Compared with the statement he made in 1965, which was more concerned with his "incorrect" artistic viewpoints, his decadent, bourgeois lifestyle, and his personal ties with Xia Yan, those written between

---

117. Shanghai Municipal Archives, B177-3-353, 3–37.
118. Lifton, *Thought Reform and the Psychology of Totalism*, 5.
119. Lifton, *Thought Reform and the Psychology of Totalism*, 41.
120. Shanghai Municipal Archives, B177-3-353, 34.
121. Lifton, *Thought Reform and the Psychology of Totalism*, 41–52.

1967 and 1973 more pointedly addressed his "crimes" in the past several decades in an attempt to meet the CCP authorities' demands. For example, he admitted in August 1971 that he had coauthored the "poisonous weed" (*ducao* 毒草) article "Night Talks beside the Hearth" with some "rightists" and "counterrevolutionaries" in order to launch a vicious attack on the party's cultural policies.[122] To respond to the campaign against Liu Shaoqi, the main target of the Cultural Revolution, Zhao confessed in 1973 that it was Liu Shaoqi's faction that had afforded him protection when *The Life of Wu Xun* came under scathing criticism nationwide. Moreover, Zhao seized the opportunity to join the party in 1957 because of Liu's suggestion, thereby tying together his and the former PRC chairman's "crimes" in a structured narrative.[123] Zhao Dan further testified that he had betrayed the CCP and later joined the Nationalist Party (GMD) during his five years in Xinjiang. As if he wished to aggravate the charge against himself, Zhao emphasized that he had never acknowledged that he had actually obtained GMD membership and thereby had kept lying to the CCP.[124]

In his confessions, Zhao parroted the castigatory language directed against him while weighing his words carefully. The sociologist Fei Xiaotong 費孝通 (1910–2005) recalled that he learned to borrow the wording and rhetoric from his critics to criticize himself in his own confessions.[125] Zhao deployed a similar tactic when, for example, he condemned himself for his role in the "scheme to debase Lu Xun." A booklet printed and released by Red Guards in 1967 had pointed the finger at Zhao for

> intentionally attacking, defaming, libeling, and debasing our great man of letters, revolutionist, and statesman Lu Xun in an attempt to . . . further oppose Chairman Mao's correct revolutionary line.[126]

In a confession penned in 1973, Zhao made a similar statement to chastise himself: "I . . . ran counter to Chairman Mao's . . . lofty appraisal of Mr. Lu Xun . . . and tampered with [his image] as a great proletarian hero. . . . That was my crime of distorting and smearing the image of the great Mr. Lu Xun."[127]

"Self-punitive tendencies" like those evidenced in Zhao's statements, according to Robert Jay Lifton, provided the writers with "pleasure from personal degradation." Producing self-disparaging confessions was an "opportunity for emotional catharsis and for the relief of suppressed guilt feelings."[128] In this sense, confession during political movements such as the Cultural Revolution was a tactic both for

---

122. Li, *Zhao Dan zishu*, 190–92.
123. Li, *Zhao Dan zishu*, 136, 173–78.
124. Li, *Zhao Dan zishu*, 121–28.
125. Fei Xiaotong 費孝通, *Wangshi chongchong* 往事重重 [The eventful past] (Shenyang: Liaoning jiaoyu chubanshe, 1998), 112.
126. *"Hunshi mowing"—Zhao Dan*, 4.
127. Li, *Zhao Dan zishu*, 178.
128. Lifton, *Thought Reform and the Psychology of Totalism*, 426.

finding temporary psychological relief and for seeking to alleviate physical torture by means of reconfirming the charges imposed upon them by the authorities. In some extreme cases, admitting or fabricating an aggravated charge and thereby demanding the severest punishment was a response to unbearable situations. When witnessing the release of many other inmates but not him, for example, the desperate Zhao Dan demanded immediate capital punishment in August 1970.[129] Despite his plea for a quick death, Zhao held tight to his bottom line: keeping his mouth shut about his once-close relationship with Madam Mao. Nowhere did Zhao mention Jiang Qing in any of his confessions, nor could the Red Guards find the faintest evidence of communication between the two.[130] It turned out that this bottom line was his best survival tactic and afforded him the opportunity to outlast the Cultural Revolution.

Conclusion

The modes of speech commonly used in communist regimes, including confessions, were not necessarily "lies, truths, or expressions of ideologies." As Botakoz Kassymbekova posits, they were "a ritual of loyalty" and "strategies" of both the rulers and the ruled.[131] Indeed, using highly formalized and ritualized language in confessions was an oft-deployed tactic to weather political storms in Mao's China. Throughout this chapter, I have shown that Zhao Dan kept adjusting his tactics to survive or thrive and minimize damage or maximize benefit when the political climate changed. He was a string-puller in favorable circumstances but a mouther of slogans and, above all, a survivor when faced with adversity. His newly acquired stardom in Mao-era China enabled him to outmuscle Chen Liting and, in no small part, led to the debacle of the making of *The Life of Lu Xun*. In this sense, Zhao's stardom bore a resemblance to what a film star in any given society is understood to possess: the ability to affect the "direction and production" of a film.[132] However, his glorified image as a superstar on the screen contrasted markedly with the sufferings inflicted upon him during the Cultural Revolution, reinforcing Zhao's martyrdom in the media narratives of post-Mao China.

My account of this film star's career thus helps explore the gap between Zhao's lived experiences in Mao's China and the more conventional narrative about Zhao that circulated in the post–Cultural Revolution era—as a victim and a dissident. Such a gap attests to Zhao Dan's biographers' unending search for "an appropriate [version of Zhao] according to their current concerns."[133] As Alexei Yurchak's study

---

129. Li, *Zhao Dan zishu*, 116–17.
130. Li, *Zhao Dan zishu*, 100.
131. Botakoz Kassymbekova, *Despite Cultures: Early Soviet Rule in Tajikistan* (Pittsburgh: University of Pittsburgh Press, 2016), 4–9.
132. Yu, "Vulnerable Chinese Stars," 222.
133. Zhao, "From Singing Girl to Revolutionary Artist," 168.

on late-Soviet society indicates, it was in such a narrative that a range of binaries—say, "oppression and resistance" and "repression and freedom"—gained currency.[134] Such artificially constructed binaries, however, shed little light on individuals' lived experiences under socialism. Therefore, I argue that the story of Zhao Dan's vicissitudes in Mao's China is by no means one about a film star's accommodation with or resistance to the party's domination because his stardom did not exist a priori but was instead the product of the politico-cultural conditions in post-1949 China. Although there is no denying that Zhao had been a prominent star before 1949, it was during the PRC era that he gained access to a broader audience in a newly integrated national market and had his prestige enhanced in a quantifiable (his status "ranking" and remuneration) and, therefore, more tangible way. Hence, Zhao Dan's story is an account of how he fashioned and refashioned himself to "work the system" to serve his best interest via his interactions with party authorities, his colleagues, and the audience, within widely recognized—albeit unspoken—limits.

---

134. Yurchak, *Everything Was Forever, Until It Was No More*, 6.

3
"Putting New Wine into Old Bottles"
Sun Yu's Filmic Career in Post-1949 China

Like Zhao Dan, Sun Yu, one of China's second-generation directors, was a principal victim of the national campaign against *The Life of Wu Xun* in the early 1950s. Although he managed to escape political persecution after submitting a 300-word confession,[1] Sun, unlike Zheng Junli, would not gain recognition from the CCP authorities in the decades to follow. Throughout the 1950s and 1960s, Sun was assigned to make only three relatively little-known films, *Brave the Wind and Waves* (1957), *The Tale of Lu Ban* (*Lu Ban de chuanshuo* 魯班的傳說, 1958), and *Qin Niangmei* (*Qin Niangmei* 秦娘美, 1960), and failed to restore his reputation as a first-tier director. In Ding Yaping's 丁亞平 words, such a preeminent director was no longer "a hero able to galvanize the audiences" in post-1949 China.[2] Sun's falling out of favor of the party and slipping into obscurity hence exemplify the marginalization of the second-generation directors, arguably "the cream of Shanghai film's 'golden era.'"[3] Tony Ryans hails the second-generation directors as the "highest achievers" in pre-1949 China because of their "talent, energy, imagination and ingenuity." Nevertheless, after 1949, many of them were consigned to tragic fates amid numerous political campaigns.[4]

The dominant narrative—in both biographies/memoirs and scholarly research published after the late 1970s—about the CCP's total suppression of old-generation filmmakers, politically as well as artistically, has been highly influential. Taiwan-based film critic Ch'en Hui-yang 陳輝揚 argues that Sun lost touch with everyday life during PRC times, and, therefore, his productions after 1949 paled in comparison with those before 1949.[5] Most historians and critics are similarly under

---

1. "Sun Yu shi shenme huose" 孫瑜是什麼貨色 [What on earth is Sun Yu], *Hongqi zhanbao* 紅旗戰報 [Red flag Battlefield Report], no. 6 (1967): 8.
2. Ding Yaping 丁亞平, *Zai lishi de bianji* 在歷史的邊際 [On the margins of history] (Beijing: Beijing shidai huawen shuju, 2015), 370.
3. Gina Marchetti, "Two Stage Sisters: The Blossoming of a Revolutionary Aesthetic," in *Transnational Chinese Cinemas: Identity, Nationhood, Gender*, ed. Sheldon Hsiao-peng Lu (Honolulu: University of Hawai'i Press, 1997), 60.
4. Tony Ryans, "The Second Generation," in *Electric Shadows: A Century of Chinese Cinema*, ed. James Bell (London: British Film Institute, 2014), 16–18.
5. Chen Huiyang (Ch'en Hui-yang 陳輝揚), *Mengying ji: Zhongguo dianying yinxiang* 夢影集：中國電影印象 [Anthology of dream and shadow: An impression on Chinese film] (Taipei: Yuncheng wenhua, 1990), 43.

the impression that Sun, unfortunately, sank into oblivion because of the lack of job opportunities in the 1950s and 1960s. Most intriguingly, Jay Leyda erroneously stated in his seminal work, *Dianying*, that he could find "no record of Sun Yu working again after the mistakes of Wu Hsun [*The Life of Wu Xun*]."[6] Some scholars even assert that, artistically, Sun had "died" in Mao-era China as the campaign against *The Life of Wu Xun* dealt him a huge blow.[7] Assertions made by Leyda and other scholars thus indicate the total obscurity of the three films directed by this experienced and reputed director during the PRC era, particularly *Brave the Wind and Waves*, another of Sun's controversial films in the 1950s.

This chapter focuses on *Brave the Wind and Waves* and Sun Yu's career in Mao's China. It highlights Sun's tactic to carve out a niche for himself in the world of film in the 1950s and tackle an identity crisis faced by all second-generation directors despite the lingering trauma he went through during the campaign of criticizing *The Life of Wu Xun*. The tactic, I argue, was "putting new wine into old bottles"—or his recourse to the familiar filmic techniques to make a film to eulogize the new sociopolitical system and the new citizenry in the PRC. To this end, Sun wholeheartedly devoted himself to producing *Brave the Wind and Waves* in 1957, to glorify China's first-generation women steamship navigators. The movie centers on Liang Ying 梁瓔 (Huang Yin 黃音) and two other female apprentices who have freshly graduated from a professional school and initially work as trainees on *The People 91* (*Renmin 91 hao* 人民91號). After overcoming all the barriers, including the captain's blatant discrimination against women, Liang is promoted as third mate within fifteen months, establishing a record in the nation. Meanwhile, Liang and her colleague Ma Jun 馬駿 (Zhongshu Huang 中叔皇 [1925–2005]) pledge their love to each other because of their shared commitment to building socialism in China.

Although this movie has been dismissed as formulaic, bland, and lacking the unique attractiveness that defines most of Sun Yu's pre-1949 films, attesting to the director's loss of his creativity,[8] *Brave the Wind and Waves* allowed Sun to experiment with a new film genre—"lyric comedy" (*shuqing xiju* 抒情喜劇), or "light comedy" (*qing xiju* 輕喜劇). Representing the realities in a light-hearted and humorous way did not considerably deviate from Sun's longstanding directorial style, for he had already emphasized his films' entertainment in the past several decades.[9] For Sun and many other directors in China who "rediscovered" comedy in 1957 and 1958, comedy provided a necessary means to illustrate a peaceful day-to-day life in the PRC without the "dramatic tension" usually seen in revolutionary and war films.[10] Although the revival of comedy in the mid- and late 1950s

---

6. Leyda, *Dianying*, 223.
7. Chen Mo 陳墨, *Yingtan jiuzong* 影壇舊蹤 [The trace in the past in the world of film] (Nanchang: Jiangxi jiaoyu chubanshe, 2000), 95.
8. Chen, *Mengying ji*, 72.
9. Sun, *Yinghai fanzhou*, 229.
10. Clark, *Chinese Cinema*, 65.

has been hailed as one of the few impressive accomplishments achieved during the Hundred Flowers Campaign,[11] scholars studying satirical comedy films and their political implications usually ignore *Brave the Wind and Waves*, in no small part because this film and Sun Yu did not officially face the CCP's political persecution in the 1950s. In comparison with satirical comedy, however, light comedy, which focused on the contradictions between "the advanced" and the "backward" political thoughts in socialist China but not on the violent clashes between the CCP and its foes,[12] would gain steam in the following decade. As this film's cameraman noted that light comedy as a genre was rare in the 1950s,[13] it would prevail in the early 1960s with the release of a number of popular and award-winning productions, such as *Li Shuangshuang* (*Li Shuangshuang* 李雙雙, dir. Lu Ren 魯韌, 1962). In this sense, *Brave the Wind and Waves* was a trailblazer in the PRC's film history. Sun thus succeeded in brewing "new wine"—light comedy—with his "old bottles"—his recognition of film as entertainment as well as a means of moral inculcation.

To give a vivid portrayal of the heroines and champion new womanhood in this historical age, Sun Yu refocused on women's images as he did in many of his 1930s films. Back in the 1930s, Sun had already earned a reputation for modeling his works after those of Josef von Sternberg (1894–1969) and turning his attention to women on the screen.[14] In a string of films in this decade, Sun endeavored to find an eclectic way to combine the "modern consciousness of patriotism with traditional strengths of Chinese women—wisdom, self-sacrifice, care, and endurance."[15] The same formula was still valid in *Brave the Wind and Waves*, in which women's self-sacrifice and perseverance enabled them to make contributions to China's socialist modernization.

The specific type of womanhood Sun Yu had established on the screen sometimes entailed displaying young women's bodies. Therefore, when treating the female body in *Brave the Wind and Waves*, Sun's tactic of putting new wine into old bottles seemed a little awkward. Paul Pickowicz argues that Sun's heroines in some of his films before 1949 radiated "a natural, spontaneous sexuality."[16] Although Sun similarly tried to exhibit women's bodies in the very beginning of *Brave the Wind and Waves*, as this chapter will show, he quickly relinquished the strategy of linking women's sexual appeal to China's modernity and subscribed to the "degendering" (*qu xingbie hua* 去性別化) approach in the remaining portion of the film. After all, as Chris Berry posits, the "viewing subject" in the PRC was not expected to

---

11. Clark, "Two Hundred Flowers on China's Screens," 75.
12. Sun, *Yinghai fanzhou*, 228.
13. Dai Weiyu 戴維宇, "Manyi wozhe 50 nian" 漫憶我這50年 [Random memories of fifty years in my life], in *Suiyue shibei* 歲月拾貝 [Collecting treasure in history], ed. Wang Xijian 王晞建 (Beijing: Zhongguo guangbo dianshi chubanshe, 2002), 253.
14. Ryans, "The Second Generation," 21.
15. Yihong Pan, "Crafting the 'New Woman' in China's Left-Wing Cinema of the 1930s: Sun Yu's Three Films," *Frontier of History in China* 6, no. 2 (2011): 279.
16. Pickowicz, *China on Film*, 52.

be "engaged in libidinally." Instead, the relationship between the camera (and, by extension, the viewers) and the female protagonist was supposed to be between the parent and the "unmarried daughter."[17] Despite this, *Brave the Wind and Waves* would soon come under criticism in the late 1950s for "lacking warm feelings toward the working class" and having "old, petit-bourgeois tendencies."[18] After the failures of his first two films released in PRC times, Suns' quest for his subjectivity as a worthy director and a contributor to the CCP's socialist cause failed.

The Storyline

Brave the Wind and Waves begins with the commencement at Chaoshan Advanced Navigation School (*Chaoshan gaoji shangchuan jishu xuexiao* 潮汕高級商船技術學校), from which the poorly disciplined female protagonists, Liang Ying and her classmates, are initially absent. They struggle to paddle a boat on the ocean when the ceremony starts and, therefore, are late for it. After graduation, the three are sent to work in Shanghai as trainees. Touring the bank of Huangpu River (*Huangpu jiang* 黃浦江), Liang Ying happens to see an inexperienced sailor falling into the river from the steamship *The People 91*. While Liang volunteers to save the young man from drowning, she comes under fire from Ma Jun, the boatswain, and Captain Zhao (Zhang Yi 張翼 [1909–1983]) for her excessive boldness. It turns out that *The People 91* is the three young women's designated workplace during their internship. For all his rich work experience and superb navigation skill, Captain Zhao has a deep-rooted prejudice against women: he believes that a male apprentice will have to spend at least eight or nine years mastering necessary skills, and the three young women's vow to become competent navigators in a short period, therefore, seems absurd.

On *The People 91*, the three female trainees kick in their new careers. Like their male colleagues, they engage in physical labor, such as pulling mooring ropes and cleaning the deck. Meanwhile, they learn nautical theories and practices day in and day out. Under the help of the party committee, the three young women manage to complete their internship in merely eight months. As the other two girls are transferred elsewhere, Liang Ying stays on *The People 91*. On one occasion, the ailing Liang attempts to steer the steamship through a difficult waterway but sends the wrong instruction. Captain Zhao thus gives her a severe reprimand. Stressed out and exhausted, Liang faints and then suffers from a high fever for a few days. On her sickbed, Liang is heard mumbling nautical terms in her somniloquy. Liang's professionalism deeply touches Political Commissar Li 李 and Captain Zhao, who

---

17. Chris Berry and Mary Farquhar, *China on Screen: Cinema and Nation* (New York: Columbia University Press, 2006), 110–13.
18. Clark, *Chinese Cinema*, 78.

are escorting the patient in the cabin. Meanwhile, the boatswain begins to show his admiration for the female protagonist's perseverance.

Liang Ying passes the test several months later and becomes the third mate. During the Labor Day break, the three women reunite in Wuhan. They put on their uniforms to participate in the celebratory procession and go to the party together. On that day, Liang Ying rejects the first mate's courtship attempt, for she despises this man's selfishness and lack of passion for work. Finally, she establishes a romantic relationship with Ma Jun, the boatswain, because of their shared political beliefs and convictions. At the end of the movie, Liang Ying is promoted to second mate and proudly becomes one of the first-generation female steamship navigators in post-1949 China.

The Production of the Film

The prototype of *The People 91* was the steamship *The People 9* (*Renmin 9 hao* 人民 9號), on which director Sun Yu and his colleagues spent nineteen days observing the everyday life and routine work of the crew on board. According to Sun, he was keenly interested in *The People 9* because of an essay he happened to read:

> I read the essays published in the fifth issue of *New Chinese Women* (*Xin Zhongguo funü* 新中國婦女) about Lin Youhua 林幼華, the first woman [steamship] navigator on the Yangzi River, in June and July 1955. [I] was deeply moved by the protagonist's fearlessness of difficulties and tenacious efforts. I believed that [the story about Lin] was a superb example of how our socialist country trains and educates the new generation.[19]

What impressed Sun most was his observation that "women had the same rights as men to take part in building the socialist country" in post-Liberation China. Hence, Sun immediately reached a decision to turn to the form of the motion picture to "create artistic images" of women who were growing up in this new society and to fulfill the goal of propagating patriotism in China.[20]

During his nineteen days on *The People 9*, Sun Yu met crew members with diverse personalities and backgrounds. Among them, Lin Youhua, a female third mate, left him with the most profound impression. Sun remembered Lin as a "frank and straightforward" young woman. Her short stature was contrasted with the tremendous enthusiasm and vigor she displayed in the workplace. This energetic and ambitious navigator typified China's first-generation female professionals and lent Sun inspiration for a new movie. Lin wound up becoming the prototype for

---

19. Sun Yu 孫瑜, "Jiangshang xing—chuangzuo *Chengfeng polang* xia shenghuo suiji" 江上行—創作《乘風破浪》下生活隨記 [Travelling on the river—Random notes on experiencing the lives of (the ship's crew) to make *Brave the Wind and Waves*], *Dazhong dianying* 大眾電影 [Mass Film], no. 9 (1957): 26.
20. Sun "Jiangshang xing," 26.

Liang Ying, the film's protagonist.[21] Huang Yin, who was to portray Liang Ying, was assigned to partner with Lin Youhua on *The People 19* during the nineteen days. Huang described Lin as a "third mate with a talent to amuse people and who was even a little bit chattering." Lin appeared uncharacteristically solemn and composed despite her brisk personality when she was at the helm.[22] In a similar fashion, Zhongshu Huang, the performer of the male protagonist, not only made friends on the steamship but also learned navigation skills and relished the opportunity to operate the ship.[23]

During the nineteen days on *The People 9*, Sun Yu was seriously contemplating drafting a screenplay. In two weeks after returning to Shanghai, Sun finished writing it under the title "Brave the Wind and Waves" and had it printed out. The Shanghai Film Bureau quickly gave the nod before Jiangnan Film Studio approved it.[24] The shortness of time to walk through the entire approval process was unprecedented. In comparison, the filmmakers of *Song Jingshi*, which was released in the same year, spent four long and grueling years making, revising, and remaking the movie, as the first chapter has shown. Without a doubt, Sun's project was easily given the green light because of the favorable policies toward intellectuals and the Hundred Flowers Movement.[25] In this new political climate, topics on everyday life, human nature, and romantic love gained renewed legitimacy in the productions of film studios nationwide.[26] The relatively mild politico-cultural policies also allowed filmmakers across the country to voluntarily form workgroups for the purpose of speeding up shooting movies. In Shanghai, for example, Shi Hui, Xu Changlin 徐昌霖 (1916–2001), Xie Jin, and other two directors created the "Society for Five Flowers" (*Wuhua she* 五花社).[27] The two directors of *Brave the Wind and Waves*, Sun Yu and Jiang Junchao 蔣君超 (1912–1991), belonged to another filmmaking group, the "Society for Five Elders" (*Wulao she* 五老社). Shen Ji 沈寂 (1924–2016), a screenplay writer and Sun's colleague, believed that making such a film was not Sun Yu's top priority at the outset. However, Jiang Junchao insisted on assisting Sun in completing the movie in order to motivate Sun, who had endured heavy pressure

---

21. Sun, "Jiangshang xing," 26.
22. Huang Yin 黃音, "Yiye riji" 一頁日記 [One page of a diary], *Dazhong dianying* 大眾電影 [Mass Film], no. 9 (1957): 28.
23. Zhongshu Huang 中叔皇, "Zai 'Minzhu jiuhao' lun shang" 在"民主九號"輪上 [On *The People 9*], 大眾電影 [Mass Film], no. 9 (1957): 27.
24. Sun, *Yinhai fanzhou*, 227.
25. Meng Liye 孟犁野, *Xin Zhongguo dianying yishu shi, 1949–1965* 新中國電影藝術史 1949–1965 [A history of film in new China, 1949–1965] (Beijing: Zhongguo dianying chubanshe, 2011), 12.
26. Jin Danyuan 金丹元, *Xin Zhongguo dianying meixue shi, 1949–2009* 新中國電影美學史 1949–2009 [A history of film aesthetics in new China, 1949–2009] (Beijing: Shenghuo dushu xinzhi sanlian shudian, 2013).
27. Zhongguo dianying nianjian she 中國電影年鑑社 [The publishing house for the Chinese film yearbook], *Zhongguo dianying nianjian 2002* 中國電影年鑑2002 [Chinese film yearbook, 2002] (Beijing: Zhongguo dianying nianjian she, 2002), 292.

following the debacle of the campaign against *The Life of Wu Xun*. Jiang's purpose was to help Sun "stage a comeback on the silver screen."[28]

Under those circumstances, Sun Yu garnered enormous support on different levels, and the film studio's growing willingness to shore up Sun's project decidedly altered the director's plan. The existing archival records show that Jiangnan Film Studio finally made a decision to change the film's nature from an "artistic film" (*yishu pian* 藝術片) to a feature film.[29] Although Sun Yu kept silent about such an alteration in his memoir, it is conceivable that his original plan was to make the movie a "documentary artistic film" (*jilu xing yishu pian* 記錄性藝術片), a film genre blending fiction and fact to represent the PRC's socialist cause. In the final years of the 1950s, such "documentary artistic films," which were usually short and entailed inconsiderable production time and small financial investment, would gain currency in the next three years to propagate the Great Leap Forward spirit on the screen. *The Evergreen Tree* (directed by Zhao Dan), as shown in Chapter 2, could fall into the category of the "documentary artistic film." Compared with a regular feature film, a "documentary artistic film" usually requires a modest budget and a notoriously short production cycle: "only two or three days to prepare."[30] Hence, it is understandable that the dramatic change to the project postponed its making. In consequence, the filming began on May 8, 1957, instead of April 1957, as had initially been planned.[31]

The film's growing importance also manifested itself in another crucial decision made by the studio at its preparatory stage: upgrading the movie from a black-and-white film to a color one.[32] Considering China's heavy reliance on imported foreign-made film stocks in this period, getting color films had long been a bottleneck in film production in China. In 1957, the three film studios in Shanghai released only four-color films in total.[33] By making *Brave the Wind and Wave*, Sun Yu thus grasped the once-in-a-lifetime opportunity to produce his only color film in his long and productive directorial career. The film studio's investment in purchasing Agfa B334 film stocks from East Germany vastly raised the cost of this movie[34] but sent an unmistakable signal that Sun Yu, an esteemed veteran but a highly controversial

---

28. Shen Ji 沈寂, *Zuoye xingcheng—wo yanzhong de yingren pengyou* 昨夜星辰——我眼中的影人朋友 [Yestreen's stars: Friends in the world of film in my eyes] (Shanghai: Shanghai renmin chubanshe, 2005), 197.
29. Shanghai Municipal Archives, B177-3-129, 11.
30. Matthew D. Johnson, "Cinema and Propaganda during the Great Leap Forward," in *Visualizing Modern China: Image, History, and Memory, 1750–Present*, ed. James A. Cook, Joshua Goldstein, Matthew D. Johnson, and Sigrid Schmalzer (Lanham, MD: Lexington Books, 2014), 205.
31. Shanghai Municipal Archives, B177-3-129, 11.
32. Liangkai 良凱, "'Chengfeng polang' gaipai caishe yingpian" "乘風破浪" 改拍彩色影片 [*Brave the Wind and Waves* will be shot as a color film], *Xinmin wanbao* 新民晚報 [Xinmin Evening News], May 5, 1957.
33. The other three were *City without Night* (Buye cheng 不夜城, dir. Tang Xiaodan 湯曉丹), *Chen San and Wuniang* (Chen San Wuniang 陳三五娘, dir. Yang Xiaozhong 楊小仲), and *Woman Basketball Player No. 5* (*Nülan wuhao* 女籃五號, dir. Xie Jin).
34. Shanghai Municipal Archives, B177-3-131, 1.

figure in the circles of filmmakers since the 1930s, had won the CCP cadres' vote of confidence at this point.[35]

The full support Sun Yu enlisted posed a new challenge. Despite his rich experience in shooting films, Sun was a neophyte in making color films. In August 1957, when the movie's rushes came under review in the film studio, the reviewers were largely critical of its lighting, color, and film exposure. For example, one reviewer stated, "In some shots, the light on the figures' faces is too bright, causing the loss of texture in highlighted [areas] and color distortion." Another critic noted, "The performers' faces are given overly bright light, while the furniture in the rooms is dark brown and purple in color. The choice of deep colors [for the furniture] creates a stark contrast to [the characters]." It was then concluded that either the quality of the film stocks or poorly executed makeup led to the overexposure of human faces in the movie.[36] Furthermore, making a color film raised safety concerns. For example, shooting the scene of the fire outbreak to vividly represent the boatswain's heroics in saving his colleagues from the fire proved far more dangerous and challenging in a color film than in a black-and-white one. Both directors on the spot reportedly appeared to be seized with anxiety and fear when the fire scene was filmed.[37]

Albeit with such technical difficulties, the crew managed to summon up the immense enthusiasm of various local governments. In Wuhan, for example, the governmental officials mobilized over 1,000 populace actors and actresses, as opposed to 100 or 200 as initially proposed, for an episode about the Labor Day parade. Of these, 500 were in the uniform of sailors. Other populace actors and actresses hailed from the local Beijing opera troupe, Hubei opera (*Chuju* 楚劇) troupe, and a drama academy. The opportunity to traverse thousands of miles across China and the upgrading of filmic technologies, particularly color film, enabled Sun Yu and his comrades to visually present to the audience the natural and cultural sceneries in different parts of China as well as the socialist industrialization campaign. In this sense, *Brave the Wind and Waves* also functioned as a "scenic film" (*fengguang pian* 風光片), highlighting the picturesque views of the Yangzi River between Wusong 吳淞 and Chongqing. For the filmmakers, the scenery of the Three Gorges (*Sanxia* 三峽) evoked poetic and philosophic sensibilities.[38] Meanwhile, it continued to play a role as a documentary and a propaganda work, as it succeeded in archiving the realities in post-1949 China. For example, the film provided the national audience with first-hand visual information about the ongoing construction of the Wuhan

---

35. Meng, *Xin Zhongguo dianying yishu shi, 1949–1965*, 171.
36. Shanghai Municipal Archives, B177-3-131, 1.
37. Zhong Shu 鍾恕, "Caise gushi pian *Chengfeng polang* shezhi fengguang" 彩色故事片《乘風破浪》攝製風光 [Anecdotes of the shooting of *Brave the Wind and Waves*, the color feature film], *Dazhong dianying* 大眾電影 [Mass Film], no. 23 (1957): 34.
38. Minyi 民宜, "*Chengfeng polang* waijing rizhi pianduan" 《乘風破浪》外景日誌片段 [Selected daily records about location shooting of *Brave the Wind and Waves*], *Dazhong dianying* 大眾電影 [Mass Film], no. 15 (1957): 26–27.

Yangzi River Bridge (*Wuhan Changjiang daqiao* 武漢長江大橋).[39] The bridge and the worksite struck a chord with Sun to such a degree that he stated four years later that the completion of this bridge evidenced the people's capacity to "become the real master of nature" in a socialist society.[40]

Criticisms and Reevaluation

As the director and playwright of *Brave the Wind and Waves*, Sun Yu set two goals to glorify the new citizenry in socialism and exhibit China's scenic beauty to the entire world. For the filmmakers, the enchanting beauty displayed in the movie was a product of at once nature, modern technology, and traditional Chinese culture, especially poetry. This nature-technology-culture matrix gave rise to a specific aesthetic feeling, "techno-poetics," as Corey Byrnes calls it. In Byrnes's analysis, as the poetic shaped humans' experiences in the natural world, technology was capable of bringing into being the poetic in the real world in post-1949 China.[41] In other words, it was the modern technologies of navigating and regulating the Yangzi River that allowed the crew to tour the Three Gorges, where the sensibilities expressed only in Tang poems were elicited and concretized. In an essay about their experiences in the Three Gorges when shooting the film, the writer emphatically articulated a poetic feeling of "people touring in a [landscape] painting" (*ren zai huazhong you* 人在畫中遊).[42] The ethos pervading the film, hence, reconfirming Sun's peculiar style of the "lyric and poetic film" he had developed back in the 1930s, for which he earned the appellation "poet-director" (*shiren daoyan* 詩人導演).[43]

Nevertheless, this highly personalized style, which underscored a poetic temperament that transcended everyday life, came under criticism even in the 1930s.[44] After 1949, the political authorities dismissively interpreted Sun's insistence on his style as a "failure to meet the ideological and artistic demands of the times and . . . inability to accumulate knowledge about the life in the new [society]."[45] The heaviest blow dealt Sun and his *Brave the Wind and Waves* was the publication of Chen Huangmei's article, "Resolutely Wrench Out the White Flags on the Silver Screen—A Critique of Wrong Ideological Tendencies in Films Produced in 1957" (*Jianjue ba diao yinmu shang de baiqi—1957 nian dianying yishupianzhong cuowu sixiang qingxiang de pipan* 堅決拔掉銀幕上的白旗—1957年電影藝術片中錯誤思想傾向的批判), in which the author pointed a finger at *Brave the Wind and Waves* and other films as follows:

---

39. Sun, *Yinhai fanzhou*, 230.
40. Shanghai Municipal Archives, C44-2-227, 235.
41. Corey Byrnes, *Fixing Landscape: A Techno-Poetic History of China's Three Gorges* (New York: Columbia University Press, 2019), 21.
42. Minyi, "*Chengfeng polang* waijing rizhi pianduan," 26.
43. Meng, *Xin Zhongguo dianying yishu shi, 1949–1965*, 171.
44. Chen, *Yingtan jiuzong*, 95.
45. Shanghai Municipal Archives, A22-2-1233, 95–96.

> The filmmakers focus only [the protagonists'] personal success and downplay the support and empowerment given by the Party organizations and leadership. [The filmmakers] even mistake unhealthy work styles and incorrect leadership as positive elements and present them [in the films]. Therefore, the images of Party members and leaders shown on the silver screen appear bland and dull or even crude, stubborn, or unreasonable.[46]

According to contemporary film reviewers, "personal success" was akin to "individualistic heroism," a marked characteristic of Sun Yu's 1930s films.[47] Meanwhile, Captain Zhao's initial prejudice against women could well corroborate Chen Huangmei's finding that filmmakers tended to portray CCP cadres in a negative light. Chen Huangmei resumed his criticism of those movies:

> [All those films] show one shared tendency, that is, trying everything to resurrect, display, and promote sentiments of the petty bourgeoisie and the capitalist class. ... This indeed reveals those filmmakers' ignorance of the Party line as well as their lack of enthusiasm for portraying the Party's activities and struggles.[48]

Chen's comment was consistent with the overall assessment of Sun Yu given by the Jiangnan Film Studio's authorities even before the essay was published: "[Sun] is insensitive to new matters and holds unimpressive [and outdated] political views."[49] In a separate report, Sun and other second-generation directors were charged with "falling behind the times, politically and artistically, ... and lacking an adequate understanding and accumulated knowledge of the new life."[50]

To respond to Chen Huangmei's critical article, Shanghai-based filmmakers, including many of Sun Yu's colleagues at Jiangnan Film Studio, convened in December 1958, further denouncing what Chen had labeled "white-flag" films. During the meeting, Sun had to speak publicly to offer a self-criticism:

> Although [I] have tried my best to depict the new life and new figures, I'm not familiar with the thoughts and feelings of the working class. Therefore, I usually *adopt the old ways* ... In the film, [I] fail to [correctly] illustrate the maturity of an educated young woman after she starts her career. Rather, [I] focus on her self-realization, highlighting [the theme] of individualistic heroism.[51]

In the same meeting, Sun's critics took issue with *Brave the Wind and Waves*:

---

46. Chen, "Jianjue badiao yinmu shang de baiqi."
47. Chen, *Yingtan jiuzong*, 95.
48. Chen, "Jianjue badiao yinmu shang de baiqi."
49. Shanghai Municipal Archives, A22-2-1478, 94.
50. Shanghai Municipal Archives, A22-2-1233, 95–96.
51. "Zai dianying chuangzuo zhong gaoju zhengzhi shuaiqi, jianchi gongnongbing wenyi fangxiang" 在電影創作中高舉政治帥旗，堅持工農兵文藝方向 [(We must) hoist the commander's flag of politics and adhere to the focus of literary and artistic creations for the workers, peasants, and soldiers], *Dazhong dianying* 大眾電影 [Mass Film], no. 12 (1958): 21. My italics.

When handling romantic love, [the film] is accused of instituting a bourgeois [filmmaking practice] of 'resorting to love to redeem a weak plot' and mistakenly transplanting the petty-bourgeois mode of romantic love into the workers, peasants, and soldiers.[52]

In various meetings organized by the Shanghai Film Bureau in the late 1950s, the film continued to be subjected to attacks from Sun Yu's fellow filmmakers. Director Gao Heng 高衡 (1917–1978) commented that the movie left the audience with the impression that the young generation in post-1949 China failed to garner support from the party and had to strive to realize individual capacities and talents. A female playwright dismissed the portrayal of the love story as "vulgar." Even worse, the boatswain, the film's male protagonist, consistently exuded a tone of melancholy and depression, the typical petty-bourgeoise sensibilities. The critics blamed Sun for having fabricated the details of the everyday life of the working-class members. For example, when Liang Ying is delirious with fever halfway through the movie, she clasps Political Commissar Li's head tightly as if it was a steering wheel. As Sun had meant to highlight such episodes to make the movie a light comedy, some reviewers considered it blasphemy against the party leadership.[53]

Aside from the film itself, Sun Yu's personality came under criticism. One of Sun's coworkers charged him for being "a dictator when making the film by demanding [his team members'] absolute submission."[54] In the context of the Hundred Flowers Movement earlier in the mid-1950s, this comment could be interpreted to embody "director-centeredness," a highly controversial filmmaking principle that had pitted quite a large number of film directors against CCP cadres since 1956. It was Sun Yu who initially called for recognizing the directors' central role in the entire process of producing films by comparing directors to the "commander-in-chief of the army" (*sanjun tongshuai* 三軍統帥) in late 1956 and early 1957.[55] At the height of the Anti-Rightist Movement, director-centeredness was condemned as an anti-CCP artistic scheme, resulting in the persecution of many esteemed filmmakers.[56] Fortunately, Sun Yu, the originator of this principle, did not personally receive punishment. The party leadership in Beijing tended to focus on *Brave the Wind and Waves*, not Sun Yu as a filmmaker, during the campaign against the "white-flag" movies. The higher authorities evidently harbored no intention to penalize Sun. Lu Dingyi 陸定一 (1906–1996), then-Minister of Culture, for example, believed that *Brave the Wind and Waves* erred merely on the side of being overly optimistic and therefore unrealistic: it was never possible for an apprentice to gain promotion to be

---

52. "Zai dianying chuangzuo zhong gaoju zhengzhi shuaiqi," 21.
53. Shanghai Municipal Archives, B177-3-333, 20–21.
54. Shanghai Municipal Archives, A23-2-1409, 120–21.
55. Sun Yu 孫瑜, "Zunzhong dianying de yishu chuantong" 尊重電影的歷史傳統 [Respect film's historical tradition], *Wenhui bao* 文匯報 [Wenhui Daily], November 11, 1956.
56. Xu Sangchu 徐桑楚, *Tabian qingshan ren weilao* 踏遍青山人未老 [Crossing all mountains adds nothing to my years] (Beijing: Zhongguo dianying chubanshe, 2006), 157.

"Putting New Wine into Old Bottles" 77

a third mate in fifteen months.⁵⁷ The kind words uttered by Minister Lu, who had been known for his hostility towards Chinese intellectuals and artists,⁵⁸ testify to the party's flexible attitude towards Sun and his work and thereby helped the director avoid further political persecution.

In all fairness, overstating the female protagonist's accomplishments was consistent with the zeitgeist of the ongoing Great Leap Forward Movement. Therefore, *Brave the Wind and Waves* would not be labeled an anti-CCP movie. For all the pressure Sun Yu had to withstand, the film differed fundamentally from the ill-fated *The Life of Wu Xun* in that it was not openly and officially banned.⁵⁹ More importantly, the criticisms leveled against the film, in most cases, remained confidential and were never disclosed to the general public.⁶⁰ Under those circumstances, the fate of the film was intriguing. As it was not outright pulled out from theaters, its distributors took the initiative to remind the prospective audiences of the political errors the movie might have committed. Some cinemas handed out "film synopses" (*dianying shuomingshu* 電影說明書), in which excerpts of some critical essays on this film were printed. This unauthorized action against Sun Yu and his film dreadfully upset this seasoned director.⁶¹ Even the movie's earliest vocal critic, Chen Huangmei, felt unsettled by the ludicrousness of such counterpropaganda:

> Putting up big-character posters in front of movie theaters and printing critical essays in the film synopses are like carrying a loudspeaker in a bookstore and telling [the customers] that a certain book is toxic because it's full of errors.⁶²

In comparison with its chaotic marketing domestically in China, *Brave the Wind and Waves* won widespread acclaim internationally. As a light comedy that displayed a vibrant socialist society in China and the picturesque landscape along the Yangzi River, the movie was exported to various foreign countries twenty times. It merits mentioning that *Liang Shanbo and Zhu Yingtai* (*Liang Shanbo yu Zhu Yingtai* 梁山伯與祝英台, 1954, dir. Sang Hu 桑弧 [1916–2004] and Huang Sha 黃沙 [1919–1988]), a path-breaking opera film that altered the image of not only the Chinese motion picture but also the newly born PRC in the international arena, was sold to merely twenty-three foreign distributors. As a matter of fact, *Brave the Wind and Waves* was behind only three films, including *Liang Shanbo and Zhu Yingtai* and *Woman Basketball Player No. 5* (*Nülan wuhao* 女籃五號, 1957, dir. Xie Jin), and

---

57. Shanghai Municipal Archives, A23-2-1409, 123.
58. Lu Dingyi was deemed a hardliner because of his opposition to pardoning the Rightists in the early 1960s. See Chen Xiaonong 陳曉農, *Chen Boda zuihou koushu huiyi* 陳伯達最後口述回憶 [Final oral memoirs of Chen Boda] (Hong Kong: Xingke'er chuban youxian gongsi, 2005), 2257.
59. *The Chronicle of Film in Shanghai* (*Shanghai dianying zhi* 上海電影志) presumes that the movie was banned because of Kang Sheng's 康生 (1898–1975) interventions, but the ban had never been issued. See Wu, *Shanghai dianying zhi*, 209.
60. Meng, *Xin Zhongguo dianying yishu shi, 1949–1965*, 172.
61. Shanghai Municipal Archives, A22-2-1045, 6.
62. Shanghai Municipal Archives, B177-1-21, 177.

surpassed all other blockbuster productions, such as the two anniversary films (*Lin Zexu* and *Nie Er*), in numbers released to the international market in the 1950s.⁶³

In July 1962, when the political climate turned again, the Minister of Culture proceeded to reevaluate many controversial films, including *Brave the Wind and Waves*, and encouraged the local authorities to reexhibit them. In light of the drastic change in party policies, the Shanghai Film Bureau publicly acknowledged, "[The bureau's cadres] lacked a deep and full understanding of the Party's Hundred Flowers policy and the policy towards the intellectuals." In consequence, the bureau affirmed that "the decision made by the bureau and distribution company to stop showing some of the movies was wrong."⁶⁴ Meanwhile, those who had directed their criticisms of *Brave the Wind and Waves* back in the late 1950s had to send Sun Yu their apologies.⁶⁵ In a buoyant mood, Sun could laugh off all the attacks from his colleagues a few years ago, but he continued to feel frustrated with the above-mentioned film synopses of *Brave the Wind and Waves* littered with critical remarks. Sun believed that his movie had received unfair treatment because of a particular ethos in the late 1950s, that is, "dismissing all films with scenes of dancing and romantic love as venomous."⁶⁶ In comparison, the Shanghai Film Bureau provided a rethink of its previous stance:

> Many reviewers tended to . . . turn a blind eye to those films' main [ideological] orientations but equated some flaws in the movies with political issues. [They] inappropriately blamed [the films] for 'opposing or attacking the Party's policies,' "championing bourgeois ideas and feelings," and so on. . . . [They] equated the characters of Party members in the movies with the Party leadership. . . . [They] elevated issues of lacking accurate artistic expressions or artistic proficiency to issues concerning political principles and the filmmakers' worldviews.⁶⁷

This comment fit well the criticisms of *Brave the Wind and Waves* in the late 1950s: Sun Yu's criticizers ignored the film's central theme, that is, the making and growth of new-generation laborers in socialism, but appeared overcritical of certain details, such as Captain Zhao's bias against women at the beginning of the film, and interpreted them as evidence of Sun Yu's political backwardness. The comic scene of the female protagonist's holding a CCP cadre's head in her dream was thus deleted. Prior to the distribution of the movie, Sun seemed to have anticipated these attacks and therefore expected that the humorous and relaxing elements would save the film from excessive and distorted political interpretations. Therefore, he and the film studio demanded the distributors give the movie a label, "color lyric-comedy" (*caishe shuqing xiju* 彩色抒情喜劇), on various occasions.⁶⁸ Sun's concern was not

---

63. Shanghai Municipal Archives, B177-3-355, 6.
64. Shanghai Municipal Archives, A22-2-1045, 7–8.
65. Shanghai Municipal Archives, B177-3-330, 5.
66. Shanghai Municipal Archives, B177-3-330, 4.
67. Shanghai Municipal Archives, A22-2-1045, 7.
68. Shanghai Municipal Archives, B177-3-156, 6.

unfounded. To escape from potential criticisms that the newly made movies purposely misrepresented the realities in socialist China, filmmakers in Mao-era China tended to resort to the genre of comedy as a relatively risk-free "vehicle for the presentation of events in ordinary citizens' lives."[69] Three decades later, Sun added that not defining *Brave the Wind and Waves* as a biographical movie allowed for a higher degree of fictionalization and artistic creation. As he was unwilling to call it a "serious film" (*zhengju* 正劇), it was reasonably categorized as "lyric-comedy."[70]

Putting New Wine into Old Bottles

Sun Yu's choice of "lyric-comedy" to define *Brave the Wind and Waves* testifies to his wariness of fleeing from possible political persecution after he fell victim to the campaign against *The Life of Wu Xun* in the early 1950s. For years, Sun behaved with extreme caution to ensure political security.[71] However, "lyric-comedy" did not deviate from Sun's filmmaking philosophy that he developed in the 1930s. In his memoir, Sun reiterated his concept of "interest" (*quwei xing* 趣味性) in all his movies:

> When I make a film, I usually pay attention to interest—namely, entertainment (*yule xing* 娛樂性). I believe that every film should be interesting. [Interest] is different from razzle-dazzle or vulgar tastes. A comic sensibility is elicited from the characters' personalities.[72]

It thus came as no surprise that the funny scenes in *Brave the Wind and Waves* embodied his longstanding style: "I further developed [the concept of] interest after the Liberation. . . . [Although] I had never made any comedies before, this film [*Brave the Wind and Waves*] was a lyric-comedy full of interest."[73]

A Comparison with Queen of Sports

Interest, as Sun Yu underscored in his memoir, prevailed in many of his filmic works in the 1930s, among which *Queen of Sports*, the pioneering sports movie in China, bore a remarkable resemblance to *Brave the Wind and Waves* in the main themes and filmic techniques applied therein. *Queen of Sports* centers on the maturity of Lin Ying 林瓔 (Li Lili 黎莉莉 [1915–2005]), a highly talented young lady from an affluent family in the countryside. Shortly after she arrived in Shanghai, Lin earned fame as an outstanding athlete as she broke two national records in a track event.

---

69. Clark, *Chinese Cinema*, 65.
70. Sun, *Yinhai fanzhou*, 227–28.
71. Ding, *Zai lishi de bianji*, 370.
72. Feng Hechen 封禾陳, "Sun Yu zishu" 孫瑜自述 [Sun Yu's account in his own words], in *Zhongguo dianying nianjian 2001* 中國電影年鑑2001 [Chinese film yearbook, 2001], ed. Zhongguo dianying nianjian she 中國電影年鑑社 [The publishing house for Chinese film yearbook] (Changsha: Yuelu shushe, 2002), 269.
73. Feng, "Sun Yu zishu," 269.

Lin soon lost her way and indulged in a luxurious lifestyle in Shanghai until she was almost assaulted by a dandy at a private party. The awakened Lin then returned to the running track to undergo intensive training under the guidance of the male protagonist (Zhang Yi). Finally, Lin came to the realization that the ultimate goal of sports was not winning championships but enhancing the popularity of sports among the general population and thereby promoting a new, healthy lifestyle in China.

Queen of Sports is closely comparable with *Brave the Wind and Waves* in numerous aspects. Both films focus on the growth of young women with the same given name, "Ying" 瓔. Both lead roles are in the apparent "bloom of health."[74] Both films link the young generation's selfhood to the Chinese nation. Or, in Vivian Shen's words, "one should cultivate the self before contributing to society and the nation," a belief Sun firmly held for decades.[75] Both movies contain facetious elements but convey political messages in line with political authorities. *Queen of Sports*, for example, makes a connection between women's bodies and the fate of the nation-state,[76] propagates the notion of "saving the nation with sports" (*tiyu jiuguo* 體育救國), and assumes, intentionally or unintentionally, the role as the booster for the ongoing New Life Movement (*Xin shenghuo yundong* 新生活運動).[77] Victor Fan finds that the female protagonist in *Queen of Sports* initially presented herself as a playful girl who resists "being taken seriously" but takes "the ideal of the New Life Movement seriously" in the end.[78] In a similar fashion, Liang Ying in *Brave the Wind and Waves* follows the same trajectory from a playful young female student to a working woman who is remolded into a new citizen in a socialist society. In this sense, Sun Yu's apologetic statement in December 1958, in which he admitted that he had resorted "to the old ways" of filmmaking, was not meant to merely parrot the critical rhetoric used by the party authorities and his colleagues but revealed the director's actual mindset.

One of the approaches to making films Sun Yu adhered to was to "combine education with recreation" (*yujiao yule* 寓教於樂). Sun insisted that the characters in his movies not "assume solemn airs" or drily "give lectures" in order to accomplish the goal of sending out political and moral messages to the film viewers: after all, the motion picture was entertainment. He later recalled that he had already experimented with inserting comic characters and entertaining plots into "serious films" or

---

74. Ding, *Zhongguo dianying tongshi 1*, 171.
75. Vivian Shen, *The Origins of Leftwing Cinema in China, 1932–37* (London: Routledge, 2005), 125.
76. Li Jiuru 李九如, "'Xin shenghuo yundong xianfeng dui': *Tiyu huanghou* yu 20 shiji 30 niandia chuqi de xiandaixing shenti huayu" "新生活運動先鋒隊"：《體育皇后》與20世紀30年代初期的現代性身體話語 [*Queen of Sports*: The body discourse in 1930s], *Dangdai dianying* 當代電影 [Contemporary Cinema], no. 7 (2014): 88–89.
77. Zhen Zhang, *An Amorous History of the Silver Screen: Shanghai Cinema, 1896–1937* (Chicago: University of Chicago Press, 2006), 36.
78. Victor Fan, "The Cinema of Sun Yu: Ice Cream for the Eye . . . But with a *Homo Sacer*," *Journal of Chinese Cinemas* 5, no. 3 (2011): 242–47.

"Putting New Wine into Old Bottles" 81

even "tragedies" ever since he made his debut film in 1928.⁷⁹ Sun ushered in such an approach to both *Queen of Sports* and *Brave the Wind and Waves*. For example, the two "Oliver Hardys" in China—Yin Xiucen 殷秀岑 (1911–1979), known as "Hardy of the Orient" (*dongfang Hadai* 東方哈代) and Guan Hongda 關宏達 (1914–1967), known as "Hardy of China" (*Zhongguo Hadai* 中國哈代)—starred in the two films. In both films, the two "Oliver Hardys" create comedic effects by throwing around their overweight bodies and displaying clumsy squeezes, collisions, and stumbles. *Brave the Wind and Waves* was, however, a post-1949 production, and the director self-consciously limited Guan Hongda's awkward and funny acts to the first several minutes of the film.

Figure 3.1: In both *Queen of Sports* and *Brave the Wind and Waves*, two "Oliver Hardy's" in China are tasked with throwing their bodies around awkwardly to amuse the audience. Screenshot from *Brave the Wind and Waves*.

---

79. Sun, *Yinhai fanzhou*, 229.

Sun Yu's lifelong quest for an eclectic approach to ideological indoctrination and entertainment had been criticized for diluting the movies' central themes and distracting the viewers' attention. As early as 1934, Sun's prime time as a productive and well-respected director in Shanghai, a reviewer made some pointed remarks on *Queen of Sports*:

> What the audiences get is nothing but some memories of a relaxing atmosphere and beautiful images. 'Manias for the championship' that the director intends to denounce and the 'massification of sports' he proposes may only exist in the corner of people's minds and leave insignificant impressions.[80]

Such incisive remarks did not radically differ from the criticisms *Brave the Wind and Waves* received in the late 1950s. Some plots that Sun designed to attain comic effects, including Captain Zhao hiding behind the clothes stand with a cat on his shoulder and Liang Ying holding the party representative's head to simulate the operation of the helm, were dismissed as "low taste," "unhealthy," and "vulgar."[81] When the critics' attention was shifted to such details, they ignored the grand historical narrative contained in the movie: the rise of laboring women as a collective in Mao-era China. Hence, it is fair to argue that, as Sun harbored an intention to carry on his filmmaking approaches and philosophies—or put new wine into old bottles—and thereby make a film to eulogize socialist modernization, the inherent flaws in his style were not only inherited but also writ large, leaving *Brave the Wind and Waves* intensely vulnerable to attacks in a new sociopolitical setting after 1949.

Womanhood and the Chinese Nation

If the film reviewers' attention only to nonessential details and supporting roles in *Brave the Wind and Waves* prevented them from celebrating the film's "main [ideological] orientations," as the Shanghai Film Bureau admitted in the early 1960s, blaming Sun Yu for highlighting the young woman's pursuit of her solo efforts, rather than following the party's instructions, was not entirely undeserving. A comparison between the female protagonists in *Queen of Sports* and *Brave the Wind and Waves* reveals the latter's heavy indebtedness to the former: both girls represent the new-generation young women, who are wholesome, fit, outgoing, ambitious, and energetic. Their earliest appearances in the movies are very similar. In *Queen of Sports*, Lin Ying is scheduled to meet with her uncle's family on the pier after arriving in Shanghai but unexpectedly disappears. It turns out the playful young woman has quietly climbed on the towering chimney. The film viewers could take the angle of the passersby in the film to stare at the woman's legs. The film's opening scene thus both portrays Lin Ying's personality and succeeds in displaying a woman's well-built

---

80. Zheng Boqi 鄭伯奇, *Liangqi ji* 兩栖集 [The anthology of the amphibious] (Shanghai: Shanghai shudian chubanshe, 1987), 220.
81. Shanghai Municipal Archives, B177-3-333, 21.

body. Such a public exhibition of the woman's body catered to the preferences of male viewers by reminding them of their "proper viewing positions."[82]

While there is no denying that putting a woman's body under the spotlight served a male-dominated film market, it is vital to arrive at a deeper understanding of the hidden, metaphoric meaning by juxtaposing the opening scenes of *Queen of Sports* and *Brave the Wind and Waves*. In the first portion of *Brave the Wind and Waves*, similarly, Liang Ying and her female classmates are absent from the commencement ceremony. Just like in *Queen of Sports*, where Lin Ying has been assigned a role as a younger female member of the family and expected to stand still waiting for her seniors, Liang Ying in *Brave the Wind and Waves* refuses to sit still inside the auditorium but chooses to row a boat on the choppy ocean. While Lin Ying wears a skirt, allowing the audience to voyeuristically see her legs, Liang Ying and her friends are in skimpy red swimsuits, showing the audience their youthful bodies. It is worth mentioning that the first several minutes of *Brave the Wind and Waves* was indeed path-breaking in film history of the PRC: it might be the first time the female protagonist wears a swimsuit on the screen in Mao's times, and its color, bright red, appears extraordinarily striking in an age when black-and-white films still dominated the market (see Figure 3.2). In this sense, both movies begin with the young women's brief absence—from both their designated areas and their prescribed roles—as a junior family member and as a student, respectively. The rediscoveries of them a few minutes later are highlighted by full-scale exhibitions of their bodies and energies, allowing the director to make a connection between the image of women and a vibrant Chinese nation.

After the first scenes, *Queen of Sports* and *Brave the Wind and Waves* diverge in their representations of feminine bodies. In *Queen of Sports*, Sun Yu felt more comfortable and confident in displaying young women's half-naked bodies in not only public spaces, such as running tracks, but also in private ones, such as dorms and shower rooms. Sun reasoned that, despite male film viewers' intense gaze, female characters' exposed limbs in certain modern institutions, including all-girls schools and stadiums, were meant to promote a modern and healthy (or asexualized) lifestyle. On the contrary, it was women's bodies tightly enveloped in a *qipao* that eroticized them.[83] Sun's self-defense was hardly convincing. Paul Pickowicz notes that the message Sun attempted to pass on simply got lost, and women's bodies in the movie "titillate[d] rather than educate[d]." Not only was "the natural, robust sexuality of the rural heroine" particularly enticing,[84] according to researchers of the

---

82. Lü Huang 呂鐄 and Li Gangbing 李鋼兵, "Chaoyue shenti de kunjing: cong Tiyu huanghou, Nülan wuhao he Sha'ou kan Zhongguo tiyu gushipian zhongde nüxing" 超越身體的困境：從《體育皇后》、《女籃5號》和《沙鷗》看中國體育故事片中的女性 [The plight of overstepping the body: Seeing the female in Chinese sports films through *Queen of Sports* (1934), *Woman Basketball Player No. 5* (1957), and *Sha Ou* (1981)], *Fünu yanjiu luncong* 婦女研究論叢 [Essays on Women's Studies], no. 4 (2009): 68.
83. Li, "'Xin shenghuo yundong xianfeng dui,'" 89.
84. Pickowicz, *China on Film*, 51.

Figure 3.2: In both *Queen of Sports* and *Brave the Wind and Waves*, Sun Yu attempted to show the young women's bodies. Screenshots from *Queen of Sports* and *Brave the Wind and Waves*.

film, but women's half-naked bodies also endowed the male audiences with a sense of superiority because of their privilege to cast their gaze.[85]

In comparison with *Queen of Sports*, *Brave the Wind and Waves* consistently features women's bodies firmly wrapped in overalls or uniforms as soon as the first scene ends. It is fair to argue that the growth of the female protagonists in this film was a process of their adoption of the gender-neutral attire, exemplifying what Meng Yue 孟悅 and Dai Jinhua 戴錦華 call "degendering"[86] or, in Mayfair Mei-hui

---

85. Wu Jun 伍俊, *Lianhua yingye gongsi fazhan beijing xia de Sun Yu zaoqi dianying (1930–1937)* 聯華影業公司發展背景下的孫瑜早期電影（1930–1937）[Sun Yu's early films in the developmental years of the United Photoplay Service (1930–1937)] (Shanghai: Shanghai jiaotong daxue chubanshe, 2018), 58–61; Lü and Li, "Chaoyue shenti de kunjing," 68.
86. Meng Yue 孟悅 and Dai Jinhua 戴錦華, *Fuchu lishi dibiao—xiandai funü wenxue yanjiu* 浮出歷史地表—現代婦女文學研究 [Emerging from the earth's surface: Studies on contemporary women's literature] (Zhengzhou: Henan renmin chubanshe, 1988), 15.

Yang's words, "gender erasure."[87] Recent studies on film in the PRC's first seventeen years have underscored a tendency in movies on the CCP's revolutionary wars and PRC times to deny and eliminate female characters' feminine traits. Shuqin Cui, for example, emphasizes the filmmakers' "degendering" of "the female body and erasing sexual difference" in the PRC's revolutionary narrative.[88] Rey Chow notes that those films tended "to downplay the gendered or sexualized specifics of women's agency" but focused "often much less on femininity as such than on the constructive roles women could play in their historical and political milieus."[89] Although "degendering" or "gender erasure" is presently under critical scrutiny,[90] there is no denying that *Brave the Wind and Waves* documented the whole process of the female protagonists' dispelling of their femininity (no matter how it is presented in a stereotyped manner) in pursuit of gender-neutral appearances. Or, in Xiao Liu's words, it was the "reorganization of labor" that reconstructed the protagonists' femininity.[91]

As soon as Liang Ying and her two friends are assigned to *The People 91* as trainees, they are required to engage in physical labor, not dissimilar to their male colleagues. Thereafter, they are usually dressed in gray, badly soiled uniforms with an unkempt appearance, standing in stark contrast to their showing-off of their bodies in bright red swimwear at the beginning of the movie. Enveloping women's bodies in cumbersome work clothes thus testifies to Sun Yu's strategy to make "new women" in post-1949 China by subsuming his passions for eulogizing youth, women, and nature to the demands of the socialist cause.[92] Likewise, in the real-life scenario, "degendering" proved a commonplace tactic when new womanhood was propagated in Mao's China. Lin Youhua, the prototype of Liang Ying, had reportedly "forgotten many things about women." "When her sister sent her a floral skirt from Guangdong, she put it on only once: a specific night after dinner."[93] In the movie, "degendering" manifested itself also in the hairstyles of the three female lead roles. During a scene in the first half of the film, all the three wear long hair, and one girl proudly shows off her two long braids. Towards the end of the film, by comparison, all of them have their long hair cut. This bodily change demonstrated the completion of the process of molding them into socialist new laborers. What

---

87. Mayfair Mei-hui Yang, "From Gender Erasure to Gender Difference: State Feminism, Consumer Sexuality, and Women's Public Sphere in China," in *Spaces of Their Own: Women's Public Sphere in Transnational China*, ed. Mayfair Mei-hui Yang (Minneapolis: University of Minnesota Press, 1999), 41.
88. Shuqin Cui, *Women Through the Lens: Gender and Nation in a Century of Chinese Cinema* (Honolulu: University of Hawai'i Press, 2003), 56.
89. Rey Chow, "Fetish Power Unbound: A Small History of 'Woman' in Chinese Cinema," in *The Oxford Handbook of Chinese Cinema*, ed. Carlos Rojas and Eileen Cheng-yin Chow (Oxford: Oxford University Press, 2013), 493.
90. For example, Rosemary Roberts points out that such a discourse creates "an essentialised notion of gender nature and gender roles." See Rosemary A. Roberts, *Maoist Model Theatre: The Semiotics of Gender and Sexuality in the Chinese Cultural Revolution (1966–1976)* (Leiden: Brill, 2010), 17. For the critique of "gender erasure," also see Liu, "*Red Detachment of Women*," 117.
91. Liu, "*Red Detachment of Women*," 118.
92. Yang, *Daoyan de puxi*, 61.
93. Sun, "Jiangshang xing," 27.

irritated Sun Yu's critics was the director's juxtaposition of the "degendering" of female protagonists and romantic love. Indeed, the love story recounted in *Brave the Wind and Waves* was comparable to that in *Queen of Sports*, too. In *Queen of Sports*, Lin Ying deals with people (such as the dandy who seduced her) and things (such as endless parties) she loathes, before grasping the essence of life and sporting ability. Hence, she dates a likeminded man, her coach. Along a similar vein, Liang Ying in *Brave the Wind and Waves* expresses her distaste at the first mate on *The People 91* because the man lacks the right political consciousness and work ethic. Therefore, Liang turns him down. Later, Liang and the boatswain fall in love because he is a conscientious and responsible worker. In both films, Sun rejected the May-Fourth-style, "hypergood" romantic love that deserved "total faith and supreme sacrifices" and subsumed "all of life's purposes."[94] Instead, both films specified the prerequisites for a happy relationship, either shared moral codes or similar political credos, testifying to Susan Glosser's observation that the CCP demanded young men and women to "gauge their compatibility with others by assessing the similarity of their political views" in post-1949 China.[95]

Although the depiction of romantic love in *Brave the Wind and Waves* had been mocked for "resorting to love to redeem a weak plot"—or an inappropriate or vulgar filler to make up for an inadequate storyline—Sun Yu's understanding was actually in compliance with the prevailing way of portraying love in literary, dramatic, and filmic works in Mao-era China: love, if "not constrained by reason," was deemed as "extremely filthy."[96] Authentic love was thus rigidly prescribed: it took place only between a man and a woman "with the same revolutionary goals" and "shared backgrounds and [political] views in the process of putting up struggles, conducting revolutions, or engaging in productive works together." Ultimately, "love must directly enhance both sides' [willingness] to devote to the revolutionary work, ideological levels, and [abilities] to participate in productive work." Therefore, politically backward individuals did not deserve love in those works.[97] Given that love was based not on individuals' desires but a shared political conviction, by the end of *Brave the Wind and Waves*, the filmmakers accordingly illustrated a romantic love between the protagonists in a "de-desiring" way: they shake hands tightly and thereby complete the metamorphosis of their relationship from colleagues to couples under the gaze of their coworkers and friends. To borrow Dai Jinhua's phrase, the making of their relationship in this movie typified "a love story without

---

94. Haiyan Lee, *Revolution of the Heart: A Genealogy of Love in China, 1900–1950* (Stanford: Stanford University Press, 2007), 15.
95. Susan L. Glosser, *Chinese Visions of Family and State, 1915–1953* (Berkeley: University of California, 2003), 184.
96. Lin Ting 林霆, *Bei guixun de xushi: shiqi nian nongye hezuohua ticai xiaoshuo yanjiu* 被規訓的敘事：十七年農業合作化題材小說研究 [The disciplined narrative: A study on novels about the rural collectivization movement in the seventeen years (of the PRC)] (Taiyuan: Beiyue wenyi chubanshe, 2014), 231.
97. Yin Hong 尹鴻 and Ling Yan 凌燕, *Xin Zhongguo dianying shi (1949–2000)* 新中國電影史（1949–2000）[A history of film in new China (1949–2000)] (Changsha: Hunan meishu chubanshe, 2002), 36.

love" (*meiyou aiqing de aiqing gushi* 沒有愛情的愛情故事) that was commonplace in many films in Mao-era China.[98]

Sun Yu in the Early 1960s

The mere fact that *Brave the Wind and Waves* did not significantly deviate from the CCP-endorsed norms of womanhood and love helped Sun Yu escape the frenzied political/ideological attacks although the film did receive scathing criticism for a while in the late 1950s. During the "Cultural Thaw" in the first half of the 1960s,[99] the film was given its long overdue credit, but Sun believed that he deserved better treatment from the party authorities in Shanghai. Hence, he continued to work hard on a number of screenplays and attempted to film at least some of them. On the surface, the CCP cadres were willing to accommodate Sun's needs because of the central government's soft-line policy toward intellectuals and artists. As a leader of the film studio admitted in 1962, Sun should have obtained permission to make more films based on the party policy, considering his standing as a May-Fourth-generation film director.[100] In reality, however, his requests were consistently met with polite rejections. In 1960, for example, Sun applied to make a film about the air force in post-1949 China. As Sun and his coworkers spent almost an entire year producing three drafts of the screenplay, they wound up not gaining the approval on the grounds that another film studio in China had already released a similar film.[101]

Bitter disappointment gripped Sun Yu two years later when he was preparing a biographical movie entitled "A Little Story of a Magic Flute" (*Shendi xiaozhuan* 神笛小傳). Following the prevailing trend of producing historical/biographical movies (as shown in Chapter 1), Sun placed high hopes on the project of "A Little Story of a Magic Flute," a story about an influential working class flute performer in China. By highlighting the vicissitudes of a musician's life and career before and after 1949, Sun intended to offer a marked contrast between the miserable "old society" before 1949 and the happy "new society" led by the CCP in China. Had this project gone through, its theme would be akin to Xie Jin's *Stage Sisters* (*Wutai jiemei* 舞臺姐妹, 1964). According to Sun, he revised the screenplay three or four times, but the stone-faced cadres only responded that the project was awaiting further scrutiny and subject to new rounds of review. Finally, the project fell apart.[102]

The other side of the story regarding the fate of "A Little Story of a Magic Flute" was slightly different. In 1962, the film studio's lower-level cadres filed reports a few times, searching for clarifications for the higher authorities' stance on Sun and his

---

98. Dai Jinhua 戴錦華, *Wuzhong fengjing* 霧中風景 [Landscape in the fog] (Beijing: Beijing daxue chubanshe, 2000), 122–24.
99. Pickowicz, *China on Film*, 213.
100. Shanghai Municipal Archives, B177-3-327, 37.
101. Shanghai Municipal Archives, A22-2-875, 16.
102. Sun, *Yinhai fanzhou*, 247.

proposed project. In principle, the studio was unwilling to accept Sun Yu's script, for the reviewers believed that it "was far from meeting the requirements" set by the film studio. Facing this comment, Sun appeared fiercely defensive and refused to make any changes. The existing archival record shows that Sun held his ground firmly and declined to create a new revision because, first of all, the opinions given by the studios differed fundamentally from his plans and designs. Second, if the screenplay were to undergo some new revisions in accordance with the reviewers' suggestions, the entire film would become a highly politicized work. Third, Sun had complete confidence in the film's popularity among the audiences. Here, Sun complained that his "romanticism" (*langman zhuyi* 浪漫主義) failed to gain his colleagues' full understanding, inviting the criticism that the storyline in "A Little Story of a Magic Flute" violated the canon of socialist realism.[103] Despite such disputes, Sun aimed at making his first film in the 1960s, by repeatedly invoking the notion of "freedom of [artistic] creation" (*chuangzuo ziyou* 創作自由). He once stated that as long as he could steer clear of taboo topics in the screenplay, the cadres needed to adopt a hands-off approach because he pledged to ensure the film's artistic values.[104]

For all Sun Yu's chest-thumping, the cadres of the studio felt confused about the approaches to handling those experienced and esteemed directors in this new political climate in the opening years of the 1960s. The CCP leader in Shanghai wondered about the line between constructive criticism of film work and interference with a director's artistic freedom. All the cadres were dwelling on a dilemma both to accommodate Sun Yu's needs, in filmmaking as well as in everyday life, and to pressure him to alter the plotline in line with the reviewers' feedback.[105] Finally, the indecisive studio made a move to report this dispute to Xia Yan, who happened to visit Shanghai in September 1962. During a talk on September 11, Xia unhesitatingly sided with the film studio. Xia confirmed that "accommodations" the party was willing to provide to Sun Yu were limited to the realms of political status and living conditions, and the film studio should never feel obligated to sacrifice the quality of the productions to please a veteran director.[106]

Conclusion

Xia Yan's remarks were a testimony to the party's overall attitudes towards experienced but elderly directors, known as the second-generation directors in Chinese film history. The government was willing to give them substantial pay and bestow political and artistic honors on them most of the time in Mao-era China. Sun Yu was ranked as a level-2 artist shortly after Liberation and received one of the highest salaries among filmmakers in Shanghai, until the outbreak of the Cultural

---

103. Shanghai Municipal Archives, B177-3-327, 36–37.
104. Shanghai Municipal Archives, B177-1-172, 143.
105. Shanghai Municipal Archives, B177-3-327, 36–37.
106. Shanghai Municipal Archives, B177-1-288, 49.

"Putting New Wine into Old Bottles" 89

Revolution.[107] However, the political authorities advanced a hidden agenda to push aside those veteran directors. As Chapter 4 will show, the Shanghai-based studios endeavored to exclude elderly directors from making mainstream films about revolutionary wars and the ongoing socialist cause. More often than not, they were tasked to direct politically safe movies, such as opera films. Unsurprisingly, Sun's last film to wrap up his decades-long career, *Qin Niangmei*, happened to be an opera film adapted from a Guizhou opera (*Qianju* 黔劇) play. Not only was the movie a black-and-white one, but Guizhou opera was also a young and relatively unknown operatic genre in China. Sun's participation in making this film itself was a manifestation of his uneasy relationship with the party authorities.

Despite the marginalization of the old-generation directors in general and Sun Yu in particular, Sun did not passively accept the fate that was befalling him. The making of *Brave the Wind and Waves* constituted his final attempt to restore his reputation and search for his identity in the new historical era. In other words, it was his subjectivizing practice. As the entire chapter has shown, Sun tried to put new wine into old bottles, turning back to filmic techniques and styles he felt familiar with to make a movie to extol socialist modernization. Indeed, this film embodied Sun Yu's specific "form of realism: poetic, ideological, revolutionary and romantic, or perhaps even 'critical realism.'"[108] Some features, such as ideological and revolutionary, were compatible with the CCP-endorsed socialist realism, whereas some others were not.

Consequently, Sun Yu's tactic was hardly a success, for he lacked awareness that his "old bottles" were the very target of this party-led sociopolitical revolution in the first place. Female bodies, romantic love, and funny jokes and acts were subject to the reviewers' critical scrutiny and were usually dismissed as "vulgar" and pandering to "bourgeois" tastes. Although the film had never been officially banned, the confidential report indicated that the studio appraised it as a work of "relatively low quality,"[109] an arresting example of the old-generation directors' inability or refusal to catch up with the new socialist era.

---

107. Shanghai Municipal Archives, B177-3-80, 2.
108. Corrado Neri, "Sun Yu and the Early Americanization of Chinese Cinema," in *Media, Popular Culture, and the American Century*, ed. Kingsley Bolton and Jan Olsson (New Barnet, UK: John Libbey Publishing, 2011), 232.
109. Shanghai Municipal Archives, A22-2-1478, 93.

4
Wu Yonggang
Opera Film, the Cinematic Cold War, and Artistic Autonomy

Opera film, a major film genre in Mao-era China, emerged with the rise of China's indigenous film industry. Before 1949, despite the participation of some superstars of Chinese opera in filmmaking, such as Mei Lanfang 梅蘭芳 (1894–1961) and Zhou Xinfang 周信芳 (1895–1975), the number of opera films remained small, and no film theorists were interested in delving into the studies of this genre. Indeed, the genre itself was undergoing a visible transformation from operatic documentaries to feature films.[1] By contrast, opera film grew into one of the major film genres in Mao-era China: in the first seventeen years of the PRC, film studios based in mainland China released 115 opera films.[2]

Such productivity has understandably sparked an intense scholarly interest. Recent studies on opera film primarily seek to explore how opera and film in China were mutually constitutive in the early years of the PRC. Weihong Bao, for example, notes that Chinese filmmakers' "preoccupations with opera films" stemmed from a desire for reaching the "widest audience" and thereby legitimating "film as a socialist mass art." Meanwhile, the making of opera films naturalized *xiqu* 戲曲—a term coined in the twentieth century—as a universal theatrical convention that transcended regional differences in China.[3] Paola Iovene finds that, while film contributed to the "standardization" of theatrical performances by limiting improvisation, opera provided the film with "a space of experimentation." This experimentation finally led to creating "the better-known film adaptations of the model operas" during the Cultural Revolution.[4] Chris Berry and Mary Ann Farquhar underscore opera film's impact beyond mainland China, by arguing that it triggered the invention of *wuxiapian* 武俠片 or "swordplay martial arts films" in Hong Kong. Both

---

1. Gao Xiaojian 高小健, *Zhongguo xiqu dianying shi* 中國戲曲電影史 [History of Chinese opera films] (Beijing: Wenhua yishu chubanshe, 2005), 17.
2. Judith T. Zeitlin, "Operatic Ghosts on Screen: The Case of *A Test of Love* (1958)," *The Opera Quarterly* 26, no. 2–3 (August 2010): 220.
3. Weihong Bao, "The Politics of Remediation: Mise-en-scène and the Subjunctive Body in Chinese Opera Film," *The Opera Quarterly* 26, no. 2–3 (August 31, 2010): 259–60.
4. Paola Iovene, "Chinese Operas on Stage and Screen: A Short Introduction," *The Opera Quarterly* 26, no. 2–3 (August 2010): 189–90.

genres were the manifestation of the "sinicization of cinema" and fell into the category of the "cinema of spectacle-attractions."[5]

Focusing exclusively on the "transmedial borrowings" between the motion picture and theater and "the mutual enrichment between stage performance and the film medium" but not conducting an investigation of opera film's political ramifications during the Cold War, that is, "the PRC's diaspora propaganda and in the globalization of Maoist ideology," according to Lanjun Xu, is inadequate to fully understand this highly popular film genre in mainland China and beyond.[6] Kwok Wai Hui posits that opera film was "the site where different political and cultural forces contest[ed] and negotiate[d] with each other" in Hong Kong.[7] Poshek Fu thus coined the term the "cinematic Cold War" to foreground China-made opera films' capacity to attain the goals of "politicization of popular culture as weapons of ideological persuasion, clandestine use of private enterprises for political propaganda, and instrumentalization of overseas Chinese communities,"[8] especially those in Hong Kong, a hotspot of the cultural Cold War. Given the spectacular market success of some high-profile opera films, such as *Liang Shanbo and Zhu Yingtai*, this highly politicized cultural and ideological fight was disguised as commercial competition.[9] The colonial authorities' embracing of opera movies but rejecting those about China's revolutions and class-based struggles in the past (such as *Song Jingshi*) stemmed from a clandestine film censorship system in Hong Kong to ensure this colonial city's "stability and prosperity."[10]

This chapter constitutes an effort to reconcile those two approaches to studying opera film in the Mao era, and to examine how the Cold War environment and cinematic and theatrical skills enabled Chinese filmmakers to pursue their personal interests and reveal their feelings. It argues that the necessity of winning the cinematic Cold War in overseas film markets—particularly that in Hong Kong—prompted the CCP authorities to loosen their control over the making of some of the opera movies and thereby allowed the filmmakers to restore a certain degree of professional autonomy, which had come under scathing criticism during the Anti-Rightist Movement in 1957. The efforts to supply opera films to the Hong Kong market culminated in the early 1960s, when Deputy Minister of Culture Xia Yan and other upper-echelon CCP leaders encouraged Chinese film studios and their leftwing partners in Hong Kong to coproduce opera films. Xia's agenda was manifold, that is, to give seasoned directors more opportunities to participate in

---

5. Berry and Farquhar, *China on Screen*, 48–53.
6. Lanjun Xu, "The Southern Film Corporation, Opera Films, and the PRC's Cultural Diplomacy in Cold War Asia, 1950s and 1960s," *Modern Chinese Literature and Culture* 29, no. 1 (Spring 2017): 239.
7. Kwok Wai Hui (Xu Guohui 許國惠), "Revolution, Commercialism and Chineseness: Opera Films in Socialist Shanghai and Capitalist-colonial Hong Kong, 1949—1966" (PhD diss., University of Chicago, 2013), 7.
8. Fu, "More than Just Entertaining," 43.
9. Fu, "More than Just Entertaining," 14.
10. Kenny K. K. Ng, "Inhibition vs. Exhibition: Political Censorship of Chinese and Foreign Cinemas in Postwar Hong Kong," *Journal of Chinese Cinemas* 2, no. 1 (2008): 23.

filmmaking activities, to export those movies in exchange for foreign currency, and, of course, to lend Hong Kong's leftwing film studios support to win the intense market competition and the cultural war. Without a doubt, Xia and his comrades were able to carry out such flexible policy thanks to a less grim political and economic situation in the first half of the 1960s, the lull before the Cultural Revolution, or what Paul Pickowicz calls the "Cultural Thaw."[11]

In this relaxing political climate, quite a few disgraced artists had their political stigmas removed. Wu Yonggang, the protagonist of this chapter, had been branded a "Rightist" in 1957 for his remarks on the lack of directorial authority and the CCP's denial of the filmmakers' artistic autonomy in post-1949 China. After that, he lost his status as a director, had his ranking downgraded, and received a substantial, punitive pay cut. Beginning in 1961, he was finally allowed to work as a director but only for opera films. As shown in Chapter 3, Wu exemplified the second-generation directors in China, who stood out "as the group of highest achievers" by making "the best Chinese films of the 1930s and 1940s" but wound up paying the exorbitant political price after 1949.[12] Back in the 1930s, Wu's initial work, *The Goddess*, was an instant critical success. William Rothman hails Wu for his "extreme technical sophistication and self-consciousness that invite comparison with films of the Hollywood director who most obviously influenced and inspired him: Josef von Sternberg."[13] Unfortunately, the remarkable success of *The Goddess* overshadowed Wu's other productions in years to follow. Taiwan-based film commentator Ch'en Hui-yang asserts that no films other than *The Goddess* in Wu's five-decade-long career were praiseworthy.[14]

Such an assessment, as I have argued in Chapter 3, testifies to a deep-seated bias against post-1949 Chinese movies, particularly those produced by second-generation directors. Artistically, the politicization of film in Mao's China stood in stark contrast to the artistic sophistication of Chinese cinema during the "Golden Era" in the 1930s and 1940s, because of "the talent, energy, imagination and ingenuity of the people who actually made the films."[15] Politically, filmmakers who had risen to prominence decades before 1949 met tragic endings in the first three decades of the PRC. Despite their willingness to adapt to the new sociopolitical settings, they never won the political authorities' complete confidence.[16]

Hence, the existing scholarship largely portrays a bleak picture of filmmakers in Mao-era China: they lost their artistic autonomy and were thereby relegated to a component part of the state propaganda apparatus before they were drawn into political maelstroms. Wu Yonggang's checkered career after 1949 seemed to

---

11. Pickowicz, *China on Film*, 213.
12. Ryans, "The Second Generation," 16–19.
13. William Rothman, *The 'I' of the Camera: Essays in Film Criticism, History, and Aesthetics* (Cambridge: Cambridge University Press, 2003), 55.
14. Chen, *Mengying ji*, 55.
15. Ryans, "The Second Generation," 16.
16. Pickowicz, *China on Film*, 210.

reconfirm such a narrative. However, as this chapter will show, the unique politico-cultural environment, domestically and internationally, in the first half of the 1960s—the cinematic Cold War—enabled Wu to carve out a space of his own to vest the opera films he directed with his long-cherished humanistic values and to deploy his film techniques, such as camera movement. A comparison between *The Goddess*, Wu's masterpiece in the 1930s, and *The Jade Hairpin*, the first opera film Wu was tasked with supplying to the Hong Kong market, reveals that Wu similarly focused on mistreated women but highlighted the possibility of redemption and conciliation at the end of both films.

More importantly, the portrayal of the female protagonist of *The Jade Hairpin*, who had fallen victim to her abusive husband, allowed Wu to publicize his keenly felt pain caused by the political persecution he had undergone and express his desire to regain the party's recognition of his worthiness. In this sense, this abused woman in the movie was an accurate mirror of Wu himself, and making opera films provided him with an otherwise unavailable subjectivizing practice in this unpredictable political climate. Without a doubt, Wu's self-expression was made possible because of a peculiar arrangement: this film, coproduced by a Shanghai-based film studio and its Hong Kong partner company, was scheduled to be screened in Hong Kong and Southeast Asian markets but not in mainland China. Unintentionally, therefore, the cinematic Cold War afforded a rare opportunity to the embattled Wu, a typical second-generation director with a high reputation but deep in political trouble in post-1949 China.

The Second-Generation Directors in Mao-Era China

It was no secret that opera films produced in Mao's times were reserved for a number of second-generation directors who started their careers in film long before 1949. Cai Ben 蔡賁 (1919–1973), then vice-director of the Shanghai Film Bureau, openly testified in 1965 that assigning elderly directors to direct opera films had been an unwritten rule in Shanghai and elsewhere in China.[17] It is thus no surprise that the forty-two opera films released by Shanghai-based film companies were made in the hands of some second-generation superstar directors, such as Wu Yonggang, Sun Yu, Yang Xiaozhong, and Ying Yunwei, who had fallen out of the new communist regime's favor. Ying Yunwei, for example, had been widely known as an accomplished film director as early as the mid-1930s because of his canonized leftwing filmic work, *Plunder of Peach and Plum* (*Taoli jie* 桃李劫, 1934). However, he never really earned the CCP's trust in post-1949 China although he briefly served as the manager of one of the three state-owned film studios in Shanghai. In the early 1950s, radical CCP cadres labeled him a "comprador bourgeois" (*maiban zichan*

---

17. Tang Xiaodan 湯曉丹, *Chenmo shijin: Tang Xiaodan dianying riji xia* 沉默是金：湯曉丹電影日記下 [Silence is golden: Tan Xiaodan's diary about film, bk. 3] (Beijing: Shangwu yinshuguan, 2016), 899.

jieji 買辦資產階級) and a "profiteer" (*touji shangren* 投機商人).[18] A 1957 internal evaluation blamed Ying for being politically backward and consistently complaining about his low "standing" and "pay."[19] Hence, Ying was deprived of any chance to direct a mainstream feature film, and all five of his filmic works between 1956 and the outbreak of the Cultural Revolution were opera films.[20] In a similar fashion, the political authorities passed a negative judgment on Wu Yonggang: his lack of self-discipline, arrogance, dissatisfaction with the party leadership, and refusal to receive thought reform in a confidential report filed in 1957.[21]

Those second-generation directors were involved in the making of opera films for both financial and political reasons. All the Shanghai-based film studios found themselves in an awful predicament of overstaffing. In 1962, for example, Xia Yan voiced his concern in a public speech that Shanghai's film companies had planned to make between nine and twelve films per year but hired many more directors (forty-six) than necessary.[22] Therefore, the directors faced stiff competition to fulfill the minimal workload (one and a half films per year)[23] and secure higher pay. Wu Yonggang's adaptation of *The Jade Hairpin* from a Yue opera play to a film screenplay allowed him to earn additional 400 yuan, an amount equivalent to his two-month salary.[24] Meanwhile, opera film provided those veteran filmmakers with shelter from ideological disputes and political struggles during the early PRC years.[25] At a time when a vast number of feature films about contemporary China—even children's movies—invariably came under critical scrutiny for political, ideological, and artistic reasons before the Cultural Revolution, opera film ensured a certain degree of safety, for all operatic plays chosen for cinematization were the end products of the CCP's decades-long opera reform[26] and were therefore deemed politically correct.[27]

The veteran film directors' participation did not guarantee their all-out efforts in producing those designated opera films. Some were reluctant contributors. Liu Qiong, for example, lamented in 1960 that the six films he directed or starred in since 1958—one opera film included—were by no means his own choices. He was

---

18. Shen Ji 沈寂, *Shen Ji renwu suoyi* 沈寂人物瑣憶 [Shen Ji's memories of figures (in the past)] (Shanghai: Shanghai shehui kexueyuan chubanshe, 2017), 127–28.
19. Shanghai Municipal Archives, A22-2-1478, 78–80.
20. They were *Song Shijie* 宋士傑 (1956, with Liu Qiong), *Legend of Fish* (*Zhuiyu* 追魚, 1959), *Pavilion of Poetry Contest* (*Doushi ting* 鬥詩亭, 1960), *Stage Arts of Zhou Xinfang* (*Zhou Xinfang de wutai yishu* 周信芳的舞臺藝術, 1961), and *Wu Song* 武松 (1963).
21. Shanghai Municipal Archives, A22-2-1233, 76.
22. Cheng Jihua 程季華, *Xiayan dianying wenji diyi juan* 夏衍電影文集第一卷 [Anthology of Xia Yan's essays on film, vol. 1] (Beijing: Zhongguo dianying chubanshe, 2000), 444.
23. Shanghai Municipal Archives, B177-1-281, 60.
24. Shanghai Municipal Archives, B177-3-363, 34.
25. Gong Yan 龔豔, *Piaoyi, gaixie yu zaizao: 20 shiji siwushi niandai Zhongguo quyu dianying zhi xingcheng* 漂移，改寫與再造－20世紀四五十年代中國區域電影之形成 [Drifting, rewriting, and reconstructing: The making of China's local films in the 1940s and 1950s] (Beijing: Zhongguo dianying chubanshe, 2013), 148.
26. Hui, "Revolution, Commercialism and Chineseness," 94.
27. Gao Xiaojian 高小健, *Xiqu dianying yishu lun* 戲曲電影藝術論 [The art of the opera film] (Beijing: Zhongguo dianying chubanshe, 2015), 118.

neither familiar with nor passionate about the themes and filmic genres he had been assigned.[28] Unlike Liu, who was outspoken, Wu Yonggang chose not to say a word in his memoir about the four opera films he directed after 1949, hinting at his disinterest in this genre.[29] For quite a number of directors, their reluctance manifested itself in their refusal to put in the effort to cinematize the operatic plays. In 1956, Xu Suling 徐蘇靈 (1910–1997), a Shanghai-based director, pointed a finger at most of his colleagues working on opera films. In Xu's opinion, many a director did nothing but shorten the length of a play to fit the movie's timeframe.[30] Zhang Junxiang 張駿祥 (1910–1996) presumed that such a pervasive lack of effort was a testimony to a thinly disguised contempt for opera film among filmmakers in China. It was under this circumstance that Zhang attempted to reconcile filmic skills and Chinese opera's theatrical techniques in making opera films. Hence, he called for a nationwide discussion on the retention of theatricality in opera films.[31]

For the directors, the degree to which they retained the theatricality of the opera films at issue was dictated by several factors, such as their understanding of China's traditional theater, types of operas, and the relationships with the opera stars they worked with. It was widely acknowledged that operas originating in southern China, such as Yue opera and Huangmei opera (*Huangmei xi* 黃梅戲), featured less stylized performance and were therefore better conducive to cinematization than were those from the north. Based on the extent to which the original operas' theatricality was preserved, hence, the opera films produced in Mao's China could be primarily categorized as the "northern school" (*beipai* 北派) and the "southern school" (*nanpai* 南派).[32]

Although Shanghai had long boasted of being the center of the "southern school," opera films made by Shanghai-based studios could well differ in style. Ying Yunwei and Liu Qiong, the directors of *Song Shijie*, for example, committed themselves to "maximally keeping and [faithfully] recording the arts of Beijing opera,"[33] whereas their colleague in Shanghai, Xu Tao, vowed to make *Searching A School* (*Sou shuyuan* 搜書院, 1956) a "classical musical" based on Cantonese opera (*Yueju*

---

28. Shanghai Municipal Archives, B177-1-238, 17–18.
29. The four opera films Wu Yonggang directed are *The Jade Hairpin*, *Third Sister You* (*You sanjie* 尤三姐, 1963), *Giving Away Xuzhou* (*Rang Xuzhou* 讓徐州, 1976), and *Tea Boy Teases the Landlord* (*Chatong xizhu* 茶童戲主, 1979).
30. Xu Suling 徐蘇靈, "Shitan xiqu yishu pian de yixie wenti" 試談戲曲片的一些問題 [On some issues of the opera art film], *Zhongguo dianying* 中國電影 [China Cinema], no. 2 (1956): 41.
31. Zhang Junxiang 張駿祥, "Wutai yishu jilu pian xiang shenme fangxiang fazhan" 舞臺藝術紀錄片向什麼方向發展 [To what direction are documentaries of stage arts steered in], in *Lun xiqu dianying* 論戲曲電影 [On opera film] (Beijing: Zhongguo dianying chubanshe, 1958), 11.
32. Ding Ning 丁寧, "Xin Zhongguo xiqu pian, meishu pian zai Gang chuanbo yanjiu" 新中國戲曲片、美術片在港傳播研究 [A study on the circulation of the PRC-made opera films and cartoons in Hong Kong], *Dianying xinzuo* 電影新作 [New Cinematic Works], no. 2 (2015): 79.
33. Ying Yuwei 應雲衛 and Liu Qiong 劉瓊, "*Song Shijie* daoyan chanshu" 《宋士傑》闡述 [The directors' statement on *Song Shijie*,] in *Dianying daoyan chanshu ji* 電影導演闡述集 [Anthology of the directors' statements], ed. Zuolin 佐臨 et al. (Beijing: Zhongguo dianying chubanshe, 1959), 32.

粵劇).³⁴ The fact that not only were the two movies made in the same year, but the two essays clarifying the directors' intentions and plans were juxtaposed in the same anthology, revealing the lack of a consensus among filmmakers regarding opera film. Stylistically, *Song Shijie* was closer to the stage performance, in no small part, because the star the film featured, Zhou Xinfang, was a towering figure in Beijing opera. Ying Yunwei, one of its two directors, had long been Zhou's dedicated fan,³⁵ and he was more than willing to yield to Zhou's demands.³⁶ In this sense, the opera films, as Anne Rebull posits, varied "from production to production" and from one studio to another.³⁷ I must add here that they differed from one director to another.

The Cinema of Attractions

Despite differing styles and ways of presentation in different opera films, these opera films, according to Chris Berry and Mary Ann Farquhar, fall into the category of the Chinese "cinema of attractions" because they are all "spun out of opera conventions" in China and attempt to display "cultural spectacles" associated with an operatic mode. Opera film took on special significance in the early PRC era, according to Berry and Farquhar, because it represented the "sinicization of cinema," an essential aspect of cultural nationalism dating to Republican times.³⁸ Xiangyang Chen further argues that opera film's penchant for spectacle over music and singing makes such a filmic genre an apt case to study a unique type of cinema of attractions in China.³⁹ Indeed, film workers had long put emphasis on the special needs for visual effects in opera films. Han Shangyi 韓尚義 (1917–1998), the art director of several opera films, for example, explicitly stated in 1956 that Chinese operas operated on the stage under "the rule of beauty" (*mei de faze* 美的法則), and therefore the set in an opera film had to be "aestheticized" (*meihua* 美化). To make those movies visually enticing, Han thus argued that only color opera films would be considered perfect.⁴⁰

---

34. Xu Tao 徐韜, "*Sou shuyuan* daoyan chanshu" 《搜書院》導演闡述 [The director's statement on *Searching a School*], in *Dianying daoyan chanshu ji* 電影導演闡述集 [Anthology of the directors' statements], ed. Zuolin 佐臨 et al. (Beijing: Zhongguo dianying chubanshe, 1959), 39.
35. Ying Dabai 應大白, *Ying Yunwei* 應雲衛 [Ying Yunwei] (Chongqing: Chongqing chubanshe, 2007), 130.
36. Ying, *Ying Yunwei*, 130; Shanghai Municipal Archives, L1-1-84, 7.
37. Anne Rebull, "Locating Theatricality on Stage and Screen: Rescuing Performance Practice and the Phenomenon of *Fifteen Strings of Cash* (*Shiwu guan*, 1956)," *CHINOPERL: Journal of Chinese Oral and Performing Literature* 36, no. 1 (July 2017): 64.
38. Berry and Farquhar, *China on Screen*, 11.
39. Xiangyang Chen, "Affect, Folklore and Cantonese Opera Film," *Journal of Chinese Cinemas* 8, no. 3 (2014): 239.
40. Han Shangyi 韓尚義, "Xiqu yingpian de zaoxing fengge" 戲曲影片的造型風格 [The opera film's visual style], in *Yinse yinji: Shanghai yingren lilun wenxuan* 銀色印記：上海影人理論文選 [The silver imprint: Selected essays on (film) theories by Shanghai filmmakers], ed. Shanghai wenxue yishu jia lianhehui, Shanghai dianyingjia xiehui 上海市文學藝術家聯合會、上海電影家協會 (Shanghai: Fudan daxue chubanshe, 2005), 12–13.

Han's call for producing only color opera films to maximize their visual effects were not overlooked by CCP authorities and his fellow filmmakers. The percentage of color opera films made in Mao's China was disproportionately high. Take the productions of the Shanghai-based studios as an example. During the seventeen years before the Cultural Revolution, Shanghai produced 177 feature films in total, of which 42 were opera films. Meanwhile, they released forty-eight color films, nineteen being color opera films.[41] It is thus evident that the ratio of color opera films to all color films (39.6%) was considerably greater than that of opera films to all feature films (23.7%). To the Hong Kong filmgoers and reviewers, opera films and films about China's ethnic minorities could fall into the same category by having similar advantages: their vivid color and their singing and dancing styles.[42]

The Hong Kong film viewers and critics were not alone in lumping together the two film types. In a report in March 1956, for example, Chen Huangmei encouraged the film workers to work on a full spectrum of movies, one category of which was "various operatic arts, all kinds of regional operas, music and dancing of all ethnic groups in China" (*Zhongguo gezhong xiqu yishu, gezhong difang xi, ge minzu de yinyue wudao* 中國各種戲曲藝術、各種地方戲、各民族的音樂舞蹈).[43] Politically, both opera film and minority film contributed to instilling a notion of a unified nation-state in the audience. The former, according to Chris Berry and Mary Ann Farquhar, allowed for the dissemination of major operatic works "beyond their former regional and linguistic boundaries,"[44] while the latter legitimized "minority peoples as part of the 'solidarity' of the Chinese nation."[45] Aesthetically, both filmic genres embarked upon orientalism to appeal to the audience. Inspired by Dru Gladney's notion of "internal orientalism," Vanessa Frangville contends that non-Han people (especially women) in minority films during Mao's times were exoticized and homogenized as an "internal Other" of the Han viewers.[46] In the same period, opera film was characterized by "a kind of orientalism/self-orientalism"[47] due to "the geopolitical dynamic during the Cold War."[48] Yang Panpan 楊槃槃, however, questions the legitimacy of the notion of self-orientalism by arguing that China-made opera films were not intended to meet the gaze of the

---

41. Wu, *Shanghai dianying zhi*, 1011–23.
42. Zhu Hong 朱虹, *Shanyao zai tongyi xingkong—Zhongguo neidi dianying zai Xianggang* 閃耀在同一星空—中國內地電影在香港 [Shining in the same starry sky—mainland-made films in Hong Kong] (Kunming: Yunnan renmin chubanshe, 2005), 32; 52–58.
43. Chen Huangmei 陳荒煤, *Chen Huangmei wenji, di 7 juan dianying pinglun shang* 陳荒煤文集第7卷：電影評論（上）[The collected writings of Chen Huangmei, vol. 7: Film reviews, bk. 1] (Beijing: Zhongguo dianying chubanshe, 2013), 6.
44. Berry and Farquhar, *China on Screen*, 47–48.
45. Yingjin Zhang, "From 'Minority Film' to 'Minority Discourse': Questions of Nationhood and Ethnicity in Chinese Cinema," *Cinema Journal* 36, no. 3 (Spring 1997): 79–80.
46. Vanessa Frangville, "The Non-Han in Socialist Cinema and Contemporary Films in the People's Republic of China," *China Perspectives*, no. 2 (2012): 62–64.
47. Xu, "The Southern Film Corporation, Opera Films, and the PRC's Cultural Diplomacy in Cold War Asia," 260.
48. Weihong Bao, "The Trouble with Theater: Cinema and the Geopolitics of Medium Specificity," *Framework*, 56, no. 2 (Fall 2015): 362.

Euro-American audience but to cater to the needs of the filmgoers in Hong Kong and Southeast Asia.[49] Nevertheless, those scholars underscore the geopolitical factor that prompted the filmmakers to resort to such a unique, exhibitionist style. In other words, the opera filmmakers' self-orientalist proclivity served the very purpose of a political struggle in Cold War Hong Kong.

The Cinematic Cold War

Dubbed the "Cold War city," Hong Kong was (and still is) characterized by the blending of people of differing nationalities, political orientations, and cultural preferences. Stacilee Ford argues that Hong Kong in the mid-twentieth century was not merely a "contact zone" but also a "unique site for the consideration of cultural production."[50] The city was more than a sizable market of various cultural products during the Cold War. As Jeremy Taylor puts it, it was a nodal point in "a chain of port cities stretching the length of East and South East Asia."[51] Hence, Poshek Fu posits that the city provided a prime example of the "cinematic Cold War" in East Asia, given the cutthroat market competition between leftist (or "patriotic") and "Free China" film studios backed by Taiwan and the United States.[52]

Poshek Fu's argument is derived from that of Tony Shaw and Denise J. Youngblood, who have observed that cinema in the Cold War world was a potent weapon because of "its purported ability" to show audiences "the 'reality' of what was for most of people a peculiarly abstract, 'virtual' conflict."[53] Indeed, the cinematic Cold War waged by the political authorities and filmmakers in the PRC was quite the opposite: in most cases, it did not intend to remind the audience of ongoing political disputes or military conflicts but purposely hid what was really going on in mainland China: economic woes, widespread famines, and political purges. The depoliticization of films exported to Hong Kong conformed to this British colony's cultural policies: only movies that "emphasized the development of the mainland" instead of illustrating the hostile international environment could "avoid provoking the censors" in British Hong Kong.[54] Therefore, the distributors and theaters in Hong Kong deliberately depoliticized PRC-made opera films by

---

49. Yang Panpan 楊槃槃, "Meng zhu chaosheng qu—'Lengzhan' geju xia de Chaoyu xiqu pian": 夢逐潮聲去——"冷戰" 格局下的潮語戲曲片 [The dream is gone with the noise of the tide—The Teochew opera film in the Cold War], *Dangdai dianying* 當代電影 [Contemporary Cinema], no. 7 (2017): 142.
50. Stacilee Ford, "'Reel Sisters' and Other Diplomacy: Cathay Studios and Cold War Cultural Production," in *Hong Kong in the Cold War*, ed. Priscilla Roberts and John M. Carroll (Hong Kong: Hong Kong University Press, 2016), 188.
51. Jeremy E. Taylor, *Rethinking Transnational Chinese Cinemas: The Amoy-Dialect Film Industry in Cold War Asia* (London: Routledge, 2011), 2.
52. Fu, "More than Just Entertaining," 2–3.
53. Tony Shaw and Denise J. Youngblood, *Cinematic Cold War: The American and Soviet Struggle for Hearts and Minds* (Lawrence: University Press of Kansas, 2010), 4.
54. Fu, "More than Just Entertaining," 17.

producing and exhibiting eye-catching posters and thereby "repackaging" them as nothing but market-oriented filmic products.⁵⁵

Under those circumstances, opera film was weaponized for the PRC authorities to win the Hong Kong filmgoers' hearts and minds, for they seemed depoliticized but served a particular political agenda of displaying a peace-loving new republic. Lanjun Xu finds that the Chinese government was eager to "change its masculine and military image" to rejoin the global community immediately after the Korean War.⁵⁶ Therefore, China-made opera films, starting from the well-known *Liang Shanbo and Zhu Yingtai*, persistently stressed "delicacy and sentiment" in the international market although the same films solicited their domestic audience in China to understand the struggle "against feudal oppression in ancient China."⁵⁷

It is worth mentioning that *Liang Shanbo and Zhu Yingtai*, for all its usefulness in the PRC's foreign affairs, was not initially designed to cater to the preferences of the Hong Kong audience. Xu Dunle 許敦樂 (b. 1925), a longtime manager of the PRC-invested Southern Film Corporation (*Nanfang yingye gongsi* 南方影業公司), recalled that this film's distributors in mainland China initially refused to add Chinese subtitles to accommodate the needs of Hong Kong's non-Wu dialect audience,⁵⁸ attesting to the CCP officers' irresponsiveness to the demands of the overseas market in the mid-1950s. Ironically, "the use of subtitling with Chinese characters" turned out to be the main reason behind opera film's success in Hong Kong and beyond.⁵⁹ *Liang Shanbo and Zhu Yingtai* scored a historic victory in the Hong Kong market: it managed to appeal to 520,505 viewers in 173 days, bringing in a whopping revenue of HK$671,578.⁶⁰ Therefore, the sensation that *Liang Shanbo and Zhu Yingtai* created prompted the Southern Film Corporation to import more opera films from the mainland. *Marriage Between a Fairy and Man* (*Tianxian pei* 天仙配, 1955, dir. Shi Hui) and *Searching a School* were among the most profitable movies in the Hong Kong market throughout the 1950s. Despite those films'

---

55. Kwok Wai Hui (Xu Guohui 許國惠), "Shangye yu zhengzhi: lengzhan shiqi Xianggang zuopai dui xin Zhongguo xiqu dianying haibao de zai chuangzao" 商業與政治：冷戰時期香港左派對新中國戲曲電影海報的再創造 [Business and politics: The left-wingers' remaking of opera film posters made in new China during the Cold War era], in *Shunliu yu niliu: chongxie Xianggang dianying shi* 順流與逆流：重寫香港電影史 [Current and counter current: Rewriting the film history of Hong Kong], ed. Poshek Fu (Fu Baoshi 傅葆石) and Su Tao 蘇濤 (Beijing: Beijing daxue chubanshe, 2020), 130.
56. Xu, "The Southern Film Corporation," 258.
57. Leyda, *Dianying*, 209. The same thing could be said about films about ethnic minorities. *Third Sister Liu* (*Liu sanjie* 劉三姐, 1963, dir. Su Li 蘇里), a film based on a popular legend of the Zhuang 壯 people, featured folksongs and the scenic beauty of Guilin 桂林. However, the CCP authorities tried to convince the audience in China that the film was made to highlight class struggle as its key theme. See Wai-fong Loh, "From Romantic Love to Class Struggle: Reflections on the Film *Liu Sanjie*," in *Popular Chinese Literature and Performing Arts in the People's Republic China, 1949–1979*, ed. Bonnie S. McDougall (Berkeley: University of California Press, 1984), 165–71.
58. Xu Dunle 許敦樂, *Kenguang tuoying* 墾光拓影 [Cultivating light and shadow] (Hong Kong: MCCM Creations, 2005), 33–35.
59. Xu, "The Southern Film Corporation," 249.
60. Xu, "The Southern Film Corporation," 223.

spectacular commercial success, as Poshek Fu notes, their role as the apparatus of "soft peddling propaganda" did not escape the attention of the contemporaries and the left-wingers' foes in Hong Kong.[61]

While Poshek Fu cites the phenomenal success of *Liang Shanbo and Zhu Yingtai* and other PRC-made opera films to bolster his argument that the cinematic Cold War in Hong Kong appeared "deceptively commercialized,"[62] the late 1950s and early 1960s marked a new phase of the cultural Cold War for the communist regime in China; that is, opera film's role as a moneymaking business loomed increasingly large in the minds of the CCP cadres. The severe famine during the Great Leap Forward and the ensuing economic crisis compelled the CCP authorities to readjust the film policies. Accordingly, opera film underwent a transformation from a showcase of China's national culture to a lucrative cinematic product catering to the tastes of the audiences in Hong Kong and Southeast Asia.

According to Xu Dunle, it was some high-ranking CCP officials, such as Liao Chengzhi 廖承志 (1908–1983) and Xia Yan, who directly took charge of film distribution in Hong Kong and thereby orchestrated such a transformation of opera film in the early 1960s.[63] To further captivate the local audience and pass the censorship imposed by the governments of Hong Kong and Southeast Asian countries, Xia Yan and Chen Huangmei,[64] along with other CCP cadres, passionately pushed for the coproduction of opera films between mainland film studios and Hong Kong–based leftwing companies, such as Great Wall (*Changcheng* 長城) Movie Enterprises Limited and Phoenix (*Fenghuang* 鳳凰) Film Corporation.[65] By 1962 and 1963, coproduced movies constituted more than half of the opera films made in China.[66] Some of those films, such as *The Jade Hairpin*, were screened exclusively in overseas markets.

It was thus obvious that coproduced opera films were an effective weapon deployed by the political authorities in mainland China and Hong Kong–based leftist filmmakers to both win the cinematic Cold War and rake in substantial revenues. Hence, high-ranking CCP cadres devoted meticulous attention to the visual effects of those movies, further giving prominence to opera film's nature as the cinema of attractions. During an oversight board meeting in 1963, for example, Chen Huangmei expressed his disappointment at the use of a mock ox and an artificial waterfall as the setting in the coproduced Huangmei opera movie, *The Cowherd and the Weaving Maid* (*Niulang zhinü* 牛郎織女, 1963, dir. Cen Fan 岑範). Chen emphasized that the mock ox was doomed to fail in the volatile Hong Kong market

---

61. Fu, "More than Just Entertaining," 20.
62. Fu, "More than Just Entertaining," 42.
63. Xu, *Kenguang tuoying*, 76.
64. Xu, *Kenguang tuoying*, 83.
65. Xu, "The Southern Film Corporation," 268.
66. Six out of twelve in 1962, and six out of ten in 1963. See He Weiguo 何衛國, *Hongloumeng yingshi wenhua yingshi wenhua lungao* 紅樓夢影視文化論稿 [Theses on motion culture and TV culture of *Dream of the Red Chamber*] (Beijing: Wenhua yishu chubanshe, 2017), 265.

because film fans there were used to viewing real tigers and lions that foreign filmmakers had brought to the screen.[67] Chen's remark thus revealed that, for many a CCP leader, the cinematic Cold War was boiled down to visual details as a key factor behind a movie's market success in this city.

The main goal of expending redoubled efforts to export opera films and facilitating coproduction was to earn foreign exchange in order to purchase much-needed film stock. As early as 1958, Xia Yan had already realized a severe shortage of film stock as the production of movies grew exponentially.[68] The inadequate supply of film stock was exacerbated one year later because of the pressing need for making films to celebrate the PRC's tenth anniversary. Consequently, Chen Huangmei personally paid visits to East Germany and the Soviet Union to tackle the problem.[69] Unfortunately, the China-Soviet rift in the late 1950s and early 1960s dealt the supply of film stock a heavy blow. The import of 35mm films, for example, dropped by 25 percent in the fall of 1960.[70] To resolve the issue, the Minister of Culture expressly demanded film studios to lower the consumption of cinefilms in the early 1960s: the spoiled cinefilm should not constitute over two-thirds of the total amount of film stock in any given film.[71] The shortage of monetary capital also hamstrung the program of localizing the production of film stock. In consequence, Marshal Chen Yi 陳毅 (1901–1972) recommended in 1964 that a Beijing opera film be made and sold to the overseas market in exchange for the funds to build a cinefilm factory.[72]

Among all upper-echelon CCP leaders, Xia Yan had a particular interest in exporting musicals and opera films to Hong Kong and Southeast Asia and urging filmmakers to participate in coproduction projects, sometimes against Chinese film studios' will and at the cost of the domestic film market. In 1964, for example, Xia suggested that the newly made musical *Ashma* (*Ashima* 阿詩瑪, 1964, dir. Liu Qiong) could be distributed in the Southeast Asian market before it was released in mainland China.[73] When the staff of Petrel Film Studio in Shanghai appeared resistant to a coproduction project recommended by Xia Yan,[74] one of his subordinates tried to appease the confused and resentful employees from Petrel by explaining

---

67. Shanghai Municipal Archives, B177-1-21, 99–100.
68. "Yishu pian fang weixing zuotanhui shang de baogao" 藝術片放衛星座談會上的報告 [A talk at the symposium on achieving prominent success in (producing) feature films], in *Zhongguo dianying yanjiu ziliao, 1949–1979 zhong* 中國電影研究資料：1949–1979 中 [Research materials of Chinese film, 1949–1979, bk. 2], ed. Wu Di 吳迪 (Beijing: Wenhua yishu chubanshe, 2006), 216.
69. Cheng, *Xia Yan dianying wenji, diyi juan*, 368–70.
70. Xu, *Tabian qingshan ren weilao*, 163.
71. Beijing Municipal Archives, 002-012-00153, 20.
72. Zhao Jingbo 趙景勃 and Ran Changjian 冉常建, *Wutai yu yinmu zhijian: xiqu dianying de huigu yu jiangshu* 舞臺與銀幕之間：戲曲電影的回顧與講述 [Between the stage and the screen: A review and narrative of opera films] (Beijing: Zhongguo wenlian chubanshe, 2007), 13.
73. Xu, *Tabian qingshan ren weilao*, 178,
74. Tang, *Chenmo shijin: Tang Xiaodan dianying riji xia*, 897.

that collaborating with their Hong Kong colleagues was meant to pledge the CCP's support of the disadvantaged leftwing filmmakers in this colonial setting.[75]

Cai Ben, vice-director of the Shanghai Film Bureau, identified himself as a practitioner of Xia Yan's agenda in his testimony in 1965. Cai summarized that Xia gave four reasons behind his endorsement for making coproduction movies: to meet the growing demands for film materials, to fulfill annual plans for movie production, to introduce China's operatic arts to the audience abroad and extend their influence beyond China, and to support progressive filmmakers in Hong Kong.[76] Evidently, economic gains had topped Xia Yan's agenda in the 1960s. Occasionally, Xia Yan's eagerness to push China-made opera films into the Hong Kong market overstepped the established government policy. In late 1962, Xia Yan was approached by Wu Xingzai 吳性栽 (1904–1919), a Shanghai émigré in Hong Kong and a freelance entrepreneur, to propose a colored remake of *Marriage Between a Fairy and Man* for the Hong Kong and Southeast Asia market. Wu's offer gained the approval of Xia and Chen Huangmei, who consigned Pegasus Film Studio to produce it. Much to Xia Yan's embarrassment, it turned out that Wu, who was not affiliated with any film company in Hong Kong, quickly sold the film rights to Shaw Bros., known as a Taiwan-backed film studio, thereby denying Pegasus's claim to it.[77]

The thrust of the controversy was that Xia Yan's personal decision overrode the party policy and the prevailing practice of the collaboration between mainland film companies and leftist filmmakers in Hong Kong. Although Shaw Bros. was labeled as "Right" during the cinematic Cold War because of its connection with Taiwan,[78] PRC-made films counted heavily on the distribution network of Shaw Bros. in Singapore and other Southeast Asian regions throughout the 1950s and 1960s.[79] In Hong Kong, the cooperation between the so-called left-wing and right-wing film studios was commonplace. The cash-strapped leftist film studios, particularly Phoenix, had to work with Shaw Bros. to secure a prepayment (one-third of the total price) before a movie was made. At the same time, Shaw Bros. was keen on acquiring rights to films made by leftwing film companies in order to amply supply its enormous network in Southeast Asia movies.[80]

---

75. "Fan gemin xiuzheng zhuyi fenzi Yang Yongzhi de shida zuizhuang" 反革命修正主義分子楊永直的十大罪狀 [Ten crimes (committed by) Yang Yongzhi, the counterrevolutionary revisionist], in *Chedi chanchu fan gemin xiuzheng zhuyi wenyi heixian ziliao huibian* 徹底鏟除反革命修正主義文藝黑綫資料彙編 [Completely eradicate the black line of the counterrevolutionary revisionist literature and arts: Compilation of materials], ed. Shanghai hongqi dianying zhipian chang hongqi gemin zaofan bingtuan 上海紅旗電影製版廠紅旗革命造反兵團 [The red flag revolutionary and rebellious corps of the Shanghai Red Flag Film Studio] (n.p., 1967), 161.
76. Tang, *Chenmo shijin: Tang Xiaodan dianying riji xia*, 899.
77. Shanghai Municipal Archives, A22-1-614, 26–28.
78. Law Kar and Frank Bren, *Hong Kong Cinema: A Cross-Cultural View* (Lanham, MA: The Scarecrow Press, 2004), 171.
79. Xu, "The Southern Film Corporation, Opera Films," 254–55.
80. Zhao Weifang 趙衛防 and Zhang Wenyan 張文燕, "Jianguo hou juyou neidi beijing de Xianggang dianying gongsi chengli chutan" 建國後具有內地背景的香港電影公司成立新探, [A new study on the establishment of Hong Kong film companies with mainland background after the founding of New China], *Shanghai daxue*

The intricate relationship—as both competitors and cooperators—between leftist and right-wing film companies in the 1960s was a testimony to the Janus-faced nature of the cinematic Cold War. For propagandists, it was a war waged between two ideological factions. In everyday life, the contention between the left-wing and right-wing filmmakers operated more like market competitions for box-office earnings.[81] To win the battles in the volatile Hong Kong market, it was of great necessity to appeal to the general, nonpartisan audience. Lau Shing Hon (Liu Chenghan 劉成漢, b. 1945), a seasoned Hong Kong filmmaker and critic, classifies the avid viewers of PRC-made movies in mid-century Hong Kong into four categories: elderly immigrants from the mainland, film workers who tried to learn cinematic skills from their mainland counterparts, left-wingers, and nonpartisans who refused to be relegated to second-class citizens.[82] Obviously, the loyal audience of mainland-produced or coproduction opera films fell into the first category.

The Jade Hairpin, a Yue Opera Film

The Hong Kong Tour

The Hong Kong citizens' "considerable nostalgia demand" for the presentations of China's traditional culture was met during the first half of the 1960s with the visits of numerous operatic troupes, including those of Beijing opera, Cantonese opera, Teochew opera (*Chaoju* 潮劇), Pingtan 評彈 storytelling, and Yue opera. While the British authorities in Hong Kong were usually tolerant of such activities with "a genuine nonpolitical nature,"[83] the audience greeted artists from the mainland with immense enthusiasm. The Teochew opera troupe's visit to Hong Kong in 1961, for example, coincided with a typhoon, but the crowd still swarmed to the theater, scrambling for tickets.[84] The Yue opera stars' visit between December 1960 and January 1961 similarly met with a rapturous reception from Hong Kong dwellers, mostly with Yangzi Delta backgrounds. It was reported that operatic fans from

---

xuebao (shehui kexue ban) 上海大學學報（社會科學版）[Journal of Shanghai University (Social Sciences Edition)] 29, no. 6 (November 2012): 29.
81. Qiaiboshi 奇愛博士, "Xianggang zuopai chuanqi—'Chang Feng Xin' de gushi" 香港左派傳奇—長鳳新"的故事 [The legend of Hong Kong's left-wing (film companies)]—The stories of Great War, Phoenix, and United Film Corporation], *Dazhong dianying* 大衆電影 [Mass Film], no. 18 (2015): 91.
82. Liu Chenghan 劉成漢 (Lau Shing Hon), "Zhongguo neidi zai dianying zai Xianggang—zongjie pian" 中國內地電影在香港—總結篇 [Mainland-made films in Hong Kong—A summary], in *Shanyao zai tongyi xingkong—Zhongguo neidi dianying zai Xianggang* 閃耀在同一星空—中國內地電影在香港 [Shining in the same starry sky—mainland-made films in Hong Kong], ed. Zhu Hong 朱虹 (Kunming: Yunnan renmin chubanshe, 2005), 283–84.
83. Xu, "The Southern Film Corporation, Opera Films," 272.
84. Ye Shuyu 葉舒瑜 (Yap Soo Ei), "Lengzhan yu Xianggang de Changcheng, Fenghuang, Xinlian—yi 1945–1967 nian wei kaocha shiduan" 冷戰與香港的長城、鳳凰、新聯—以1945–1967年為考察時段 [A study of the Hong Kong leftist film companies during the Cold War (1945–1967)] (MA thesis, National University of Singapore, 2011), 55.

the Americas and Southeast Asia expressly flew in for the performances.[85] Such a passion attests to the lasting impact of what Poshek Fu calls the "Shanghai-Hong Kong nexus," which had played a central role in the popular culture and entertainment industry between the 1930s and the founding of the PRC.[86]

For the CCP authorities, the sensation created during the Hong Kong tour provided an impetus to popularize the arts of Yue opera, to proclaim the PRC as a successor to and reviver of China's traditional culture,[87] and most importantly, to display an affluent and prosperous Chinese nation at a time when rumors were flying about the ongoing Great Leap Forward famine and severe economic difficulties in China. Hence, all Yue opera performers were obligated to take on glamorous appearances in public during the tour. Xu Yulan 徐玉蘭 (1921–2017) recalled that all actresses and actors gathered in Shamian Island 沙面, Guangzhou, to receive special training about how to cope with the Hong Kong audience and media properly. She and her colleagues were asked to wear *qipao* and wool coats before heading for Hong Kong, trying to convince Hong Kong fans into believing that the rumored shortage of daily necessities in mainland China was completely fabricated.[88] Elsewhere, Xu remembered that all the Yue opera stars stepped down off the train at the railway station in Hong Kong with high-heeled shoes, *qipao*, and permed hair.[89]

The need to visually impress the Hong Kong citizens both on and off the stage indicated that the political authorities had cast the Yue opera as exhibitionistic and thereby highly politicized art to win the hearts and souls of local theatergoers and ordinary city-dwellers. This tour constituted part and parcel of the CCP's newly enacted policy of foreign affairs in the wake of the Great Leap Forward. This policy, characterized by the willingness to compromise with the governments of non-communist countries and cater to the tastes of the local audience, would come under scathing criticism during the Cultural Revolution. Xia Yan and Chen Huangmei, two of the engineers and practitioners of this politico-cultural agenda, were later accused of "ingratiating [themselves] with imperialists and revisionists" (*meidi meixiu* 媚帝媚修) and "sabotaging the world revolution" (*pohuai shijie gemin* 破壞世界革命). Xia Yan, in particular, allegedly kept exporting programs about "emperors, kings, generals, ministers, scholars, and beauties" (*diwang jiangxiang caizi jiaren* 帝王將相才子佳人) to foreign markets until 1964.[90]

---

85. Yuan Xuefen 袁雪芬 et al., "He Xianggang tongbao xiangchu de rizi" 和香港同胞相處的日子 [(Our) days with the Hong Kong compatriots], *Xiju bao* 戲劇報 [The Drama Journal], no. 4 (1961): 14.
86. Poshek Fu, *Between Shanghai and Hong Kong: The Politics of Chinese Cinemas* (Stanford: Stanford University Press, 2003), xii–xiii.
87. Hui, "Revolution, Commercialism and Chineseness," 188.
88. "Yueju Honglou meng qingqian 50 zai" 越劇紅樓夢情牽50載 [The Yue operatic (play) of *Dream of the Red Chamber*: Sentiment that lingers for half a century], Shanghai TV Station, March 15, 2008.
89. Xu Yulan 徐玉蘭 and Dong Yu 董煜, *Renru baiyu xi ru lan* 人如白玉戲如蘭 [The person is like white jade, and the play orchid] (Shanghai: Shanghai shiji chuban gufen youxian gongsi, 2013), 145.
90. "Fan gemin xiuzheng zhuyi fenzi Xia Yan de shida zuizhuang" 反革命修正主義分子夏衍的十大罪狀 [Ten crimes (committed by) Xia Yan, the counterrevolutionary revisionist], in *Chedi chanchu fan gemin xiuzheng zhuyi wenyi heixian ziliao huibian* 徹底剷除反革命修正主義文藝黑線資料彙編 [Completely eradicate the

For the radicals during the Cultural Revolution, the commercial success of this tour was a telltale sign of Xia Yan's anti-Maoist cultural policy. It allegedly drew admiration from "revisionists" in China and the Soviet Union and reaped enormous profits in Hong Kong.[91] Therefore, the tour was blamed for pandering to the corrupted Hong Kong audience's preferences and performing the task of "gathering currency" (*huobi huilong* 貨幣回籠), that is, achieving commercial success.[92] The criticism revealed a hidden agenda behind organizing the Hong Kong tour, earning foreign exchange for a cash-strapped country deep in economic trouble. Of all the plays staged at the Astor Theatre (*Puqing xiyuan* 普慶戲院), the blockbuster *Dream of the Red Chamber* (*Honglou meng* 紅樓夢) and the relatively low-profile *The Jade Hairpin* (*Biyu zan* 碧玉簪) captured the rapt attention of Hong Kong filmmakers and investors, such as Run Run Shaw (Shao Yifu 邵逸夫, 1907–2014).[93] A plan was thus brewing to make the two films for the Hong Kong market.

The Jade Hairpin

The byproducts of the Yue opera performers' Hong Kong tour, *Dream of the Red Chamber* and *The Jade Hairpin*, were later remembered as "twin excellences" (*liangjue* 兩絕) of opera films for their spectacular box-office success in Hong Kong.[94] They wound up creating a new wave of sensation of China-made opera films in general and Yue opera films in particular in this British colony in the mid-1960s. A Hong Kong writer proclaimed in 1962 that Yue opera movies had gained the most enormous popularity, but the Chinese authorities were obviously concerned that Yue opera stars might have devoted themselves exclusively to filmmaking and therefore spent no time on stage in China. Therefore, the CCP cadres decided to reverse the trend of producing too many blockbuster Yue opera films for the Hong Kong market and demanded that they refocus onstage performances in 1963.[95] *Dream of Red the Chamber*'s success was reasonably predictable, considering

---

black line of the counterrevolutionary revisionist literature and arts: Compilation of materials], ed. Shanghai hongqi dianying zhipian chang hongqi gemin zaofan bingtuan 上海紅旗電影製片廠紅旗革命造反兵團 [The revolutionary and rebellious corps of the Shanghai Red Flag Film Studio] (n.p., 1967), 71.

91. Shangyue bayi gongshe changying 上越八一公社長纓 [The long spear of the August 1 commune at Shanghai Yue opera troupe], "Yueju *Honglou meng* bixu chedi pipan" 越劇《紅樓夢》必須徹底批判 [We must thoroughly criticize *Dream of the Red Chamber*, the Yue opera play], in *Yueju zhanbao* 越劇戰報 [Yue opera war report], ed. Shanghai Yueju yuan bayi gongshe *Yueju zhanbao* bianji bu 上海越劇院八一公社《越劇戰報》編輯部 [Editorial office of Yue opera war report of the August 1 commune at Shanghai Yue opera troupe] (n.p., 1967), 11.
92. "Hu Yeqin shi Yueju yuan dangnei touhao zou ziben zhuyi daolu de dangquan pai" 胡野檎是越劇院黨內頭號走資本主義道路的當權派 [Hu Yeqin is the number one capitalist establishment inside the communist party in the Yue opera troupe], in *Yueju zhanbao* 越劇戰報 [Yue opera war report], ed. Shanghai Yueju yuan bayi gongshe *Yueju zhanbao* bianji bu 上海越劇院八一公社《越劇戰報》編輯部 [Editorial office of Yue opera war report of the August 1 commune at Shanghai Yue opera troupe] (n.p., 1967), 13.
93. Xu, *Kenguang tuoying*, 83–84.
94. Wu, *Shanghai dianying zhi*, 341.
95. Shanghai Municipal Archives, B177-3-419, 18–19.

its all-star cast and record-breaking budget.[96] By comparison, *The Jade Hairpin*'s relatively modest budget and unimpressive casting made its market success more noteworthy.

The Jade Hairpin reportedly raked in a considerable box-office revenue of HK$750,000, a record for all Chinese-language movies in 1963.[97] A Hong Kong–based newspaper accredited the film's success to Jin Caifeng's 金采風 (b. 1930) superb performing skills and, more importantly, breathtakingly beautiful appearance. According to the author of this newspaper essay, Jin, who had been humbled to play a supporting role in *Dream of the Red Chamber*, shone brilliantly in this film. She was considered able to rival any film stars in Hong Kong who earned their reputations for their good looks. Meanwhile, the filmmakers' outstanding skills of shooting the movie and the rich color applied to its scenes overcame a universal shortcoming in nearly all PRC-made films, subpar cinematography.[98] Without a doubt, the visual effect in this movie was accomplished because of the first-class film stock imported from Hong Kong. It is thus fair to argue that it was the star Yue opera performer's enchanting beauty and exquisite artificial scenes presented by the moviemakers, but not necessarily its plotline, that ensured the film's high popularity in the Hong Kong market. In other words, it typified a Chinese "cinema of attractions" as recognized by Chris Berry and Mary Ann Farquhar.

The film's storyline, by comparison, not only lacked complexity but also sparked widespread controversy. In the words of its inspector, Xia Yan, *The Jade Hairpin* was short of correct "ideological principles" (*sixiang xing* 思想性) because it portrayed a woman in imperial China who was willing to put up with her husband's physical and mental abuses. The disgruntled Xia complained that he was unable to find any anti-feudal implications in the film. Instead, he believed that the film became the apologist of the feudal system in ancient China.[99] Xia's negative assessments were not unfounded. Set in the Ming dynasty, *The Jade Hairpin* pivoted on the unfortunate marriage between Ms. Li Xiuying 李秀英, a daughter of the Minister of Personnel, and Wang Yulin 王玉林. Wang suspected that his newlywed wife had an affair with her cousin and therefore mentally tormented Xiuying for a long while. At night, Yulin refused to share a bed with Xiuying but chose to put his head on his desk to sleep. Concerned that Yulin might catch a cold but frustrated by his

---

96. The archival record shows that the cost of *Dream of the Red Chamber* amounted to 836,078.53 yuan (about HK$1.9 million). See Shanghai Municipal Archives, B177-3-371, 3–6. By comparison, the cost of a Hong Kong–made film was between HK$200,000 and HK$300,000 in the mid-1960s. See Law and Bren, *Hong Kong Cinema*, 162.
97. Xu Yuan 許元, "Yueju dianying fazhan shi kaolun" 越劇電影發展史考論 [Investigation and analysis of the history of Yue opera films], in *Xiju xue di 5 ji* 戲劇學第5輯 [Studies on drama, number 5], ed. Shanghai xiju xueyuan xiju xue yanjiu zhongxin 上海戲劇學院戲劇研究中心 [Research center of drama studies at the Shanghai Theater Academy] (Shanghai: Wenhua yishu chubanshe, 2017), 51.
98. "Xianggang *Xinsheng wanbao* zaiwen zanshang wo Yueju yingpian *Biyu zan*" 香港《新生晚報》載文讚賞我越劇影片《碧玉簪》[Hong Kong Xinsheng Evening publishes an essay to praise our Yue opera film, *The Jade Hairpin*], *Cankao xiaoxi* 參考消息 [Reference News], April 25, 1963.
99. Shanghai Municipal Archives, B177-1-288, 51.

longtime mistreatment, Xiuying hesitated whether she should cover her husband with a coat to keep him warm. In the movie as well on the stage, Jin Caifeng put on an emotional but self-restrained performance to underscore the protagonist's intense internal conflict, making this portion of the operatic play one of the best-recognized episodes known as "Covering Clothes Three Times" (*San gaiyi* 三蓋衣). All the misunderstandings were cleared up at the end of the film, but Xiuying refused to pardon her husband. Finally, it took Yulin's success in obtaining the first rank in the upcoming Civil Service Exam to win Xiuying's heart again.

A woman's low status in her marriage, her submission to humiliation, and the necessity of a man to succeed in the Civil Service Exam, among other things, all supported Xia Yan's position that this ideologically backward film contributed to defending China's feudal legacy. On the eve of the Cultural Revolution, *The Jade Hairpin* would be cited as an example of Xia's promotion of "the privileges and rights of the feudal class" (*fengjian faquna* 封建法權).[100] This accusation was based on Xia's approval of the movie's release despite his dissatisfaction. However, *The Jade Hairpin* was allowed to be screened in the market outside mainland China only. As I have stated, Xia's eagerness to sell *The Jade Hairpin* to Hong Kong and Southeast Asia stemmed from the PRC's enormous demands for foreign currency. In a report to the Ministry of Culture, the Shanghai government anticipated that the investment from Hong Kong could meet the expenditure of importing filmic devices and machinery for Chinese film studios.[101] The coproducer from Hong Kong, Giant Roc Film Company (*Dapeng yingye gongsi* 大鵬影業公司), an alternative name for Phoenix Film Corporation, ended up paying its partner in Shanghai, Petrel Film Studio, HK$200,000, the same amount of investment for *Dream of the Red Chamber* despite the latter's far greater cost. The contract signed between the two coproducers specified that the former was entitled to receive all the revenue from markets of capitalist countries or regions, such as Hong Kong, Macau, Singapore/Malaysia, Indonesia, and Burma.[102] Upon further deliberation, however, the Chinese authorities decided to take back the rights in the Cambodian, Burmese, and Indonesian markets, considering that the three countries had established diplomatic relations with the PRC.[103] This dispute was a testimony to the Chinese authorities' keenness on maximally retaining opera films' profits in the overseas market in this Cold War era.

Wu Yonggang

The status of *The Jade Hairpin* as a film exclusively for the market outside mainland China unintentionally allowed its filmmakers to achieve a high degree of autonomy,

---

100. Shanghai Municipal Archives, B177-1-172, 74.
101. Shanghai Municipal Archives, A22-2-1055, 19.
102. Shanghai Municipal Archives, A22-2-1055, 25–26.
103. Shanghai Municipal Archives, A22-2-1055, 18.

artistically and ideologically. The female protagonist's excessive tolerance and patience and the final conciliation between the spouses in the film are consistent with the topics of practically all films Wu Yonggang directed before and after it. Although Rey Chow attributes the success of Wu's *The Goddess* to the welding of "the historical content of social oppression and the innovative formal elements that are specific to the film medium,"[104] it is worth mentioning that "social oppression" or class struggle as a central theme of *The Goddess* was not pushed for by Wu but by the leftwing filmmakers, including Xia Yan, behind the screen. On the contrary, Wu strove to downplay bitter struggles in the external world and preferred to highlight the main character's psychological condition.[105] In his essay published in 1935, Wu acknowledged that his portrayal of the lives of lower-class members and class-based clashes was inadequate. As he intended to show the goodness of human nature, he created the persona of the school headmaster with "a good conscience" to incarnate "justice" in Chinese society.[106]

In all his films in the 1930s and 1940s, Wu Yonggang displayed a solid tendency to deemphasize class struggle and reiterate the notion of class conciliation by heaping praise on a sublime personality and pursuing the universal virtues of humankind.[107] Because of his prioritization of presenting human nature on the screen, his relationship with leftwing filmmakers quickly soured.[108] Wu's humanistic bent did not vanish after 1949. His final work, *Evening Rain* (*Bashan yeyu* 巴山夜雨, 1980), similarly lauded the noble human nature without laying the blame on the Cultural Revolution despite the political purge he underwent in the past decades.[109] While scholars were inclined to label Wu as a humanist (*rendao zhuyi zhe* 人道主義者), Kristine Harris suggests that this humanism be interpreted within the "Confucian framework";[110] but Paul Pickowicz traces Wu's humanism to his education in a Christian middle school in Henan and defines it as "Christian humanism."[111]

---

104. Rey Chow, *Primitive Passions: Visuality, Sexuality, Ethnography, and Contemporary Chinese Cinema* (New York: Columbia University Press, 1995), 24–25.
105. Shao Wenyan 邵雯豔, *Huayu dianying yu Zhongguo xiqu* 華語電影與中國戲曲 [Sinophone films and Chinese operas] (Shanghai: Fudan daxue chubanshe, 2013), 46.
106. Wu Yonggang 吳永剛, "Shennü wancheng zhihou" 神女完成之後 [After completing *The Goddess*], *Lianhua huabao* 聯華畫報 [UPS Pictorial] 5, no. 1 (1935): 2–3.
107. Lian Xiufeng 連秀鳳, "Cengjing canghai nanwei shui—pouxi Wu Yonggang de dianying meixue guan" 曾經滄海難為水—剖析吳永剛的電影美學觀 [Having ever seen a vast ocean, one may not content himself with a pond of water: An analysis of Wu Yonggang's ideas of cinematic aesthetics] (MA thesis, Beijing dianying xueyuan, 1992), 3–12.
108. Chen Mo 陳墨, "Gungun bujin Langtaosha" 滾滾不盡《浪淘沙》 [A review of *Gold and Sand*], *Dangdai dianying* 當代電影 [Contemporary Cinema], no. 2 (2005): 85.
109. Gao Xiaojian 高小健, "Wu Yonggang: zhuisuo bujin de huati—yige dianying zhishi fenzi de jingshen yu yishu" 吳永剛：追索不盡的話題—一個電影知識份子的精神與藝術 [Wu Yonggang: An eternal topic—The spirit and arts of a cinematic intellectual], *Dangdai dianying* 當代電影 [Contemporary Cinema], no. 5 (2004): 50.
110. Kristine Harris, "The Goddess," in *Chinese Films in Focus II*, ed. Chris Berry (London: BFI/Palgrave MacMillan, 2008), 129.
111. Pickowicz, *China on Film*, 62.

The female protagonist's willingness to tolerate and finally pardon her abusive husband in *The Jade Hairpin* once again sheds light on Wu Yonggang's humanism, as one can see in all his other films. Nevertheless, Wu's colleagues and friends were keen on placing Xiuying's conciliatory attitude in the film in the context of the hostile political situation and the wretched political plight Wu had faced in Mao-era China and thereby interpreting it in a different light. Yu Ling, former director of the Bureau of Culture in Shanghai, asserted in 1983 that making *The Jade Hairpin* allowed the embattled Wu Yonggang to publicize his positive attitudes in times of dreadful hardship since the late 1950s; that is, "not losing heart, not complaining, and not becoming dispirited" (*bu sangqi, bu baoyuan, bu tuishang* 不喪氣，不抱怨，不頹傷) and "steeling himself to wait for [his] loyalty and goodwill to be revealed" (*moli yi xu jian zhongliang* 磨礪以須見忠良).[112]

What Yu Ling referred to here was Wu Yonggang's victimhood in the midst of the Anti-Rightist Movement in 1957 that dealt Wu a heavy blow, politically, artistically, and financially. In the first half of the 1950s, Wu gained the CCP authorities' recognition as a veteran artist and a productive director. Therefore, he was given an official rank as a level 2—one of the highest in the world of film in Shanghai—artist.[113] Despite this, as I have mentioned, the party authorities behind closed doors dismissed Wu as a self-conceited and poorly motivated filmmaker who was consistently critical of the CCP in the mid-1950s. Wu, who was clearly aware of such negativity, began to have a few essays published in late 1956, openly questioning the CCP's leading role in filmmaking. For example, he stated that film was by nature an art form rather than an instrument of ideological edification.[114] In a separate essay, Wu demanded that the party give freer rein to filmmakers in moviemaking.[115]

Wu's viewpoints soon came under harsh criticism. Wu's colleague, Ai Mingzhi 艾明之 (1925–2017), for example, not only blamed Wu for whipping up "anti-CCP" (*fandang* 反黨) feeling but also accused Wu's pre-1949 productions of having "poisoned" (*mazui* 麻醉) the audience and contributed to Chiang Kai-shek's conciliatory policies and capitulationism on the eve of the Anti-Japanese War (1937–1945).[116] The publication of Ai's essay in *The People's Daily*, the party's mouthpiece, forbode the political maelstrom Wu Yonggang was drawn into: he was stigmatized as a "Rightist." In all fairness, Ai's castigatory essay rightly summed up a central thread running from the 1930s to the 1940s in most of Wu's films; that is,

---

112. Yu Ling 于伶, "Yonggang, yongbie le!" 永剛，永別了！[Yonggang, farewell!], in *Zhongguo dianying nianjian 1983* 中國電影年鑒1983 [Chinese film yearbook, 1983], ed. Zhongguo dianying jia xiehui [China Film Association] (Beijing: Zhongguo dianying chubanshe, 1984), 124.
113. Shanghai Municipal Archives, B177-3-80, 2.
114. Wu Yonggang 吳永剛, "Zhenglun buneng daiti yishu" 政論不能代替藝術 [Political commentary should not usurp arts], *Wenhui bao* 文匯報 [Wenhui Daily], December 7, 1956.
115. Wu Yonggang 吳永剛, "Chunfeng jiedong yougan" 春風解凍有感 [Some thoughts (inspired by) thawing by the spring breeze], *Xinmin wanbao* 新民晚報 [Xinmiin Evening News], May 5, 1957.
116. Ai Mingzhi 艾明之, "Bo Wu Yonggang" 駁吳永剛 [Refuting Wu Yonggang], *Renmin ribao* 人民日報 [People's Daily], November 27, 1957.

the possibility of maintaining the harmonious relationships among individuals of differing gender, class, and ideological backgrounds, and the emphasis of humanistic universalism. Hence, the predicament Wu faced stemmed, in part, from the incompatibility between his humanism and the theory of class struggle endorsed by the CCP. In the following five years, Wu suffered a demotion and a substantial pay cut: his ranking was lowered from level 2 in 1956 to level 9 in 1961, and his salary was halved accordingly.[117] He was stripped of the opportunity to direct a film and spent years in exile in the department of art designing.[118]

In a changing political climate in the early 1960s, the party authorities showed benevolence to veteran filmmakers in an attempt to regain the latter's support. Under this circumstance, Wu Yonggang finally took an opportunity to direct a movie, which turned out to be *The Jade Hairpin*. A declassified document revealed that cadres of the film studio were dwelling on a dilemma then: Wu's political stigma should be removed because of a relatively relaxing political atmosphere, but the studio could not afford to run the risk of allowing Wu to direct a regular feature film. Once again, as described, opera film became a shelter for seasoned directors, such as Wu.[119] More intriguingly, *The Jade Hairpin* was poised to supply the overseas market as a weapon amid the cinematic Cold War and was not expected to be screened in China. In this sense, assigning Wu Yonggang to direct this opera film led to the segregation of this politically questionable director from the massive audience in mainland China. Xia Yan's authorization of the film's release despite his questioning of its political correctness was a testimony to his recognition of such segregation. Depriving the audience in mainland China of the opportunity to see the film unintentionally afforded Wu a niche to practice the much-sought-after professional autonomy he had cried for back in 1956 and 1957. It was thus understandable that Wu's lifelong pursuit of a harmonious relationship among individuals of diverse backgrounds was encapsulated in Xiuying's final forgiveness for her tyrannical husband in *The Jade Hairpin*.

In the film, the female protagonist's effort to maintain kindness and good faith despite her husband's physical and mental abuses culminated in the aforesaid episode of "Covering Clothes Three Times," a fifteen-minute long shot in the second half of the film. To highlight Xiuying's hesitation, confusion, apprehension, and resentment, Wu deftly made use of the camera to its fullest. Indeed, Wu's camera has long been a subject of scholarly inquiry. For example, Kristine Harris notes that Wu Yonggang's use of the camera in *The Goddess* served the purposes of "visual domination and physical violation."[120] William Rothman argues that Wu differed

---

117. Shanghai Municipal Archives, B177-7-363, 6.
118. Ye Ming 葉明, "Wu Yonggang daoyan yishu de daolu" 吳永剛導演藝術的道路 [The path of Wu Yonggang's directorial arts], in *Wode tansuo he zhuiqui* 我的探索和追求 [My exploration and pursuits], ed. Wu Yonggang 吳永剛 (Beijing: Zhongguo dianying chubanshe, 1986), 9.
119. Shanghai Municipal Archives, A22-2-1233, 96.
120. Harris, "*The Goddess*," 132.

from D. W. Griffith (1875–1948) and Josef von Sternberg in their cameras' relationships with their female stars. For Griffith and von Sternberg, the camera related to their female protagonists as the father, but for Wu, the camera provided an angle from the goddess's son, who kept growing up but retained "his filial piety."[121] In the post-1949 era, Wu's self-conscious manipulation of the camera gave way to a more "objective" use of the camera, that is, the concealment of the director as the subjective gazer. The fifteen-minute long shot of "Covering Clothes Three Times" was cited as an example of Wu's transition to a more "naturalistic" way of shooting films in PRC times.[122] Given *The Jade Hairpin* as a locus for Wu Yonggang's self-expression,[123] nonetheless, it was unavoidable that he would once again manipulate the camera to serve his purpose. To shoot the fifteen-minute long shot of "Covering Clothes Three Times," as Wu's former colleague believed, Wu borrowed a wagon from a funeral parlor to function as a dolly.[124] It is difficult to verify or falsify this claim, but the horizontal camera movement was frequently used within this fifteen-minute timeframe. In the climax of this episode, the indecisive Xiuying was lifting the coat and contemplating offering assistance to her husband she both loved and bore a grudge against. Torn between the two conflicting sentiments, Xiuying slowly but steadily moved from the left to the right. Here, Jin Caifeng's superb stage techniques of taking small steps while maintaining a motionless upper body were given a full presentation because of Wu's horizontal camera movement. After the performer completed her small-step movement, the camera was abruptly raised to offer a high-angle shot to spotlight this mistreated and vulnerable woman. In *The Goddess*, Wu's high-angle shot was interpreted as his imposition of "coercion and force" upon the miserable woman.[125] In contrast, the high-angle shot in *The Jade Hairpin* served as an invitation to beg film viewers to bear witness to this hesitant victim's final decision to help and salve her victimizer (see Figure 4.1).

Wu Yonggang's camera movement thus enhanced Xiuying's image as a woman who attempted to redeem the injustice she undeservedly received with her warm-heartedness and sincerity. For Wu's colleagues and friends, the hesitant, resentful, but still caring wife was the incarnation of Wu himself in this adverse political environment. It thus came as no surprise that Yu Ling depicted Wu's mentality in the 1950s and 1960s as "not losing heart, not complaining, and not becoming dispirited" with the hope that the political authorities—his victimizers—would correct all misunderstandings and dispel all doubts about his allegiance. As in many of his films, Wu was anxious to build a conciliatory relationship between the victim and the victimizer, between himself and the CCP. To this end, Wu experimented with a new relationship between the camera and the female star in *The Jade Hairpin*; not

---

121. Rothman, *The 'I' of the Camera*, 59–62.
122. Gao, "Wu Yonggang," 55.
123. Gao, "Wu Yonggang," 55.
124. Ye, "Wu Yonggang daoyan yishu de daolu," 10–11.
125. Harris, "*The Goddess*," 132.

Figure 4.1: When shooting the long episode "Covering Clothes Three Times," Wu Yonggang used medium shots and close-ups to show the resentful and hesitant wife. By the end of this long episode, the camera is hoisted to give a high-angle shot to demonstrate the actress's horizontal movement and invite the audience to cast their gazes on a more determined Xiuying, who finally decides to pardon her husband by covering the man with a coat to keep him warm. Screenshot from *The Jade Hairpin*.

that between the mother and the son as in *The Goddess* three decades before, but that between Wu and himself: Xiuying was Wu's mirror image at this moment. Film researchers in post-Mao China thus rightly commented that Xiuying's performance, singing and bodily movements included, gave full expression of Wu's pent-up resentment and acute depression after he was branded a "Rightist."[126] Without a doubt, it was the necessity of winning the market in Hong Kong and Southeast Asia

---

126. Gao, "Wu Yonggang," 52.

at the height of the cinematic Cold War that afforded Wu the luxury of attaining the goal of artistic autonomy and allowed for more unrestrained self-expression.

Conclusion

The Jade Hairpin was not the only opera film Wu Yonggang directed to give vent to a sense of grievance and express his desire for the party's understanding, if in an indirect way. A year later, Wu produced *Third Sister You*, a Beijing opera movie. It similarly centered upon a female protagonist who was eager to clear herself when her fiancé threw her chastity into doubt. Film scholars have been keenly aware of Wu's self-activating agency to inject his own feelings into both films he made in the 1960s.[127] By comparison, *The Jade Hairpin* has garnered greater attention both in Hong Kong and in post–Cultural Revolution China. *The Jade Hairpin*'s success, just like that of *Liang Shanbo and Zhu Yingtai* and many other Yue opera films, resided in Yue opera's conduciveness to cinematization. As Jin Jiang finds, the motion picture, particularly those from Hollywood, had long exerted an impact on Yue opera performers "in search of their own acting style" before 1949.[128] It is the proximity between cinema and Yue opera and other operas in southern China that defines the "southern school" of opera film, whose less stylized performance allows for a greater degree of intervention from the directors.[129]

It thus came as no surprise that the malleability and manipulability of Yue opera enabled Wu Yonggang to cinematize *The Jade Hairpin* and make it a locus to unleash his feelings. Meanwhile, the imperative of the cinematic Cold War in Hong Kong and Southeast Asia impelled the political authorities to tolerate, if not encourage, Wu to produce such a politically incorrect and ideologically dubious film. For Xia Yan and his likeminded CCP cadres, *The Jade Hairpin*'s immense popularity in Hong Kong helped to fulfill multiple goals: to absorb investments from Hong Kong and overseas film companies, to earn invaluable foreign exchange in support of China's fragile economy, to exhibit a prosperous and affluent nation with a rich cultural heritage to an international audience, to promote China's cultural tradition, and to nurture a left-leaning audience in Hong Kong. Ultimately, the CCP officials took aim at maximally appealing to the audience in Hong Kong and thereby winning the cinematic Cold War in this colonial city. It was under such exceptional politico-cultural circumstances that Wu Yonggang produced *The Jade Hairpin* and enjoyed the rare opportunity to imprint the film with a mark of his filmmaking style, humanistic bearings, and personal sensibilities, something he had struggled mightily for but failed to obtain back in the late 1950s.

---

127. Gao, "Wu Yonggang," 50.
128. Jiang, *Women Playing Men*, 81.
129. Ding, "Xin Zhongguo xiqu pian, meishu pian zai Gang chuanbo yanjiu," 79.

5

The Making of Xie Jin in the PRC

Womanhood, Melodrama, and Co-authorship

Xie Jin, arguably the "single most important film-maker during the first half-century of the PRC"[1] and one of the most influential artists in China in the second half of the twentieth century,[2] enjoyed a high reputation both domestically and internationally. Film viewers, critics, and scholars of different backgrounds have sung high praise of Xie and his film productions for different reasons. For example, he is lauded as a gifted director who could successfully negotiate "the political demands of the new Chinese cinema and the aesthetic traditions of pre-1949 Shanghai cinema."[3] More specifically, Xie is remembered to have been "at the forefront of the exploration of different representations of women within socialist cinema"[4] and have experimented with a new type of comedy in response to the ongoing political mass mobilization in Mao's China.[5] In short, Xie Jin's success in post-1949 China resided in both his effort to absorb foreign filmic ideas and practices[6] and his willingness to embrace the socialist ideologies. Hence, for some critics, Xie exemplified a new generation of Chinese filmmakers who succeeded in adopting "a set of language and knowledge [based upon] a new worldview."[7]

In the 1980s, the assessment of this experienced and accomplished director became polarized. On the one hand, a new breed of scholars, Zhu Dake 朱大可 (b.

---

1. Robert Chi, "The Red Detachment of Women: Resenting, Regendering, Remembering," in *Chinese Films in Focus: 25 New Takes*, ed. Chris Berry (London: BFI Publishing, 2003), 155.
2. Yu Qiuyu 余秋雨, "Xu" 序 [Preface], in *Lun Xie Jin dianying* 論謝晉電影 [On Xie Jin's films], ed. Zhongguo dianying jia xiehui 中國電影家協會 [China Film Association] (Beijing: Zhongguo dianying chubanshe, 1998), 1.
3. Lu, *Moulding the Socialist Subject*, 55.
4. Marchetti, "Two Stage Sisters," 60.
5. Lu, *Moulding the Socialist Subject*, 47.
6. Zhong Dianfei believed that Xie Jin kept making progress because he immersed himself in "new filmic concepts" from foreign countries, especially Italy. See Zhong Dianfei 鍾惦棐, "Xie Jin dianying shisi" 謝晉電影十思 [Ten thoughts on Xie Jin's films], in *Lun Xie Jin dianying* 論謝晉電影 [On Xie Jin's films], ed. Zhongguo dianying jia xiehui 中國電影家協會 [China Film Association] (Beijing: Zhongguo dianying chubanshe, 1998), 100.
7. Li Yiming 李奕明, "Xie Jin dianying zai Zhongguo dianying shi shang de diwei" 謝晉電影在中國電影史上的地位 [The standing of Xie Jin's films in Chinese film history], in *Lun Xie Jin dianying* 論謝晉電影 [On Xie Jin's films], ed. Zhongguo dianying jia xiehui 中國電影家協會 [China Film Association] (Beijing: Zhongguo dianying chubanshe, 1998), 72.

1957) in particular, blamed Xie Jin for being a "cinematic Confucianist" who used "blatant emotional manipulation to put across dated moral points."[8] On the other hand, as Xie's fame as a first-rate filmmaker in China continued to grow throughout the decade, his making of several movies set in the Cultural Revolution, particularly *Hibiscus Town* (*Furong zhen* 芙蓉鎮, 1986), enabled him to assume a leading role in representing the traumatic experiences during the Cultural Revolution and as a vocal critic of the CCP. In those films, some CCP cadres are singled out as the victimizers who inflict trauma upon the intellectuals and artists during this tumultuous decade.[9]

Ironically, what Xie Jin has been acclaimed for and blamed for is essentially the same thing: his ability to emotionally appeal to (or manipulate) the audiences or his "signature melodramatic imagination."[10] Although Zhu Dake, Xie's loudest critic, falls short of using any terms similar to "melodrama" in his analysis of the "Xie Jin mode of cinema," he notes pointedly that the four core components, that is, "good people in trouble," "the discovery of [moral] values," "moral exhortation," and "the triumph of the good over the evil," prevail in virtually all Xie's movies.[11] Here, the four elements in Xie's films are consistent with those in a "classical" melodrama, such as "a mode of high emotionalism and stark ethical conflict" and "[t]he polarization of good and evil."[12] While for Zhu Dake, the moral-emotion matrix in Xie Jin's melodrama films has been a hindrance to generating a "modern consciousness,"[13] the same formula, according to Paul Pickowicz, is conducive to a "blunt criticism of aspects of Communist Party history."[14] Pickowicz continues to argue that Xie's melodrama, particularly *Hibiscus Town*, can be seen as a natural continuation of "the classic nonleftist and leftist melodramas that were so popular in the Republican era."[15]

While I harbor no intention of tracing Xie Jin's melodramatic mode to the 1930s and 1940s, this chapter focuses on three of his major film works in Mao-era China, *Woman Basketball Player No. 5*, *The Red Detachment of Women* (*Hongse niangzi jun* 紅色娘子軍, 1961), and *Stage Sisters*,[16] to examine the rise of Xie Jin as a standout among the young-generation filmmakers and finally a leading film director in

---

8. Tony Ryans, "Breakthroughs and Setbacks: The Origins of the New Chinese Cinema," in *Perspectives on Chinese Cinema*, ed. Chris Berry (London: BFI Publishing, 1991), 109.
9. Ren Zhonglun 任仲倫, "Lun Xie Jin dianying" 論謝晉電影 [On Xie Jin's films], in *Lun Xie Jin dianying* 論謝晉電影 [On Xie Jin's films], ed. Zhongguo dianying jia xiehui 中國電影家協會 [China Film Association] (Beijing: Zhongguo dianying chubanshe, 1998), 4.
10. Lu, *Moulding the Socialist Subject*, 47.
11. Zhu Dake 朱大可, "Xie Jin dianying moshi de quexian" 謝晉電影模式的缺陷 [The flaw in Xie Jin's cinematic mode], in *Lun Xie Jin dianying* 論謝晉電影 [On Xie Jin's films], ed. Zhongguo dianying jia xiehui 中國電影家協會 [China Film Association] (Beijing: Zhongguo dianying chubanshe, 1998), 91.
12. Peter Brooks, *The Melodramatic Imagination: Balzac, Henry James, Melodrama, and the Mode of Excess* (New Haven, CT: Yale University Press, 1995), 12–13.
13. Zhu, "Xie Jin dianying moshi de quexian," 91–92.
14. Pickowicz, *China on Film*, 7.
15. Pickowicz, *China on Film*, 92.
16. All three films were produced by Shanghai Pegasus Film Studio.

Mao-era China and beyond. Although those movies have captured close attention in academia, this chapter explores the processes of their making and thereby argues that Xie Jin's spectacularly successful career, the high popularity of his films, and his unique directorial style did not just result from Xie Jin's artistic ingenuity and personality but stemmed from peculiar sociocultural conditions in the first seventeen years of the PRC, including the policy of building a national film market and the political authorities' hidden agenda of sidelining old-generation directors, as Chapters 3 and 4 have shown.

Woman Basketball Player No. 5

Woman Basketball Player No. 5 differs from most of its contemporary films in that it does not center on a conventional socialist hero or heroine, peasants, workers, or soldiers. The backgrounds of the protagonist, Tian Zhenhua 田振華 (Liu Qiong), and his long-separated sweetheart, Lin Jie 林潔 (Qin Yi 秦怡 [b. 1922–2022]), are ambivalent, if not questionable. Tian was once a basketball star playing for a sports club in 1930s Shanghai. As he rejected his boss's match-fixing demand, he was brutally beaten by hooligans and was therefore forced into retirement. Lin Jie, the boss's daughter, ended up marrying a rich man. Eighteen years later, Tian assumes the position of the coach of the Shanghai Women's Basketball Team, where he bumps into a young basketball player, Lin Xiaojie 林小潔 (Cao Qiwei 曹其緯). Xiaojie turns out to be Lin Jie's daughter. Tian is committed to training Xiaojie, a highly talented athlete, to be a basketball star with a genuine passion for the game. In the end, Tian and Lin Jie reunite, and Xiaojie is called up for the national team.

Although Xie Jin had been designated as the director of a few films before the mid-1950s, *Woman Basketball Player No. 5* was remembered as his actual debut in his animated filmmaking career. Xie sensed that the party authorities had no "complete faith in" him before the project of shooting *Woman Basketball Player No. 5* unfolded. Therefore, he was chosen to direct some "minor works," for which he "didn't have a hand in selecting the scripts."[17] In this sense, *Woman Basketball Player No. 5* was Xie's first work because of his heavy involvement in the entire process of producing this movie. In his interview with Marco Müller (b. 1953) in 1980, Xie acknowledged that he was permitted to participate in drafting the screenplays beginning from the project of *Woman Basketball Player No. 5*. Before that, by contrast, he was merely a passive recipient of filmmaking assignments.[18] In a separate interview, Xie even claimed that he took the initiative to select the screenplay of *Woman Basketball Player No. 5* and exerted complete control over its making.[19]

---

17. Chris Berry, *Speaking in Images: Interviews with Contemporary Chinese Filmmakers* (New York: Columbia University Press, 2005), 27.
18. Xiaer Taisong 夏爾·泰松 (Charles Tesson) et al., *Jiuba li de dushi ren* 酒吧裡的讀詩人 [Poem readers in bars] (Kaifeng: Henan daxue chubanshe, 2019), 115.
19. Berry, *Speaking in Images*, 28.

Xie Jin's memory had clearly misled him. Making *Woman Basketball Player No. 5* constituted a part of a government-sponsored program to participate in the World Festival of Youth and Students in 1957. Given the nature of this international event, the party authorities demanded making a film for and by the younger generation. In consequence, Premier Zhou Enlai proceeded to seek a director of the age of thirty to fulfill the task, and Xie Jin happened to be the chosen one.[20] Xie Jin's candidacy stemmed from a strategic plan to promote younger directors in various film studios across China in the first half of the 1950s. In 1954, three assistant directors in their thirties, including Xie, moved up to be directors. More importantly, Xie was the only one who did not have a background as a People's Liberation Army cadre.[21] Therefore, it was conceivable that Xie's promotion mainly resulted from his work experiences and competence in filmmaking skills. A Shanghai-based screenwriter and Xie's longtime colleague recalled that Xie was known for his unique ability to stitch seamlessly political messages in cinematic narratives and characterizations. Xie impressed the leadership as well as ordinary members of the Shanghai-based studios with his artistic "savvy" (*wuxing* 悟性).[22] Another of his former colleagues was impressed by Xie's energy, passion, and ability to coordinate with other departments in the same studio.[23] Xie himself was proud of his unique capability of transforming a mediocre script into a high-quality film when he was still a rookie director.[24]

The nomination of Xie Jin, a young director in whom the party did not have complete faith, was also an outgrowth of a mild political climate in the mid-1950s. Xie admitted in an interview that he was able to make *Women Basketball Player No. 5* "during a relatively lax interlude, just before the Antirightist Campaign."[25] As the CCP briefly eased its control over the film in the mid-1950s, directors in Shanghai were encouraged to team up with one another to ramp up film production. Under this circumstance, Xie Jin cooperated with his fellow directors, such as Shi Hui, Xu Changlin, and Bai Chen 白沉 (1922–2002), in 1956, and the team was known as the "Society of Five Flowers."[26] Their collaboration resulted in the production of a few films, including Xie's *Woman Basketball Player No. 5*. Shen Ji, also a member of the Society of Five Flowers, recalled that every member, especially Bai

---

20. Song Xiaobin 宋小濱, *Jiali jiawai hua Xie Jin* 家裡家外話謝晉 [On Xie Jin both in and outside his family] (Beijing: Zhongguo shehui chubanshe, 2013), 81.
21. Luo Yijun 羅藝軍, "Xie Jin, wode tonglu ren" 謝晉，我的同路人 [Xie Jin, my fellow traveler], in *Lun Xie Jin dianying* 論謝晉電影 [On Xie Jin's films], ed. Zhongguo dianying jia xiehui 中國電影家協會 [China Film Association] (Beijing: Zhongguo dianying chubanshe, 1998), 9–10.
22. Zhou Xia 周夏, Chen Mo 陳墨, and Qizhi 啟之, *Haishang yingzong (Shanghai juan)* 海上影蹤（上海卷）[The trace of film in Shanghai (the volume of Shanghai)] (Beijing: Minzu chubanshe, 2011), 75.
23. Zhou, Chen, and Qizhi, *Haishang yingzong (Shanghai juan)*, 351.
24. Berry, *Speaking in Images*, 28.
25. Berry, *Speaking in Images*, 29.
26. Yi Quan 易荃, "Shangying chang junzuo xiaozu ru yuhou chunsun" 上影廠劇作小組如雨後春筍 [Playwriting teams in Shanghai-based film studios spring up like mushrooms], *Dianying yishu* 電影藝術 [Cinematic Arts], no. A2 (1956): 58.

Chen, contributed to completing the film's screenplay, and Shi Hui, the soon-to-be martyr of the Anti-Rightist Movement, provided Xie with firm guidance.[27]

While the members of the team benefited from their mutual support, most of them would fall prey to the political storm during the campaign against "Rightists" a year later. It turned out that Xie Jin was the sole survivor.[28] Xie's success in escaping political persecution was thus considered miraculous because his mentors, friends, and teammates, such as Shi Hui and Bai Chen, had all been charged for their anti-CCP activism. Other than the favoritism he received from Premier Zhou and the Shanghai-based CCP cadres, Xie's preoccupation with the production of *Woman Basketball Player No. 5* prevented him from uttering any controversial remarks. When the campaign came to an end, some cadres wondered aloud why Xie, who was usually full of "nonsense" (*hushuo badao* 胡説八道), inconceivably left no record about his criticisms of the party policies during the Hundred Flowers Campaign.[29]

Untouched by the Anti-Rightist Movement, Xie Jin's standing as a rising star was further enhanced because of the popularity of *Woman Basketball Player No. 5*. A contemporary film reviewer expressly associated the film's success with the ongoing political campaign. The reviewer stated, "*Woman Basketball Player No. 5* began its production in early 1957, when . . . a revisionist countercurrent was assaulting the Party-led film industry." As an entertaining movie, the reviewer continued, *Woman Basketball Player No. 5* should have been prone to the influence of unhealthy ideological orientations, but its director took the film with utmost seriousness by conveying important political messages to the audiences.[30] The essay thus conveyed an impression that Xie Jin had been proactively toeing the party line despite his colleagues' scathing criticisms against the CCP shortly before the Anti-Rightist Movement unfolded. Xie thus became the beneficiary of this eventful period: he was immune to political persecution but took advantage of the favorable political climate to produce a widely acclaimed film in early 1957.

This lax period offered enormous freedom to Xie Jin. In Paul Clark's words, Xie succeeded in working "within the new cultural boundaries" with "an ability to stretch them."[31] Hence, Xie took the liberty to resort to Hollywood films, particularly those dealing with "love, sports, and all the rest,"[32] as his source of inspiration. When his interviewer, Marco Müller, suggested in 1980 that *Woman Basketball Player No. 5* bore a resemblance to an American sitcom, Xie conceded that Hollywood films

---

27. Zhou, Chen, and Qizhi, *Haishang yingzong (Shanghai juan)*, 42–43.
28. Zhou, Chen, and Qizhi, *Haishang yingzong (Shanghai juan)*, 43.
29. Song, *Jiali jiawai hua Xie Jin*, 81–82.
30. Yijun 藝軍, "Ping 'Nülan 5 hao'" 評 "女籃5號" [Review of "*Woman Basketball Player No. 5*"], in *Zhongguo dianying pinglun ji di 2 ji* 中國電影評論集第2集 [Collection of reviews of Chinese films, bk. 2], ed. Zhongguo dianying chubanshe 中國電影出版社 (Beijing: Zhongguo dianying chubanshe, 1959), 46–47.
31. Clark, "Two Hundred Flowers on China's Screens," 75.
32. Berry, *Speaking in Images*, 29.

had a profound influence on his works.³³ As a relatively inexperienced director, Xie also enjoyed the rare privilege of selecting the actress to play the lead role. When Xie nominated Cao Rulin's 曹汝霖 (1877–1966) granddaughter, he ran into bitter opposition both because the young woman had no professional acting experience and because Cao was denounced as a traitor of China and was the main target of patriotic students during the May Fourth Movement (1919). Fortunately, Xie won the full support of upper-echelon leaders in Beijing, and his nomination finally obtained approval.³⁴

The favoritism Xie Jin gained from Beijing enabled him to take a unique angle and select an appealing topic to narrate the story about the making of a new-generation female athlete in the PRC era. Jin Danyuan 金丹元 argues that the movie's success lies in the director's inclusion of all necessary elements to cater to the tastes of urban film viewers: film stars, romantic love, the passion for building a new China, a highly popular sport, and light music (as opposed to hard-core revolutionary music in virtually all other contemporary films).³⁵ Ding Yaping further notes that the filmic representations of "marginal figures" (*bianyuan renwu* 邊緣人物)—those who were not workers, peasants, or soldiers—and the disclosure of their private lives on the silver screen were capable of arousing the filmgoers' curiosity. Focusing on such figures' emotive world in Xie's filmic works, hence, gave him and other Shanghai-based filmmakers the opportunities to identify them with intellectuals and artists in pre-1949 Shanghai.³⁶

Therefore, despite the film's pronounced intention to display the bodies of female athletes as a metaphor for the "prosperity and strength of the new socialist state," Xie Jin succeeded in piecing together the grand narrative of socialist nationalism and the portrayal of the everyday life in mid-century Shanghai.³⁷ Xie Jin's approach to reminding the audiences of Shanghai's urban culture before Liberation resonated well with some audience members. Chen Naishan 陳乃珊 (b. 1946), for example, felt fascinated by the stardom of Liu Qiong and Qin Yi and paid close attention to such details as the personae's attire in the movie. Chen proclaimed that she liked to revisit every tiny detail shown in the film because it faithfully represented urban life in 1950s Shanghai.³⁸ Chen's reaction testifies to Jason McGrath's observation that viewers of propaganda films in Mao's China tended to "concentrate

---

33. Xiaer Taisong et al., *Jiuba li de dushi ren*, 115.
34. Chen Lixu 陳立旭, "He Long paiban Cao Rulin sunnü zhuyan *Nülan wuhao*" 賀龍拍板曹汝霖孫女主演《女籃五號》 [He Long gave the nod to (allow) Cao Rulin's granddaughter to feature in *Woman Basketball Player No. 5*], *Dangshi zonglan* 黨史縱覽 [Survey of the CCP's History], no. 7 (2020): 36. Cao Rulin was the Minister of Transportation in 1919.
35. Jin, *Xin Zhongguo dianying meixue shi, 1949–2009*, 68.
36. Ding Yaping 丁亞平, *Zhongguo dianying lishi tuzhi 1896–2015 shang* 中國電影歷史圖志 1896–2015 上 [A pictorial history of Chinese cinema, 1896–2015, part 1] (Beijing: Wenhua yishu chuabanshe, 2015), 432–34.
37. Amanda Shuman, "No Longer 'Sick': Visualizing 'Victorious' Athletes in 1950s Chinese Films," *Historical Social Research* 43, no. 2 (2018): 227.
38. Chen Naishan 陳乃珊, *Shanghai TASTE* 上海TASTE [Shanghai TASTE] (Shanghai: Shanghai cishu chubanshe, 2008), 125.

on seemingly inconsequential details" because of "sheer boredom" of ideological indoctrination.[39] The same details, however, did not escape the vigilant eye of some critics. Xia Yan, for example, raised a question about the luxurious furnishings in the female protagonist's home. Xia feared that such a portrayal of the young athlete's extravagant living conditions only led the viewers to wonder whether she grew up in a family of a "great capitalist" or a "great landlord," hence hurting the positive public perceptions of her.[40] Here, what Chen Naishan appreciated was precisely what Xia found disturbing: *Woman Basketball Player No. 5*'s "obvious references" to pre-1949 Shanghai films.[41] Some other reviewers complained that the love story of the two older protagonists "held such an emotional sway over audiences that it overshadowed the other narrative on the young women basketball team in the new China."[42]

Red Detachment of Women

Those who had significant reservations about *Woman Basketball Player No. 5* were concerned that the movie prioritized the domestic space over a collective, the CCP-dominated one. In this sense, the making of *Red Detachment of Women* has been viewed as Xie Jin's response to such a critique.[43] *Red Detachment of Women* begins with the encounter between Hong Changqing 洪常青 (Wang Xingang 王心剛, b. 1932), the party representative, and Wu Qionghua (Zhu Xijuan 祝希娟, b. 1938), Nan Batian's 南霸天 (Chen Qiang 陳強, 1918–2012) bondservant. Changqing manages to rescue the brutally tortured Qionghua, and the latter finally joins the Red Detachment of Women led by Changqing. A series of incidents, including Changqing's death, impel Qionghua to mature from a hotheaded rookie soldier into a self-conscious communist warrior.

The movie proved to be a phenomenal success, both critically and commercially. It won multiple awards in the first Hundred Flowers Awards (*Dazhong dianying baihua jiang* 大眾電影百花獎, 1962) and won recognition internationally. Because most voters of the Hundred Flowers Awards were young urbanites,[44] the film's popularity among urban viewers was out of question. Seven months after it was initially released, the film appealed to 20.18 million audience members, making it the single most viewed film across the country.[45] It enjoyed popularity in both

---

39. Jason McGrath, "Cultural Revolution Model Opera Films and the Realist Tradition in Chinese Cinema," *The Opera Quarterly* 26, no. 2–3 (September 2010): 344.
40. Ren Hui 任晦, "Cong *Nülan wuhao* xiangdao de yixie wenti 從《女籃5號》想起的一些問題 [Some thoughts provoked by (watching) *Woman Basketball Player No. 5*], *Renmin ribao* 人民日報 [People's Daily], January 3, 1958.
41. Liu, "*Red Detachment of Women*," 127.
42. Lu, *Moulding the Socialist Subject*, 57.
43. Liu, "*Red Detachment of Women*," 127.
44. Clark, "Closely Watched Viewers," 76.
45. Shanghai Municipal Archives, B177-1-262, 51.

Figure 5.1: Lin Jie is putting on make-up at an elegant dressing table before reuniting with Tian Zhenhua in *Women Basketball Player No. 5*. Such details as the furnishings in the female protagonist's home raised doubts about her class background. Meanwhile, the portrayal of an upper-class lifestyle was a reminder of Shanghai's urban culture in pre-1949 China. Screenshot from *Women Basketball Player No. 5*.

urban and rural areas. A 1962 report indicated that the distributors sold 213 35mm copies and 400 16mm copies in China, topping the list of films made in Shanghai.[46] Considering that 16mm copies were specifically reserved for the rural market,[47] *Red Detachment of Women* thus conceivably achieved remarkable success similarly in the countryside.

The film's extraordinary capacity to galvanize a massive audience offers a marked contrast to the negative internal reviews it had received right before its

---

46. Shanghai Municipal Archives, B177-1-298, 92.
47. Clark, "Closely Watched Viewers," 80.

exhibition. Jay Leyda, for example, dismissed it as a "superficial film" and blamed the filmmakers for producing "a film for children—an adventure story with abstract time, abstract place, stereotyped characters and illogical action."[48] What Ledya denounced was precisely what average film viewers felt fascinated about. A film fan later recalled that although *Red Detachment of Women* was a "propaganda film, pure and simple," he felt "it dramatically entertaining" because the movie had "a feel for adventure" and was "emotionally arousing."[49] Facing the film's spectacular success among the audience, Leyda lamented, "the Film Bureau must have lost any trust they may have had in my judgment."[50] In a similar fashion, an officer from the Shanghai Film Bureau pointed a finger at Xie Jin in June 1960, because Xie was allegedly more interested in causing excitement among filmgoers and highlighting a "sentimental emotion" in *Red Detachment of Women*. More seriously, some cadres denounced Xie for his reluctance to revise the movie in line with the reviewers' suggestions.[51]

What the internal reviewers took issue with was what finally defines the film: "a typical revolutionary melodrama" that "reenacts the official history of a CCP-led revolution" by underscoring "nonnegotiable class conflicts," clear-cut moral polarization, and excessive emotionalism.[52] The thrust of criticisms voiced by Leyda and the Shanghai Film Bureau's reporters was the menace posed to socialist realism by a melodramatic mode of representation (although neither of them used any phrases related to it). Robert Chi notes that such a threat led to "the dismissal of the film as exaggerated and unrealistic (as well as exoticist, being set on a tropical island)."[53] Chi further points out that melodrama is "not in itself gendered as feminine," but *Red Detachment of Women* is decidedly a "women's war film."[54]

Being a "women's war film," *Red Detachment of Women* would later come under the critical scrutiny of film scholars for its (mis)construction of womanhood. Dai Jinhua posits that in all pre-1978 movies directed by Xie Jin, women do not refer to an actual gender but function as a metaphor in history, that is, the oppressed "people" (*renmin* 人民) who live their miserable lives at the bottom rung of society.[55] Ma Ning adds that women are deemed to be the representative of the "most revolutionary" people and "made the bearers of law and order of the New China"

---

48. Leyda, *Dianying*, 303.
49. Timothy Tung, "The Work of Xie Jin: A Personal Letter to the Editor," in *Film and Politics in the Third World*, ed. John D. H. Downing (New York: Praeger, 1987), 201.
50. Leyda, *Dianying*, 303.
51. Shanghai Municipal Archives, A22-2-875, 34.
52. Liu, "*Red Detachment of Women*," 116.
53. Chi, "The Red Detachment of Women," 153.
54. Chi, "The Red Detachment of Women," 156.
55. Dai Jinhua 戴錦華, "Lishi yu xushi—Xie Jin dianying yishu guanjian" 歷史與敘述——謝晉電影藝術管見 [History and narrative—A brief view of Xie Jin's cinematic arts], in *Lun Xie Jin dianying* 論謝晉電影 [On Xie Jin's films], ed. Zhongguo dianying jia xiehui 中國電影家協會 [China Film Association] (Beijing: Zhongguo dianying chubanshe, 1998), 146–47.

because they are the most oppressed.⁵⁶ Rey Chow similarly argues that women in socialist films are merely "a genderless collectivity," and the individual woman in films like *Red Detachment of Women* "could not be objectified into an independent or self-sufficient ontological entity."⁵⁷

Such denial of women's agency in Mao-era films has recently drawn criticism. In her studies on *Red Detachment of Women*, Zheng Wang questions the legitimacy of the scholarly assumption that "the representation of revolutionary heroines demonstrates the patriarchal socialist state's 'masculinization' of women." Wang thus questions "the methodological and conceptual adequacies in the conventional field of film studies when applied to socialist cinema" and calls for "an investigation of the specific political context and the actual filmmakers and production crews."⁵⁸ In the political context of Mao's China, Xiaomei Chen recalls, female warriors' feminine beauty did not dissolve because they were absorbed into a collectivity. Rather, they became the "embodiments of youth, beauty, grace, passion, and energy" and were gazed at by young men and women "with the same intensity as images of Rita Hayworth and Marilyn Monroe."⁵⁹ Jason McGrath likewise mentions anecdotal accounts that male viewers were sexually aroused by another version of *Red Detachment of Women*.⁶⁰ McGrath's findings thus reveal the yawning gap between the scholarly assumption of the Mao-era spectator—"a nonindividualized, communal subject" in Chris Berry's words⁶¹—and the real-life audiences' lived experiences at this particular historical time.

In a similar fashion, the audiences in the context of China in the 1950s and 1960s could be well aware of the romantic relationship between Changqing and Qionghua, an episode deleted right before the movie was shown. As Xiao Liu indicates, the filmgoers of the day "had the feeling that it was going to be a love scene even though what she saw was already a *clean* version with no explicit love plot." Liu ascribes such a hunch to viewers' familiarity with "the conventions of onscreen love scenes, which had already become a fixed set of cinematic idioms fully developed by both Hollywood movies and pre-PRC Shanghai films."⁶² Liu's analysis is only half right. The "conventions" were in actuality a common practice in almost

---

56. Ma Ning, "Spatiality and Subjectivity in Xie Jin's Film Melodrama of the New Period," in *New Chinese Cinemas: Forms, Identities, Politics*, ed. Nick Browne et al. (Cambridge: Cambridge University Press, 1994), 22.
57. Chow, "Fetish Power Unbound," 492.
58. Zheng Wang, *Finding Women in the State: A Socialist Feminist Revolution in the People's Republic of China, 1949–1964* (Berkeley: University of California Press, 2017), 15.
59. Xiaomei Chen, *Acting the Right Part: Political Theater and Popular Drama in Contemporary China* (Honolulu: University of Hawai'i Press, 2002), 36–37.
60. Jason McGrath, "Communists Have More Fun! The Dialectics of Fulfillment in Cinema of the People's Republic of China," *World Picture* 3 (Summer 2009): 14.
61. Chris Berry, "Neither One Thing Nor Another: Toward a Study of the Viewing Subject and Chinese Cinema in the 1980s," in *New Chinese Cinema: Forms, Identities, Politics*, ed. Nick Browne et al. (Cambridge: Cambridge University Press, 1994), 89.
62. Liu, "*Red Detachment of Women*," 132.

all revolutionary movies where love stories were insinuated, but love scenes were missing. In Dai Jinhua's words, they were "love stories without love."[63]

The earliest "love stories without love" arguably appeared in two films in the early 1950s, *From Victory to Victory* (*Nanzheng beizhan* 南征北戰, dir. Cheng Yin 成蔭 [1917–1984] and Tang Xiaodan 湯曉丹 [1910–2012], 1952) and *Reconnaissance Across the Yangzi River* (*Dujiang zhencha ji* 渡江偵察記, dir. Tang Xiaodan, 1954). Both films are set in the final stage of the Chinese Civil War (1946–1949). In those movies, the filmmakers manipulatively displayed the meaningful gazes, yearning looks, and ambivalent remarks of the heroes and the heroines to meet the filmgoers' demands for the narrative of romantic love.[64] It is thus no surprise that when Xie's colleagues and CCP cadres were debating the necessity of retaining love scenes in *Red Detachment of Women* before its release, Chen Huangmei suggested telling a more vivid love story and expressly cautioned against the approach taken in *Reconnaissance Across the Yangzi River* to hiding the love story.[65]

Unfortunately, the scenes about the romantic relationship between Changqing and Qionghua were excluded from the final product of the movie. Xie Jin recalled decades later that he and the screenwriter both intended to keep the love story, but "a decision came down from the higher-ups," leaving them "with no choice."[66] The removal proved awkward. Although Wang Hui 汪暉 presumes that the filmmakers succeeded in refashioning scenes and props that were previously designed to drop a hint of the romantic relationship between Changqing and Qionghua into filmic elements that confirm the female protagonist's loyalty to the party,[67] in the real-life scenario, the movie's internal reviewers found that they were still able to see some traces of this romantic relationship.[68] Filmgoers nationwide harbored the same feeling.[69] Xie Jin, who was unable to openly discuss the deletion of such scenes shortly after the film was screened, publicly apologized that the movie seemed unbalanced: the plots in the first half, which centers on Qionghua's resistance to Nan Batian and her impulsive temperament, play out better than those in the second half—the two protagonists' destinies.[70]

---

63. Dai, *Wuzhong fengjing*, 124.
64. Yin and Ling, *Xin Zhongguo dianying shi (1949–2000)*, 35–36.
65. Shanghai Municipal Archives, B177-3-551, 17.
66. Berry, *Speaking in Images*, 32.
67. Wang Hui 汪暉, "Zhengzhi daode jiqi zhihuan de mimi—Xie Jin dianying fenxi" 政治與道德及其置換的秘密——謝晉電影分析 [Politics, morality, and the secret of their displacement—An analysis of Xie Jin's films], in *Lun Xie Jin dianying* 論謝晉電影 [On Xie Jin's films], ed. Zhongguo dianying jia xiehui 中國電影家協會 [China Film Association] (Beijing: Zhongguo dianying chubanshe, 1998), 183–84.
68. Shanghai Municipal Archives, B177-3-551, 17.
69. Yin and Ling, *Xin Zhongguo dianying shi (1949–2000)*, 36.
70. Xie Jin 謝晉, "Cong daoyan de ganshou dao guanzhong de ganshou—*Hongse niangzi jun* daoyan sanji" 從導演的感受到觀眾的感受—《紅色娘子軍》導演散記 [From the director's feelings to the audience's experiences—Some random notes on directing *Red Detachment of Women*], *Renmin ribao* 人民日報 [People's Daily], August 23, 1961.

Figure: 5.2: The reunion between Qionghua and Changqing has been seen as a scene where the female protagonist's love for the man is played out in *Red Detachment of Women*. However, the deletion of the love story in the movie's final edition makes this scene highly ambivalent. Screenshot from *The Red Detachment of Women*.

The deletion of the two protagonists' love story testifies to the multiple authorship of the film, as opposed to what Xiao Liu calls "multilayered authorship." While I highlight the forceful and decisive intervention of the political authorities, who unknowingly became another author, Liu emphasizes the existence of various editions of the story, such as the reportage and a local dialect opera.[71] Liu's invoking of different editions of the story contributes to her argument that the film continued a tradition of family melodrama in the early years of the PRC. Here, the family was referred to as "a big revolutionary family" that integrated "domestic space into communal space." Liu posits that Xie's prioritization of a "communal space" over a private one constituted this director's response to the criticisms of his *Woman Basketball Player No. 5* he received a few years earlier.[72] In a sense, it is such a prevailing assumption that Xie's cinematic melodrama before the 1980s placed a premium on a collectivity at the cost of individuals that prompts Dai Jinhua to argue that Xie

---

71. Liu, "*Red Detachment of Women*," 132.
72. Liu, "*Red Detachment of Women*," 127.

was interested in addressing issues related to history/society rather than desire and individual.⁷³

Such an assessment misses a key point of multiple authorship. The presumed Xie Jin style that focuses on the collective instead of the individual and the communal rather than the domestic, I argue, was more a creation of Xie's political supervisors. He was hardly a collaborator but a reluctant recipient at best. Before the making of the film, Xie and the screenplay writer made a decision to expand the roles of Qionghua and Changqing. More importantly, how the movie differed from the earlier edition of the story, including the reportage and a local opera, was Xie's highlighting of Qionghua's story as "a personal paradigm" rather than presenting her as merely one member of the collectivity.⁷⁴ To underscore Qionghua's private life, Xie thus struggled mightily to keep the love story—the private space—of the two protagonists. A 1965 report reveals that Xie Jin's initial plan was to include a scene of the dating between the two protagonists when the party authorities place Qionghua in confinement as a penalty for her mistake. As the plan was called off, the frustrated Xie complained that romantic love as an essential part of the human being's life would have highlighted the genuine human feelings and contributed to dramatizing the plotlines. In the process of making the film, Xie kept bargaining with the party authorities and therefore came under criticism for "being obsessive about personal tastes" and "failing to reform [his] petty-bourgeois feelings." A reporter thus concluded that the film could not have accomplished such a remarkable achievement without the party's intervention, reconfirming the movie's multiple authorship.⁷⁵

Stage Sisters

The report about the tug of war between Xie Jin and the CCP cadres regarding the removal of the love scene in *Red Detachment of Women* tellingly showed Xie's enhanced standing in Pegasus in the late 1950s. It was the relatively mild political environment in the mid-1950s that allowed Xie to exercise his artistic autonomy when making *Woman Basketball Player No. 5*, an essentially made-to-order movie supposedly out of Xie's control. By comparison, Xie's growing reputation enabled him to not only choose the screenplay of *Red Detachment of Women* but also negotiate with, if not directly challenge, the party's authorities. The market and critical success of *Red Detachment of Women* allowed Xie to gain laurels as a stellar director. In the midst of the Cultural Thaw in the early 1960s, an official publicly apologized to Xie on behalf of Pegasus for having deleted the love scenes against the director's

---

73. Dai, "Lishi yu xushi," 146.
74. Kristine Harris, "Re-makes/Re-models: *The Red Detachment of Women* between Stage and Screen," *The Opera Quarterly* 26, no. 2–3 (2010): 321–22.
75. Shanghai Municipal Archives, B177-3-551, 18–22.

will, further boosting Xie's confidence.[76] When directing *Stage Sisters* in 1963 and 1964, Xie's discord with the studio's CCP leadership escalated into open conflict.

Stage Sisters features two Yue opera actresses, Chunhua 春花 (Xie Fang 謝芳, b. 1935) and Yuehong 月紅 (Cao Yindi 曹銀娣, b. 1939), both of whom hail from the rural area in Shaoxing, Zhejiang, in the mid-1930s. As local tyrants bully them, they are brought to Shanghai. Very soon, they establish unrivaled reputations as Yue opera superstars. Their paths begin to diverge after that. Chunhua rejects Manager Tang's 唐 (Li Wei 李緯 [1919–2005]) proposal of staging indecent plays and begins to come under the heavy influence of a left-wing journalist, Jiang Bo 江波 (Gao Fang 高放, b. 1939). In consequence, Chunhua coordinates with other Yue opera performers to stage Lu Xun's *The New Year's Sacrifice* (*Zhufu* 祝福). Meanwhile, Yuehong cannot resist the seduction of the luxurious lifestyle in Shanghai and agrees to marry Manager Tang. After Manager Tang plots to blind Chunhua, and the scheme fails, he passes Yuehong off as the culprit. After Liberation, Chunhua reunites with Yuehong in the countryside, and both resume their performing careers.

The film was long in the making. A loyal Yue opera fan,[77] Xie's foray into the operatic motion picture can be dated to 1949, when he assisted Zheng Xiaoqiu 鄭小秋 (1910–1989) in directing *Opera Heroes* (*Liyuan yinglie* 梨園英烈).[78] Xie reportedly began to entertain the idea of producing a movie about Chinese opera performers as early as 1956. Although Xie was preoccupied with directing two films, including *Red Detachment of Women*, in the next several years, he never gave up on this project.[79] It happened that the Shanghai Yue Opera Troupe was staging an opera under the name of *Stage Sisters* (*Wutai jiemei* 舞臺姐妹), which instantly captured Xie's interest.[80] In a newspaper essay dated March 11, 1962, Xie announced in public that he was painstakingly brainstorming the plotlines and themes of *Stage Sisters*, the film.[81] In the same year, the film studio also approved the proposal of the project. A detailed outline of the film did not come out until April 1963, and it soon riveted the attention of officials from the Ministry of Culture in Beijing, Xia Yan and Chen Huangmei. Chen mandated a month later that *Stage Sisters* be branded a "key film" (*zhongdian yingpian* 重點影片) and be made into a color film. In October 1963, Xia personally called the cadres of the Shanghai Film Bureau and recommended collaboration with the Hong Kong–based Southern Film Corporation to draw up a plan to sell the movie abroad. To supply the film to both the domestic and international

---

76. Xu, *Tabian qingshan ren weilao*, 165.
77. Tung, "The Work of Xie Jin," 200.
78. Yomi Braester, "Farewell My Concubine: National Myth and City Memories," in *Chinese Films in Focus: 25 New Takes*, ed. Chris Berry (London: BFI Publishing, 2003), 94.
79. Shanghai Municipal Archives, A22-1-914, 29–30.
80. Bao Shiyuan 鮑世遠, *Xishui changliu* 戲水長流 [The stream of theater flows long] (Shanghai: Shanghai wenyi chubanshe, 2011), 80.
81. Xie Jin 謝晉, "Yao shenme yang de juben" 要什麼樣的劇本 [What screenplays do (we) want], *Guangming ribao* 光明日報 [Guangming Daily], March 11, 1962.

markets, Xia Yan further proposed that the production crew prepare two different endings—one for the domestic market and the other for the overseas audience.[82]

The full support Xie Jin secured from Xia Yan and Chen Huangmei was by no means a blessing. Xie later came to realize that the film would become a prime target of waves of denunciation before and during the Cultural Revolution because of his connection with Xia Yan.[83] At one point, Xie remembered, over 100,000 people condemned him in public during the campaign against the film.[84] In reality, the trouble had already broken out as soon the project was set in motion. The entire process of making *Stage Sisters* was weighed down by a series of controversies, clashes, and political struggles, including the animosity between Xia Yan and the Shanghai CCP leadership and the ensuing political persecution of Xia. Three months before Xie submitted the film's detailed outline, Ke Qingshi 柯慶施 (1902–1965), first secretary of the CCP Shanghai committee and mayor of Shanghai, had officially called for "making a great effort to write about the thirteen years" (*daxie shisan nian* 大寫十三年)—producing literary, theatrical, and filmic works exclusively about post-1949 China.[85] In this sense, Xie Jin took a grave political risk of running counter to the party committee's decision by filming *Stage Sisters*, a movie predominantly set in pre-1949 China. A 1966 report revealed that the Shanghai CCP leadership was kept in ignorance of Xie Jin's interactions with the Beijing-based authorities, particularly Xia Yan, until the crew began to shoot the movie.[86]

The project of *Stage Sisters* was thus drawn into a feud between the Ministry of Culture in Beijing and Shanghai-based CCP officials, especially Ke Qingshi and Zhang Chunqiao. The tension began to build as early as 1961, when Premier Zhou Enlai's remarks on softening the party's stance on filmmaking were toned down in Shanghai. The animosity later intensified to such a degree that Ke Qingshi personally urged Xia Yan not to interfere in the internal affairs of the film studios in Shanghai.[87] By 1963 and 1964, the disagreement between the two became an open secret in the film circles.[88] It is thus understandable that Shanghai's high-ranking officials would unleash a fusillade of criticisms of *Stage Sisters* to preclude its final release. One cadre from the Propaganda Department of the Municipal Committee in Shanghai seemed to be offended by Chunhua's maxim, "leading clean lives and staging serious plays" (*qingqing baibai zuoren, renren zhenzhen changxi* 清清白白做人，認認真真唱戲), and interpreted it as the embodiment of bourgeois individualism.[89]

---

82. Shanghai Municipal Archives, A22-1-914, 30–31.
83. Xiaer Taisong et al., *Jiuba li de dushi ren*, 116.
84. Berry, *Speaking in Images*, 33.
85. Meng, *Xin Zhongguo dianying yishu shi, 1949–1965*, 484.
86. Shanghai Municipal Archives, A22-1-914, 31.
87. Chen Huangmei 陳荒煤 and Chen Bo 陳播, *Zhou Enlai yu dianying* 周恩來與電影 [Zhou Enlai and film] (Beijing: Zhongyang wenxian chubanshe, 1995), 39.
88. Tan, *Zhongguo dianying ren koushu lishi yinhai chenfu lu Luo Yijun koushu lishi*, 94–100.
89. Shanghai Municipal Archives, A22-1-914, 33.

The opinion was not entirely unfounded. At a time when violent revolutions and bitter class struggle were the mainstream, "leading clean lives and staging serious plays" conveyed a message not in line with the class theory endorsed by the party. More importantly, the film suggests that the heroine's life and career are praiseworthy and respectable not thanks to the party leadership but because of her firm belief in "leading clean lives and staging serious plays." One of the few persons who embody the CCP is the female journalist, but she shows up as late as the film's second half.[90] More recently, Jin Jiang takes issue with Stage Sisters by arguing that the film "denies agency to the people the CCP claims to have liberated."[91] In all fairness, the filmmakers had attempted to downplay the party's influence (at least in the first half of the film) to the best of their abilities and illustrate Chunhua's personal struggles and individual fulfillment, thus drawing some reviewers' scathing criticisms.

The campaign against Stage Sisters and Xie Jin culminated when Zhang Chunqiao joined the chorus blaming the movie. In August 1964, Zhang pointed out that the film was guilty of peddling the "theory of class conciliation" (jieji tiaohe lun 階級調和論). In the following four months, the entire film studio was mobilized to review the movie in hopes that some major revisions could be made before it was granted permission for a public exhibition.[92] Xie's colleagues and the studio's cadres thus advanced numerous comments. For example, some reviewers complained the episode about Manager Tang's seduction of Yuehong was excessively lengthy and sexually suggestive. Some others felt uneasy about the stifling atmosphere shown in the movie. In other words, the director was said to have focused on displaying the ordeals the protagonists undergo but refused to illustrate the party's leadership that would decidedly alter the women's ideological orientations.[93]

The hope that Xie Jin would be cooperative enough to present a revised edition of the film was dashed both because of the director's noncompliance and the swiftly changing political climate. Indeed, Xie's clash with the studio's cadres had already surfaced in early 1964, when the filming project had just started. Xie reportedly unleashed an outpouring of anger facing a studio manager's opinion that the movie set looked awkwardly oversized. Xie even publicly attacked the manager by labeling him a bureaucratist. In the next several months, Xie's resentment continued to flare up, and he refused to interact with the cadres in the studio. Meanwhile, Xie brought his coworkers and friends in the film studio, such as Wang Lingu 王林谷 (1919–1995), the film's screenwriter, and Chen Liting, into the confrontation with the studio's leadership.[94] In December 1964, Pegasus's cadres decided to produce an additional 200 shots and thereby substantially change the film to meet the demands

---

90. Meng, Xin Zhongguo dianying yishu shi, 1949–1965, 482.
91. Jiang, Women Playing Men, 190.
92. Shanghai Municipal Archives, A22-1-914, 34.
93. Shanghai Municipal Archives, B177-3-476, 4–6.
94. Shanghai Municipal Archives, B177-3-476, 1–8.

of the CCP Committee in Shanghai. By comparison, Xie Jin took the issue lightly and believed that all the problems resided in the heroine's maxim, "leading clean lives and staging serious plays." Its deletion could suffice to satisfy the party authorities.[95]

In April 1965, the film studio and Xie Jin reached an agreement to revise the film by using "scissors"; that is, to re-edit *Stage Sisters*. As such, the studio leadership compromised and recommended insubstantial change to the movie,[96] but the last-ditch effort to rescue it pleased nobody. Director Xie later believed that he reworked the film "against his will," and the final part of the movie, which was intended to raise the audiences' ideological consciousness, was hollow and superfluous.[97] For the film fans that had the opportunity to see the movie more than a decade later, the quality of the film's second half—the portion that underwent a major change—fell considerably.[98] For film scholars, the political intervention precluded the already sophisticated Xie Jin from pushing his filmic arts to new heights.[99]

More importantly, the filmmakers' strenuous effort proved futile. The months leading up to the outbreak of the Cultural Revolution were bitterly hostile to Xie Jin and *Stage Sisters*, dispelling any possibility of publicly showing this film. Later Xie came to realize that the hidden agenda of denouncing *Stage Sisters* was to target not just Xia Yan but also Premier Zhou Enlai.[100] Xie's interpretation of the ongoing political struggle was based on the well-publicized relationship between Premier Zhou and Xia Yan. Chen Huangmei recalled later that Xia became Zhou's protégé and agent in the Nationalist Party-occupied area in China since their secret meeting in Shanghai in 1937.[101]

The painful process of making, debating on, and revising *Stage Sisters* made it a typical co-authored film checkered with contradictions. Gina Marchetti notes that as much as *Stage Sisters* was purported to "fervently support the party and revolution," the radicals during the Cultural Revolution could easily "unearth a bourgeois, Western sensibility."[102] The "Western sensibility" refers to the influence of Hollywood films on *Stage Sister*. In the 1980s, Xie openly admitted that the film "has a Hollywood quality to it . . . especially in its structure."[103] Some of Xie's fans hold the firm belief that Xie's works had their "seeds in the *Waterloo Bridges* [sic]

---

95. Shanghai Municipal Archives, A22-1-914, 33–35.
96. Shanghai Municipal Archives, A22-1-914, 35.
97. Zhu Anping 朱安平, "*Wutai jiemei* 'taiwai youtai'" 《舞臺姐妹》 "臺外有臺" [*Stage Sisters*, a stage outside the stage], *Dazhong dianying* 大眾電影 [Mass Film], no. 2 (2006): 39.
98. Tung, "The Work of Xie Jin," 201.
99. Zhang Mingtang 張銘堂, "Xie Jin dianying zhimi" 謝晉電影之謎 [The enigma of Xie Jin's films], in *Lun Xie Jin dianying* 論謝晉電影 [On Xie Jin's films], ed. Zhongguo dianying jia xiehui 中國電影家協會 [China Film Association] (Beijing: Zhongguo dianying chubanshe, 1998), 38–39.
100. Berry, *Speaking in Images*, 33.
101. Zhou Bin 周斌, *Yingshi xiju sibian lu* 影視戲劇思辨錄 [An intellectual inquiry into film, TV, and theater] (Shanghai: Dongang chuban zhongxin, 2019), 44.
102. Marchetti, "Two Stage Sisters," 77.
103. George S. Semsel, "Interviews," in *Chinese Film: The State of the Art in the People's Republic*, ed. George Stephen Semsel (New York: Praeger, 1987), 107.

and *Gone with the Winds* [sic]."[104] To be more specific, *Stage Sisters* could be readily comparable with a "Hollywood backstage melodrama." Marchetti finds that it "has all the classic elements of that genre," such as "the hard struggle to the top of the theatrical profession, the bitterness of the aging actress's lot, the inevitability of decline, sour romances, misguided ambitions, competition, romantic needs vying with the dream of theatrical success, the hardships of exploitation by unsympathetic bosses."[105]

Meanwhile, *Stage Sisters* has been viewed as a tribute to Shanghai films in the 1930s. Ding Yaping comments that it bears a resemblance to *Woman Basketball Player No. 5* in that both foreground the marginalized figures (athletes and actresses) in the new society and thereby allowed the similarly marginalized Shanghai-based artists and intellectuals to articulate their will to revolution.[106] However, Marchetti acknowledges that the overall style of *Stage Sisters* still conforms to the norm of socialist realism because each character occupies "a certain class position" and represents "the contradictions associated with a specific historical period." To reconcile the Hollywood and Soviet modes she sees in the same film, Marchetti thus argues that *Stage Sisters* "remained at the edge" of both forms.[107] Such generic hybridity has prompted some film historians to wonder whether Xie intentionally moved away from the melodramatic mode when making *Stage Sisters*. For example, Meng Liye 孟犁野 posits that Xie seemed to have jettisoned his "red romanticism" (*hongse langman* 紅色浪漫) as shown in *Red Detachment of Women* and self-consciously returned to a simpler aesthetical and ideological mode—humanism and realism—in making *Stage Sisters*.[108]

The Xie Jin Mode Reconsidered

As film scholars take pains to clarify different threads of film theories and practices stitched in a single film of *Stage Sister*—Hollywood, Soviet, and 1930s Shanghai— careful scrutiny of the entire filmmaking process only reveals that the coexistence of the differing, sometimes mutually conflicting, cinematic modes is not necessarily a manifestation of the complexity of Xie Jin's directorial style. This hybridity stems from the uneasy co-working of different parties, and Xie was just one of them. The political interventions in the making of *Stage Sisters* were forceful from day one of this project. Xie somehow enjoyed less autonomy this time than he did in the task of shooting *Woman Basketball Player No. 5*: Xia Yan, not Xie Jin, took the initiative to temporarily transfer Xie Fang from Beijing to Shanghai as the leading actress. While Xie appreciated the help Xia Yan offered to him when he was still working

---

104. Tung, "The Work of Xie Jin," 200.
105. Marchetti, "Two Stage Sisters," 70.
106. Ding, *Zhongguo dianying lishi tuzhi 1896–2015 shang*, 434.
107. Marchetti, "Two Stage Sisters," 71.
108. Meng, *Xin Zhongguo dianying yishu shi, 1949–1965*, 483.

on the screenplay,[109] CCP officials from the other side of the political spectrum, such as Zhang Chunqiao, dealt a fatal blow to it before and during the Cultural Revolution. It is not an overstatement that *Stage Sisters* became an arena where the upper-echelon CCP cadres wrestled with one another in the mid-1960s.

The imprint left by the political and cultural war surrounding the movie and the co-authorship between Xie Jin and the political authorities were precisely what Zheng Wang calls "the fierce struggles behind the scenes" unbeknownst to film viewers and scholars alike. Wang calls for a historical approach, rather than "projecting researchers' own values and aesthetic standards shaped in a specific location and political moment onto a visual text," to foster a fuller understanding of films in Chinese socialism.[110] Following this line of thought, this chapter has placed the production of Xie Jin's films in the context of the ever-changing political climate in Mao-era China and his relations with the party leadership at different levels. In so doing, I seek to understand the Xie Jin (melodramatic) mode not as static and given but as dynamic.

The Xie Jin mode, as coined by Zhu Dake, though dismissed as a vague or ill-defined term,[111] centers on Xie's ability to manipulate morality and emotion, a film formula imported from Hollywood. Therefore, Zhu hints that the Xie Jin mode is, in essence, a classical Hollywood melodrama.[112] Xie Jin's melodrama, according to Charles Hayford, is located in "the literary historical sense of a mode that emerged in the aftermath of the Enlightenment." This mode emphasizes the Chinese people's heroic struggles against feudalism and imperialism.[113] Hence, this mode of melodrama has been known as "political melodrama." Nick Browne posits that the term "political melodrama" helps to broaden the scope of "Western theory of melodrama" because the latter privileges the private sphere and loses "sight of the broader social conditions of the meaning of the form."[114] It is the nature of Xie Jin's filmic works as political dramas that leads to the conclusion that "works like *Two Stage Sisters*" "fervently support the party and the revolution."[115]

While there is no denying that Xie Jin's films, just like virtually all other films produced in Mao-era China, are political, my question is: are they political enough, and are all Xie Jin's films equally political? As mentioned, *Woman Basketball Player No. 5*'s popularity resides in Xie Jin's ability to meet the needs of Shanghai urbanites

---

109. Xier Taisong et al., *Jiuba li de dushi ren*, 116.
110. Wang, *Finding Women in the State*, 16.
111. Yu Ji 余紀, "Jiefang de sixiang yu sixiang de jiefang" 解放的思想與思想的解放 [The emancipatory thoughts and thought emancipation], in *Lun Xie Jin dianying* 論謝晉電影 [On Xie Jin's films], ed. Zhongguo dianying jia xiehui 中國電影家協會 [China Film Association] (Beijing: Zhongguo dianying chubanshe, 1998), 110.
112. Zhu, "Xie Jin dianying moshi de quexian," 91–92.
113. Charles W. Hayford, "*Hibiscus Town*: Revolution, Love and Bean Curd," in *Chinese Films in Focus: 25 New Takes*, ed. Chris Berry (London: BFI Publishing, 2003), 120.
114. Nick Browne, "Society and Subjectivity: On the Political Economy of Chinese Melodrama," in *New Chinese Cinema: Forms, Identities, Politics*, ed. Nick Browne et al. (Cambridge: Cambridge University Press, 1994), 43.
115. Marchetti, "Two Stage Sisters," 77.

by displaying romantic love, sports, light music, and a petty-bourgeois lifestyle and highlighting the visible influences of Hollywood and Shanghai's urban culture.[116] The façade of the grand narrative of revolution and nationalism conceals the director's intention to privilege the private space over the public one. In other words, its inadequate politicalness made the film stand out among its peers and allowed Xie to gain both a domestic and an international reputation. In a similar fashion, *Stage Sisters* came under frenzied attacks in part because it paled in comparison with another movie Shanghai-based filmmakers were working on almost at the same time: *Sentinel under the Neon Lights* (*Nihongdeng xia de shaobing* 霓虹燈下的哨兵, 1964, dir. Wang Ping 王蘋 [1916–1990] and Ge Xin 葛鑫 [1917–2000]).[117] *Sentinel under the Neon Lights* presented a hard-core revolutionary narrative in accordance with the campaign of "making a great effort to write about the thirteen years."

Indeed, the making of *Sentinel under the Neon Lights* itself exemplifies a rumbling tension between the Shanghai-based filmmakers and the left-leaning political authorities in Shanghai. Back in 1960, when a proposal to write a screenplay about the People's Liberation Army soldiers was brought forward to the leadership of various film studios in Shanghai, it did not come to fruition. The proposer then turned to the military for help, and the story was staged in the form of drama in 1963. This play's remarkable success once again opened up a new opportunity to make the story a motion picture product. However, the filmmaking team assembled in 1963 was a mix of the staff from both Shanghai and the People's Liberation Army. To be more precise, although Pegasus was presented as the producer of the movie, its director and leading actors all came from the army. Shanghai filmmakers played a marginal role as providers of technological support.[118] In a sense, the marginalization of Shanghai-based film artists necessitated the film's political correctness. In this political climate, hence, Xie Jin's *Stage Sisters* was politically dubious.

A comparison of the three films under review in this chapter reveals that Xie Jin was subject to political pressure and constantly fine-tuned his style accordingly. As *Woman Basketball Player No. 5* raised eyebrows because it prioritized the domestic/private sphere, essentially a bourgeois family and a romantic interpersonal relationship, *Red Detachment of Women* obliterated the signs of the love story. In other words, the cinematic narrative is entirely deprived of the private sphere. The pendulum swung back to the narrative of individual struggles and personal feelings in *Stage Sisters* when Xie gained the full support of Xia Yan and Chen Huangmei. It is worth mentioning that both *Woman Basketball Player No. 5* and *Stage Sisters* were intended to supply the international market at the earliest stage of their production. Therefore, the prioritization of the private over the public and the individual over

---

116. Jin, *Xin Zhongguo dianying meixue shi, 1949–2009*, 68.
117. Zhu, "*Wutai jiemei* 'taiwai youtai,'" 39.
118. Song Zhao 宋昭, *Mama de yisheng: Wang Ping zhuan* 媽媽的一生—王蘋傳 [My mom's life—Wang Ping's biography] (Beijing: Zhongguo dianying chubanshe, 2006), 157–62.

the collective/revolutionary in those two movies strategically catered to the audience's preferences outside China.

When it came to *Hibiscus Town* in the 1980s, Xie Jin's "political melodrama" once again turned inward to the sphere of the family. Paul Pickowicz finds that *Hibiscus Town* is similar to melodramas in Republican times in that they "focus so narrowly on the family unit" and do not address "anything significant about social and political forces that are at work outside the family."[119] Xie's recourse to the experiences of individuals and families in all his films made after the Cultural Revolution are consistent with the trajectory of his life and career. In his own words, his film career "went through the same trajectory of ups and downs" of the PRC. His eagerness to illustrate the trauma he and his colleagues suffered during the Cultural Revolution stemmed from his desire to "learn what lessons" one could learn from the calamitous decade. Obviously, the lessons could only be taught at the individual level because of Xie's firm belief that individuals' fates could not be divorced from that of the nation, and his own style matured through the process.[120]

However, it is noteworthy that Xie Jin hardly had full control over his films in pre–Cultural Revolution times. I have argued that all the three films under review in this chapter resulted from both Xie's creativity and political interventions. They were all co-authored works, but the levels of co-authoring varied. The project of making *Woman Basketball Player No. 5* was spoon-fed to Xie because of his age and qualifications. Given the nature of the film as a gift to the international event and a hospitable political climate in the mid-1950s, Xie came under less political interference, enabling him to absorb the Hollywood narrative mode and Shanghai's urban culture into the film. In the late 1950s, Xie, whose fame was on the rise, suffered intense political pressure when making *Red Detachment of Women*. The troubled relationship between Xie and the CCP authorities resulted in the castration of the film by deleting the love story between the protagonists. Finally, in the mid-1960s, when Xie's career reached its zenith, he lost control over *Stage Sisters* because of fierce power struggles between Shanghai and Beijing. The "co-authorship" of Xie, the Minister of Culture, and the Shanghai authorities reoriented the project several times, and the film finally collapsed under the weight of unbearable political pressures.

Xie Jin was thus both a beneficiary of the political authorities' favoritism toward younger directors and a victim of his clashes with the party leadership, especially that in Shanghai. As a beneficiary of the times, Xie saw his films reach "the public in a way unmatched by the Fifth Generation" because of the CCP government's endeavor to establish a national film market since the early 1950s.[121] Xie's promotion to directorship in the early 1950s signaled the approval he won from the leadership

---

119. Pickowicz, *China on Film*, 94.
120. Berry, *Speaking in Images*, 34–35.
121. Xudong Zhang, *The Modernism in the Era of Reforms: Cultural Fever, Avant-Garde Fiction, and the New Chinese Cinema* (Durham, NC: Duke University Press, 1997), 221.

during the opening years of the PRC. For the same reason, he became the lone filmmaker from the "Society of Five Flowers" who survived the Anti-Rightist Movement. The CCP cadres justified well their selection of Xie Jin instead of older and more experienced directors to direct films about the communist revolution and contemporary China because veteran directors, such as Yang Xiaozhong, Chen Liting, and Sun Yu, were too physically weak to "go deep into the lives [of the masses]" (*shenru shenghuo* 深入生活) and obtain necessary information and materials for filmmaking projects.[122] As I have argued, other older-generation directors usually assumed a marginal role after 1949. More often than not, they were assigned to produce the least politicized opera movies. Hence, Xie was in an unmatched position to be one of the few directors ready to make highly politicized films, paving the way for him to be a specialist in political drama. It was under such a circumstance that all the three movies under review in this chapter were color films, indicating the enormous privilege Xie Jin could enjoy at a time when color film stock was rare nationwide.

As a victim, Xie Jin tended to disagree with the cadres. The intensity of Xie's conflicts with the party authorities increased with the growth of the director's prestige, particularly after he scored enormous success in making *Woman Basketball Player No. 5*. When the film studio moved to delete the love scenes in *Red Detachment of Women*, Xie's clash with the CCP cadres began to surface. Xie was accused of "having not reformed [his] petty-bourgeois thoughts" and "ideologically wavering."[123] For that reason, the party leadership in the film studio as well as in Shanghai harbored an agenda to lower Xie's public profile despite his unsurpassed accomplishments. In April 1961, when a film academy in Vietnam solicited some photos of famed Chinese filmmakers, the Shanghai Film Bureau refused to send those of Xie Jin on the grounds that he was "politically and historically" questionable and was not the best candidate for promoting the image of Chinese film in the international arena.[124] In 1962, some observers felt it unimaginable that Xie was barred from entering the 220-person roster of the "Literary Federation" (*Wenlian* 文聯) in Shanghai.[125] In contrast, some filmmakers favored by the CCP authorities sat quite high in this federation. For example, Zhao Dan and Shen Fu were elected as vice-chairs in May 1962.

Given the mutual distrust of the party leadership in Shanghai and the nature of Xie Jin's films about the Chinese revolution and post-1949 society, all his films were subject to intense scrutiny. Therefore, all his films were shaped by multiple factors—his love of Shanghai films back in the 1930s, socialist realism, Hollywood influences, Western critical realism,[126] Italian neorealism, and classical Chinese

---

122. Shanghai Municipal Archives, B177-3-475, 7–15.
123. Shanghai Municipal Archives, B177-3-551, 21–30.
124. Shanghai Municipal Archives, A22-2-958, 68.
125. Shanghai Municipal Archives, B177-3-330, 33.
126. Gina Marchetti posits that *Stage Sisters* "has a chamber quality of a literature influenced by Ibsen and Western critical realism." See Marchetti, "Two Stage Sisters," 69.

literature.¹²⁷ Among them, the party's intervention was all too clear. Both Xie and some of his audiences had revealed the disjointedness between the first and second halves in *Red Detachment of Women* and *Stage Sisters*, hinting at the party's might to override the director's decisions and plans.

An unintended consequence was creating a melodramatic style named after Xie Jin, or the "Xie Jin mode of cinema." Nick Browne notes that the key to Xie Jin's melodrama is "the nexus between public and private life." *Woman Basketball Player No. 5* shows that Xie was inclined to foreground the private and decrease the dosage of ideological indoctrination. The same thing could be said about the uncensored edition of *Red Detachment of Women*, whose love scenes were supposed to be Xie's favorite. In this sense, Xie's melodrama still conformed to a classical melodramatic mode that privileges family and the "private sphere." It was the CCP authorities that compelled Xie to refocus on broader sociopolitical conditions, creating what Browne calls "political melodrama."¹²⁸ Moreover, despite Xie's reputation for his conflicts with the film studio's cadres, deep in his mind, Xie was willing to compromise when necessary. One of his colleagues even complained that Xie kept in step with contemporary politics too closely. Likewise, Xie's wife admitted later that Xie had always been willing to reform his thoughts during Mao's times.¹²⁹

Conclusion: The Making of Xie Jin

Xie Jin exemplifies a new breed of film directors who built their careers almost entirely during the PRC era. Therefore, although Xie has usually been categorized as a third-generation director, he undoubtedly belongs to the first generation in post-1949 China.¹³⁰ The new PRC regime and its various politico-cultural movements thus left indelible imprints on him and his directorial style. The entire chapter has explored how Xie negotiated with the political authorities and how political forces variously altered his filmic works. Xie's "political melodrama," hence, was an outgrowth of the intersection of the influences of Hollywood films, Shanghai's urban culture in Republican times, socialist realism, and Italian neorealism. While the demands from the overseas market and the preferences of Premier Zhou Enlai and Xia Yan impelled him to foreground individuals' feelings, censors in Shanghai and beyond required Xie's movies to portray the heroes and heroines as a collective one—"the People."¹³¹

Such a tug of war contributed to the creation of Xie's melodramatic mode that negotiated "the personal and the political, the private and the public."¹³² More

---

127. Semsel, "Interviews," 113.
128. Browne, "Society and Subjectivity," 43.
129. Lu Shoujun 陸壽鈞, *Haishang yingren* 海上影人 [Filmmakers in Shanghai] (Shanghai: Shanghai shudian chubanshe, 2013), 56.
130. Li, "Xie Jin dianying zai Zhongguo dianying shi shang de diwei," 72–73.
131. Chi, "The Red Detachment of Women," 156.
132. Liu, "*Red Detachment of Women*," 135.

importantly, Xie's interactions with the political authorities also shaped his own subjectivity over the decades. He later admitted that the "political roller coaster" he and his colleagues/friends had experienced helped him to understand the changing political situations and mature "through the process."[133] Indeed, Xie's positions shifted even in the post–Cultural Revolution years, when he won widespread acclaim as a maestro of making "trauma" films. Immediately after the Cultural Revolution, Xie felt the urge to let the audiences know about the terrible fates his friends had suffered. Therefore, he made a string of trauma films. During the 2000s, by contrast, he defended his collaboration with the PRC regime to produce films "about the contrast between the old society and the new society" because he sincerely believed that the present (post-1949 China) and the past were diametrically different times. Because, in his view, the 1950s was such a prosperous time, his films made in this period accordingly portrayed "a much brighter side of life."[134] Torn between a desire to criticize "social deformation in the past" and an awareness of the sociopolitical context provided by the CCP in which his subjectivity as a world-famous film director took shape, Xie's post–Cultural Revolution films are thus defined by "neither excus[ing] the Party nor support[ing] a call for dismantling it."[135]

The intricate process of making Xie Jin's subjectivity, hence, invited Zhu Dake's criticism that Xie's movies popularized an unmodern, conservative moral code of forbearance, conciliation, and subservience. Meanwhile, Zhu dismissed Xie's melodramatic approach to highlighting the moral-emotion matrix as a manifestation of "cultural colonialism" (*wenhua zhimin* 文化殖民主義).[136] As such, Zhu dwelled on a dilemma between defining Xie as a Confucian moralist who vigorously resisted modern culture and condemning him for excessively absorbing Western influences. Such a self-contradiction itself indicates the complexity of Xie's directorial style and subjectivity, both of which were constantly subject to change and refashioning over the decades in PRC times.

---

133. Berry, *Speaking in Images*, 34.
134. Berry, *Speaking in Images*, 31–35.
135. Browne, "Society and Subjectivity," 54.
136. Zhu, "Xie Jin dianying moshi de quexian," 92–93.

6
Conclusion

Both Louis Althusser and Slavoj Žižek address the "double meaning" of an individual's subjectivity—a person as a "free agent, instigator of its activity" and as someone "subject to political rule."[1] In Althusser's words, "[t]here are no subjects except by and for their subjection."[2] This "double meaning" manifests itself in what Alexei Yurchak calls the "Lefort Paradox" in the socialist context: "achieving the full liberation of the society and individual (building of communism, creation of the New Man) by means of subsuming that society and individual under full party control."[3] In this sense, the filmmakers' quest for their subjectivities in post-1949 China and their subjection to the party-state in Mao-era China were implicated in each other in an irreducible way, as two sides of the same coin. In other words, their resistance to and accommodation with the party policies did not stem from their a priori identities as resisters or collaborators but resulted from the subjectivizing processes they underwent in the seventeen years before the Cultural Revolution.

In the post–Cultural Revolution period, memoirists and (auto)biographers tended to portray them as victims or even martyrs in Mao-era China. Such retrospectively constructed "facts," which usually deviated from the lived experiences of those film directors, as I have argued, sprang from a collective action taken by the survivors of the Cultural Revolution from the late 1970s onward, to trenchantly criticize various CCP-led political movements. Such critiques were not only emotional but also dictated by the political environment of the day. For example, Zheng Junli's wife, Huang Chen, publicly testified in a 1978 essay against Jiang Qing for the latter's "appalling crime" of murdering Zheng and angrily called for severely punishing

---

1. Slavoj Žižek, *The Sublime Object of Ideology* (London: Verso, 1989), 229.
2. Louis Althusser, *Lenin & Philosophy and Other Essays* (New York: Monthly Review Press, 2001), 183.
3. Yurchak, *Everything Was Forever, Until It Was No More*, 11. The Lefort paradox is derived from Claude Lefort's analysis of the contradiction of the rule in any given society: "The rule must be abstracted from any question concerning its origin; thus, it goes beyond the operations that it controls." Meanwhile, the rule must also prove its validity through usage; it is constantly subject to the demonstration of its effectiveness, and is thus contradictorily represented as a convention." Finally, the "authority of the master" could conceal the contradiction. See Claude Lefort, *The Political Forms of Modern Society: Bureaucracy, Democracy, Totalitarianism* (Cambridge, MA: The MIT Press, 1986), 212–13.

Jiang, her longtime friend.⁴ This essay, without a doubt, constituted a concerted effort to defame the Gang of Four and to hold its members accountable for all the tragedies that had occurred during the Cultural Revolution before the official trial of Jiang Qing proceeded. Thirty-five years later, a calmer and more sober Huang Chen began to portray the same Madam Mao in a very different fashion. In her memoir published in 2013, Huang, who finally achieved peace of mind, recalled the firm friendship of Jiang Qing, Zheng Junli, and Zhao Dan before and after 1949 and portrayed Madam Mao in a more positive light: a cheerful and amicable Jiang Qing in the 1950s as well as a gloomy and nervous Jiang Qing under unbearable political pressure on the eve of the Cultural Revolution.⁵ The marked contrast highlighted in Huang's memoir thus creates an impression that Jiang Qing herself was the victim of the precarious political climate in Mao-era China.

This autobiographer's shifted grounds over the three decades provide a reminder about the risk of uncritically accepting such accounts. They also raise questions regarding the legitimacy of memoirs and personal accounts as reliable sources in studying the lived experiences in Mao-era China. At a time when the entire society was eager to exorcise the foul influences of the Cultural Revolution and, by extension, the Mao Zedong era, narratives about the filmmakers' victimhood and martyrdom took on special political significance. It was under this circumstance that Zhao Dan was enshrined as a noble warrior against the CCP's control over China's film industry. In a similar fashion, the post-1949 film works of old-generation directors, such as Wu Yonggang and Sun Yu, slipped into oblivion as if they were entirely futile because of the party's oppression. Even Xie Jin, who managed to escape all political persecutions before the mid-1960s, downplayed the benefits he reaped during the first seventeen years of the PRC but became better known as a critic and exposer of the evils of the Cultural Revolution.

What this narrative misses is the other side of the story. Zheng Junli enjoyed an excellent reputation as a specialist in historical/biographical movies in the 1950s and 1960s because of, not despite, the party's censorship of the motion picture. More importantly, he became a self-conscious contributor to and promoter of party-endorsed historiography. Zhao Dan broke records for the speediness of shooting a film during the Great Leap Forward and thereby earned enormous political capital. This political capital was further translated into his success as a film superstar in the late 1950s and early 1960s. Likewise, Sun Yu was a propagandist of the Great-Leap speed by highlighting the accelerated promotion track of the protagonist in *Brave the Wind and Waves* from a trainee to the third mate within fifteen months. Wu Yonggang, who had never been involved in making any films related to China's traditional opera before 1949, established his fame internationally as a maestro of

---

4. Huang, "Kongsu 'Siren bang' dui Zheng Junli tongzhi ji qita dianying gongzuozhe de canku pohai," 203.
5. Huang and Zheng, *Wo he Junli*, 80–95.

opera film in the 1960s, prompting Hong Kong investors to expressly designate him in 1962 as the director of a new edition of *Marriage Between a Fairy and Man*.[6]

It is worth mentioning that Wu Yonggang's willingness to cooperate with the party authorities did not result from the political persecution he suffered in 1957 and beyond. As early as 1955, Wu produced *Hasen and Jiamila* (*Hasen yu Jiamila* 哈森與加米拉), a film featuring an all-Kazakh cast.[7] The CCP's organ newspaper, *The People's Daily*, lauded this film for authentically representing the lives and struggles of Kazakh in northwestern China and publicizing the notion of "collectivism."[8] In hindsight, *Hasen and Jiamila* was recognized for its contribution to instilling into the massive audience the CCP's policies on China's ethnic minorities.[9] Finally, Xie Jin rose to prominence quickly not just because of his outstanding filmmaking abilities but also thanks to the CCP's hidden agenda to cultivate and promote young-generation film workers. An unintended consequence was the creation of Xie's unique, melodramatic directorial style, helping him spread his fame both at home and abroad.

It is tempting to define those directors' collaboration with the party as what Gleb Tsipursky calls "conformist agency"—"the conscious and willing decision, stemming primarily from one's internal motivations and desires, to act in ways that closely follow top-level guidelines."[10] However, the notion of "conformist agency" still operates within the resistance-accommodation paradigm. Throughout this book, I have called for transcending this paradigm by placing emphasis on understanding those star directors as ordinary people with universal human needs: substantial pay, improved living conditions, more job opportunities, and higher political standing. Their career success under the new sociopolitical system, if possible, would certainly help to meet all those private needs. Therefore, it is vital to understand that those directors worked along the party lines—however ambivalent and ever-changing—to serve dual purposes: to exploit their position to pursue their personal interests[11] and to make contributions to propagating China's socialism on the screen.

---

6. Shanghai Municipal Archives, A22-1-614, 27.
7. Liu, *Moulding the Socialist Subject*, 77.
8. Zhang Yue 章越, "Kan gushi pian 'Hasen yu Jiamila'" 看故事片 "哈森與加米拉" [Watching the feature film, *Hasen and Jiamila*], *Renmin ribao* 人民日報 [People's Daily], August 2, 1955.
9. Li Miao 李淼, *Yunnan shaoshu minzu ticai dianying yanjiu: bianjiang xiangxiang, minzu renting yu wenhua jiangou* 雲南少數民族題材電影研究：邊疆想像、民族認同與文化建構 [Studies on minorities films in Yunnan: The imagination of the frontier, ethnic identities, and cultural construction] (Kunming: Yunnan daxue chubanshe, 2016), 31.
10. Gleb Tsipursky, *Socialist Fun: Youth, Consumption, and State-Sponsored Popular Culture in the Soviet Union, 1945–1970* (Pittsburgh: University of Pittsburgh Press, 2016), 8.
11. Vladimir Shlapentokh calls this process "privatization" or even "destatization." He believes that the process of "privatization," in which individuals took advantage of the public services they were involved in to seek private profits, constituted the most important part of social development in all socialist regimes, China included. See Shlapentokh, *Public and Private Life of the Soviet People*, 154.

Their efforts to turn their public services into their private gains and their toeing the party line in their filmmaking activities were not mutually contradictory. Instead, the intertwining of the two constituted the very essence of those filmmakers' everyday lives in Mao-era China, and it is futile to disentangle the two. In the process of working under the new sociopolitical system in Mao-era China, the filmmakers' strenuous efforts to find new niches for their film careers (successfully or not), make private gains, and reconfirm their positions in the film circles served as their subjectivizing practices. As such, they were eager to write themselves into the new social and political order. To rephrase Althusser and Žižek, they developed their subjectivities by both taking the initiatives in their careers and subjecting them to the party-state. Their entanglement with the political authorities shaped their new identities. By resorting to their most essential and most skillful subjectivizing practice—filmmaking—the filmmakers tried their best to *work* the system to maximize the benefits and minimize the damages.

Bibliography

Ai Mingzhi 艾明之. "Bo Wu Yonggang" 駁吳永剛 [Refuting Wu Yonggang]. *Renmin ribao* 人民日報 [People's Daily], November 27, 1957.
Althusser, Louis. *Lenin & Philosophy and Other Essays*. New York: Monthly Review Press, 2001.
Andrews, Julia F. *Painters and Politics in the People's Republic of China, 1949–1979*. Berkley: University of California Press, 1994.
Andrews, Julia F. "Traditional Painting in New China: Guohua and the Anti-Rightist Campaign." *The Journal of Asian Studies* 49, no. 3 (August 1990): 555–77.
Arvidsson, Stefan, Jakub Beneš, and Anja Kirsch. "Introduction: Socialist Imaginations." In *Socialist Imaginations: Utopias, Myths, and the Masses*, edited by Stefan Arvidsson, Jakub Beneš, and Anja Kirsch, 1–17. London: Routledge, 2019.
Bao Shiyuan 鮑世遠. *Xishui changliu* 戲水長流 [The stream of theater flows long]. Shanghai: Shanghai wenyi chubanshe, 2011.
Bao, Weihong. "The Politics of Remediation: Mise-en-scène and the Subjunctive Body in Chinese Opera Film." *The Opera Quarterly* 26, no. 2–3 (August 31, 2010): 256–90.
Bao, Weihong. "The Trouble with Theater: Cinema and the Geopolitics of Medium Specificity." *Framework*, 56, no. 2 (Fall 2015): 350–67.
Bender, Mark. *Plum and Bamboo: China's Suzhou Chantefable Tradition*. Urbana: University of Illinois Press, 2003.
Berry, Chris. "Neither One Thing Nor Another: Toward a Study of the Viewing Subject and Chinese Cinema in the 1980s." In *New Chinese Cinema: Forms, Identities, Politics*, edited by Nick Browne, Paul G. Pickowicz, Vivian Sobchack, and Esther Yau, 88–113. Cambridge: Cambridge University Press, 1994.
Berry, Chris. *Speaking in Images: Interviews with Contemporary Chinese Filmmakers*. New York: Columbia University Press, 2005.
Berry, Chris, and Mary Farquhar. *China on Screen: Cinema and Nation*. New York: Columbia University Press, 2006.
Bian, Morris L. *The Making of the State Enterprise System in Modern China: The Dynamics of Institutional Change*. Cambridge, MA: Harvard University Press, 2005.
"Bianzhe de hua" 編者的話 [The editors' remarks]. *Xin shixue tongxun* 新史學通訊 [Newsletter of New Historical Studies] 1, no. 5 (1951): 2.

Braester, Yomi. "Farewell My Concubine: National Myth and City Memories." In *Chinese Films in Focus: 25 New Takes*, edited by Chris Berry, 89–96. London: BFI Publishing, 2003.

Braester, Yomi. "A Genealogy of Cinephilia in the Maoist Period." In *The Oxford Handbook of Chinese Cinema*, edited by Carlos Rojas and Eileen Cheng-yin Chow, 98–115. Oxford: Oxford University Press, 2013.

Braester, Yomi. *Witness Against History: Literature, Film, and Public Discourse in Twentieth-Century China*. Stanford: Stanford University Press, 2004.

Braester, Yomi, and Tina Mai Chen. "Film in the People's Republic of China, 1949–1979: The Missing Years?" *Journal of Chinese Cinemas* 5, no. 1 (2011): 5–12.

Brooks, Peter. *The Melodramatic Imagination: Balzac, Henry James, Melodrama, and the Mode of Excess*. New Haven, CT: Yale University Press, 1995.

Browne, Nick. "Society and Subjectivity: On the Political Economy of Chinese Melodrama." In *New Chinese Cinema: Forms, Identities, Politics*, edited by Nick Browne, Paul G. Pickowicz, Vivian Sobchack, and Esther Yau, 40–65. Cambridge: Cambridge University Press, 1994.

Byrnes, Corey. *Fixing Landscape: A Techno-Poetic History of China's Three Gorges*. New York: Columbia University Press, 2019.

Chatterjee, Choi, David Ransel, Mary Canender, and Karen Petrone. "Introduction: The Genesis and Themes of Everyday Life in Russia Past and Present." In *Everyday Life in Russia Past and Present*, edited by Choi Chatterjee, David Ransel, Mary Canender, and Karen Petrone, 1–13. Bloomington: Indiana University Press, 2015.

Cheek, Timothy. "Historians as Public Intellectuals in Contemporary China." In *Chinese Intellectuals between State and Market*, edited by Edward Gu and Merle Goldman, 204–22. London: Routledge, 2004.

Cheek, Timothy. *Propaganda and Culture in Mao's China: Deng Tuo and the Intelligentsia*. Oxford: Clarendon Press, 1997.

Chen Baichen 陳白塵. "Chen Baichen dianying ju xuan" 陳白塵電影劇選 [Selected film and dramatic scripts of Chen Baichen]. *Dushu* 讀書 [Reading], no. 7 (1982): 99–104.

Chen Baichen 陳白塵. "Ganxie yu zhufu—wei *Song Jingshi* shangying zuo" 感謝與祝福—為宋景詩上映作 [Gratitude and best wishes—for the exhibition of *Song Jingshi*]. *Tianjin ribao* 天津日報 [Tianjin Daily], June 23, 1957.

Chen Baichen 陳白塵. "Nongmin geming yingxiong Song Jingshi ji Heiqi jun—'Song Jingshi lishi diaocha baogao tiyao.'" 農民革命英雄宋景詩及其黑旗軍——"宋景詩歷史調查報告" 提要 [The peasant revolutionary hero Song Jingshi and the Black Flag Army—Abstract of "the investigation report on the history of Song Jingshi"]. *Renmin ribao* 人民日報. [People's Daily], November 11, 1952.

Chen Baichen 陳白塵. *Song Jingshi lishi diaocha ji* 宋景詩歷史調查記 [The investigation report on the history of Song Jingshi]. Beijing: Renmin Chubanshe, 1957.

Chen Baichen 陳白塵, Ye Yiqun 葉以群, Tang Tao 唐弢, Ke Ling 柯靈, Du Xuan 杜宣, and Chen Liting 陳鯉庭. *Dianying wenxue juben Lu Xun* (shangji) 電影文學劇本魯迅 (上集) [The script of (*The Life of*) *Lu Xun*, part 1]. Shanghai: Shanghai wenyi chubanshe, 1963.

Chen Hong 陳虹. *Chen Baichen pingzhuan* 陳白塵評傳 [Critical biography of Chen Baichen]. Chongqing: Chongqing chubanshe, 1998.

Chen Hong 陳虹. "Fuqin de gushi" 父親的故事 [(My) father's story]. In *Wutai yu jiangtai: xiju jia Chen Baichen* 舞臺與講臺：戲劇家陳白塵 [The stage and the podium: The dramatist Chen Baichen], edited by Chen Hong 陳虹, 9–22. Nanjing: Nanjing daxue chubanshe, 2003.

Chen Hong 陳虹. *Wutai yu jiangtai: Xiju jia Chen Baichen* 舞臺與講臺：戲劇家陳白塵 [The stage and the platform: Chen Baichen, the dramatist]. Nanjing: Nanjing daxue chubanshe, 2003.

Chen Huangmei 陳荒煤. *Chen Huangmei wenji di 3 juan: sanwen (xia)* 陳荒煤文集第3卷：散文（下）[The collected writings of Chen Huangmei, vol. 3: Essays, bk. 2]. Beijing: Zhongguo dianying chubanshe, 2013.

Chen Huangmei 陳荒煤. *Chen Huangmei wenji, di 7 juan dianying pinglun (shang)* 陳荒煤文集第7卷：電影評論（上）[The collected writings of Chen Huangmei, vol. 7: Film reviews, bk. 1] Beijing: Zhongguo dianying chubanshe, 2013.

Chen Huangmei 陳荒煤, and Chen Bo 陳播. *Zhou Enlai yu dianying* 周恩來與電影 [Zhou Enlai and film]. Beijing: Zhongyang wenxian chubanshe, 1995.

Chen Huiyang (Ch'en Hui-yang 陳輝揚). *Mengying ji: Zhongguo dianying yinxiang* 夢影集：中國電影印象 [Anthology of dream and shadow: An impression on Chinese film]. Taipei: Yuncheng wenhua, 1990.

Chen Liting 陳鯉庭. "Daoyan yinggai shi shengchan de zhongxin huanjie" 導演應該是生產的中心環節 [The director should take the center stage in film production]. *Wenhui bao* 文匯報 [Wenhui Daily], November 23, 1956.

Chen Lixu 陳立旭. "He Long paiban Cao Rulin sunnü zhuyan *Nülan wuhao*" 賀龍拍板曹汝霖孫女主演《女籃五號》[He Long gave the nod to [allow] Cao Rulin's granddaughter to feature in *Woman Basketball Player No. 5*]. *Dangshi zonglan* 黨史縱覽 [Survey of the CCP's History], no. 7 (2020): 36.

Chen Mo 陳墨. "Gungun bujin Langtaosha" 滾滾不盡《浪淘沙》[A review of *Gold and Sand*]. *Dangdai dianying* 當代電影 [Contemporary Cinema], no. 2 (2005): 83–87.

Chen Mo 陳墨. *Yingtan jiuzong* 影壇舊蹤 [The trace in the past in the world of film]. Nanchang: Jiangxi jiaoyu chubanshe, 2000.

Chen Naishan 陳乃珊. *Shanghai TASTE* 上海TASTE [Shanghai TASTE]. Shanghai: Shanghai cishu chubanshe, 2008.

Chen Qingquan 陳清泉. *Yuebai fengqing: Shanghai yingtan wangshi ji qita* 月白風清：上海影壇往事及其他 [The moon is bright and the air serene: The past in the film circles in Shanghai and other matters]. Shanghai: Shanghai wenyi chubanshe, 2015.

Chen Shuyu 陳漱渝. "*Dazhong dianying* kandeng de yipian bushi zhi wen" 《大眾電影》刊登的一篇不實之文 [A misleading article published in *Mass Film*]. *Lu Xun yanjiu dongtai* 魯迅研究動態 [The Trend of Studies on Lu Xun], no. 3 (1986): 7–10.

Chen Xiangyang. "Affect, Folklore and Cantonese Opera Film." *Journal of Chinese Cinemas* 8, no. 3 (2014): 226–43.

Chen Xiaomei. *Acting the Right Part: Political Theater and Popular Drama in Contemporary China*. Honolulu: University of Hawai'i Press, 2002.

Chen Xiaonong 陳曉農. *Chen Boda zuihou koushu huiyi* 陳伯達最後口述回憶 [Final oral memoirs of Chen Boda]. Hong Kong: Xingke'er chuban youxian gongsi, 2005.

Cheng Jihua 程季華. *Xiayan dianying wenji diyi juan* 夏衍電影文集第一卷 [Anthology of Xia Yan's essays on film, vol. 1]. Beijing: Zhongguo dianying chubanshe, 2000.

Cheng Mo 程沫. "Makesi zhuyi shiguan xia de dianying lisih yanjiu—jiyu dui *Xiandai Zhongguo dianying shilue* de fenxi" 馬克思主義史觀下的電影歷史研究—基於對《現代中國電影史略》的分析 [Historical studies on film under the Marxist conception of history—An analysis of *Brief History of Contemporary China*]. *Shiting* 視聽 [Seeing and Hearing], no. 4 (2019): 231–32.

Cheng Yinghong. *Creating the "New Man": From Enlightenment Ideals to Socialist Realities*. Honolulu: University of Hawai'i Press, 2009.

Chi, Robert. "The Red Detachment of Women: Resenting, Regendering, Remembering." In *Chinese Films in Focus: 25 New Takes*, edited by Chris Berry, 152–59. London: BFI Publishing, 2003.

Chow, Rey. "Fetish Power Unbound: A Small History of 'Woman' in Chinese Cinema." In *The Oxford Handbook of Chinese Cinema*, edited by Carlos Rojas and Eileen Cheng-yin Chow, 490–506. Oxford: Oxford University Press, 2013.

Chow, Rey. *Primitive Passions: Visuality, Sexuality, Ethnography, and Contemporary Chinese Cinema*. New York: Columbia University Press, 1995.

Clark, Paul. *Chinese Cinema: Culture and Politics since 1949*. Cambridge: Cambridge University Press, 1987.

Clark, Paul. "Closely Watched Viewers: A Taxonomy of Chinese Film Audiences from 1949 to the Cultural Revolution Seen from Hunan." *Journal of Chinese Cinemas* 5, no. 1 (2011): 73–89.

Clark, Paul. "Two Hundred Flowers on China's Screens." In *Perspectives on Chinese Cinema*, edited by Chris Berry, 66–96. Ithaca, NY: China-Japan Program, Cornell University, 1985.

Cui Shuqin. *Women Through the Lens: Gender and Nation in a Century of Chinese Cinema*. Honolulu: University of Hawai'i Press, 2003.

Dai Jinhua 戴錦華. "Lishi yu xushi—Xie Jin dianying yishu guanjian" 歷史與敘述—謝晉電影藝術管見 [History and narrative—A brief view of Xie Jin's cinematic arts]. In *Lun Xie Jin dianying* 論謝晉電影 [On Xie Jin's films], edited by Zhongguo dianying jia xiehui 中國電影家協會 [China Film Association], 142–60. Beijing: Zhongguo dianying chubanshe, 1998.

Dai Jinhua 戴錦華. *Wuzhong fengjing* 霧中風景 [Landscape in the fog]. Beijing: Beijing daxue chubanshe, 2000.

Dai Weiyu 戴維宇. "Manyi wozhe 50 nian" 漫憶我這50年 [Random memories of fifty years in my life]. In *Suiyue shibei* 歲月拾貝 [Collecting treasure in history], edited by Wang Xijian 王晞建, 251–57. Beijing: Zhongguo guangbo dianshi chubanshe, 2002.

Dai Zhixian 戴知賢. *Wentan san gong'an* 文壇三公案 [Three complicated cases in the literary circles]. Zhengzhou: Henan renmin chubanshe, 1994.

DeMare, Brian James. *Mao's Cultural Army: Drama Troupes in China's Rural Revolution*. Cambridge: Cambridge University Press, 2015.

Ding Ning 丁寧. "Xin Zhongguo xiqu pian, meishu pian zai Gang chuanbo yanjiu" 新中國戲曲片、美術片在港傳播研究 [A study on the circulation of the PRC-made opera films and cartoons in Hong Kong]. *Dianying xinzuo* 電影新作 [New Cinematic Works], no. 2 (2015): 77–82.

Ding Yaping 丁亞平. *Zai lishi de bianji* 在歷史的邊際 [On the margins of history]. Beijing: Beijing shidai huawen shuju, 2015.

Ding Yaping 丁亞平. *Zhongguo dianying tongshi 1* 中國電影通識1 [The common knowledge of Chinese cinema 1]. Beijing: Zhongguo dianying chubanshe, 2016.

Ding Yaping 丁亞平. *Zhongguo dianying lishi tuzhi 1896–2015 shang* 中國電影歷史圖志 1896–2015 上 [A pictorial history of Chinese Cinema, 1896–2015, part 1]. Beijing: Wenhua yishu chuabanshe, 2015).

Dirlik, Arif. "The Problem of Class Viewpoint versus Historicism in Chinese Historiography." *Modern China* 3, no. 4 (October 1977): 465–88.

Dobrenko, Evgeny. *Stalinist Cinema and the Production of History: Museum of the Revolution*. Translated by Sarah Young. Edinburgh: Edinburgh University Press, 2008.

Donald, Stephanie Hemelryk. *Public Secrets, Public Spaces: Cinema and Civility in China*. Lanham, MD: Rowman & Littlefield, 2000.

Edmunds, Clifford. "The Politics of Historiography: Jian Bozan's Historicism." In *China's Intellectuals and the State: In Search for New Relationship*, edited by Merle Goldman, Timothy Cheek, and Carol Lee Marmin, 65–106. Cambridge, MA: Harvard University Press, 1987.

Enyedi, György. "Urbanization under Socialism." *Cities after Socialism: Urban and Regional Change and Conflict in Post-Socialist Societies*, edited by Gregory Andrusz, Michael Harloe, and Ivan Szeleny, 100–118. Oxford: Blackwell, 1996.

Esherick, Joseph W. *The Origins of the Boxer Uprising*. Berkeley: University of California Press, 1987.

Fan Cuiting 樊粹庭. *Fan Cuiting wenji jumu chuangzuo xia* 樊粹庭文集·劇目創作下 [Fan Cuiting's anthology—Playwriting part 2]. Zhengzhou: Henan daxue chubanshe, 2012.

"Fan gemin xiuzheng zhuyi fenzi Xia Yan de shida zuizhuang" 反革命修正主義分子夏衍的十大罪狀 [Ten crimes (committed by) Xia Yan, the counterrevolutionary revisionist]. In *Chedi chanchu fan gemin xiuzheng zhuyi wenyi heixian ziliao huibian* 徹底剷除反革命修正主義文藝黑線資料彙編 [Completely eradicate the black line of the counterrevolutionary revisionist literature and arts: Compilation of materials], edited by Shanghai hongqi dianying zhipian chang hongqi gemin zaofan bingtuan 上海紅旗電影製片廠紅旗革命造反兵團 [The revolutionary and rebellious corps of the Shanghai Red Flag Film Studio], 67–72. n.p., 1967.

"Fan gemin xiuzheng zhuyi fenzi Yang Yongzhi de shida zuizhuang" 反革命修正主義分子楊永直的十大罪狀 [Ten crimes (committed by) Yang Yongzhi, the counterrevolutionary revisionist]. In *Chedi chanchu fan gemin xiuzheng zhuyi wenyi heixian ziliao huibian* 徹底鏟除反革命修正主義文藝黑綫資料彙編 [Completely eradicate the black line of the counterrevolutionary revisionist literature and arts: Compilation of materials], edited by Shanghai hongqi dianying zhipian chang hongqi gemin zaofan bingtuan 上海紅旗電影製片廠紅旗革命造反兵團 [The revolutionary and rebellious corps of the Shanghai Red Flag Film Studio], 158–75. n.p., 1967.

Fan, Victor. "The Cinema of Sun Yu: Ice Cream for the Eye . . . But with a *Homo Sacer*." *Journal of Chinese Cinemas* 5, no. 3 (2011): 219–51.

Fang Xiangdong 房向東. *"Hengzhan": Lu Xun yu zuoyi wenren* 〝橫站〞：魯迅與左翼文人 ["Standing horizontally": Lu Xun and left-wing writers]. Shanghai: Shanghai sanlian shudian, 2014.

Fei Xiaotong 費孝通. *Wangshi chongchong* 往事重重 [The eventful past]. Shenyang: Liaoning jiaoyu chubanshe, 1998.

Feng Hechen 封禾陳. "Sun Yu zishu" 孫瑜自述 [Sun Yu's account in his own words]. In *Zhongguo dianying nianjian 2001* 中國電影年鑒2001 [Chinese film yearbook, 2001], edited by Zhongguo dianying nianjian she 中國電影年鑒社 [The publishing house for Chinese film yearbook], 267–71. Changsha: Yuelu shushe, 2002.

Fitzpatrick, Sheila. *Everyday Stalinism: Ordinary Life in Extraordinary Times: Soviet Russia in the 1930s*. Oxford: Oxford University Press, 2000.

Ford, Stacilee. "'Reel Sisters' and Other Diplomacy: Cathay Studios and Cold War Cultural Production." In *Hong Kong in the Cold War*, edited by Priscilla Roberts and John M. Carroll, 183–210. Hong Kong: Hong Kong University Press, 2016.

Frangville, Vanessa. "The Non-Han in Socialist Cinema and Contemporary Films in the People's Republic of China." *China Perspectives*, no. 2 (2012): 61–69.

Fu Poshek. *Between Shanghai and Hong Kong: The Politics of Chinese Cinemas*. Stanford: Stanford University Press, 2003.

Fu Poshek. "More than Just Entertaining: Cinematic Containment and Asia's Cold War in Hong Kong, 1949–1959." *Modern Chinese Literature and Culture* 30, no. 2 (Fall 2018): 1–55.

Gao Xiaojian 高小健. "Wu Yonggang: zhuisuo bujin de huati—yige dianying zhishi fenzi de jingshen yu yishu" 吳永剛：追索不盡的話題—個電影知識份子的精神與藝術 [Wu Yonggang: An eternal topic—The spirit and arts of a cinematic intellectual]. *Dangdai dianying* 當代電影 [Contemporary Cinema], no. 5 (2004): 48–55.

Gao Xiaojian 高小健. *Xiqu dianying yishu lun* 戲曲電影藝術論 [The art of the opera film]. Beijing: Zhongguo dianying chubanshe, 2015.

Gao Xiaojian 高小健. *Zhongguo xiqu dianying shi* 中國戲曲電影史 [History of Chinese opera films]. Beijing: Wenhua yishu chubanshe, 2005.

Gilley, Bruce. *China's Democratic Future: How It Will Happen and Where It Will Lead*. New York: Columbia University Press, 2004.

Glosser, Susan L. *Chinese Visions of Family and State, 1915–1953*. Berkeley: University of California, 2003.

Goldman, Merle. *China's Intellectuals: Advise and Dissent*. Cambridge, MA: Harvard University Press, 1981.

Gong Yan 龔豔. *Piaoyi, gaixie yu zaizao: 20 shiji siwushi niandai Zhongguo quyu dianying zhi xingcheng* 漂移，改寫與再造—20世紀四五十年代中國區域電影之形成 [Drifting, rewriting, and reconstructing: The making of China's local films in the 1940s and 1950s]. Beijing: Zhongguo dianying chubanshe, 2013.

Guo Moruo 郭沫若. "Du *Wu Xun lishi diaocha ji*" 讀《武訓歷史調查記》 [On the Investigation report of the history of Wu Xun]. *Renmin ribao* 人民日報 [People's Daily], August 4, 1951.

Guo Xiaohui 郭曉惠. *Jiantao shu: shiren Guo Xiaochuan zai zhengzhi yundong Zhong de linglei wenzi* 檢討書: 詩人郭小川在政治運動中的另類文字 [The confession: The poet Guo Xiaochuan's alternative literature during political movements]. Beijing: Zhongguo gongren chubanshe, 2001.

Han Shangyi 韓尚義. "Xiqu yingpian de zaoxing fengge" 戲曲影片的造型風格 [The opera film's visual style]. In *Yinse yinji: Shanghai yingren lilun wenxuan* 銀色印記：上海影人理論文選 [The silver imprint: Selected essays on [film] theories by Shanghai filmmakers], edited by Shanghai wenxue yishu jia lianhehui, Shanghai dianyingjia xiehui 上

海市文學藝術家聯合會、上海電影家協會, 10–14. Shanghai: Fudan daxue chubanshe, 2005.

Hang, Krista Van Fleit. "Zhong Xinghuo: Communist Film Worker." In *Chinese Film Stars*, edited by Mary Farquhar and Yingjin Zhang, 108–18. London: Routledge, 2010.

Harris, Kristine. "The Goddess: Fallen Woman of Shanghai." In *Chinese Films in Focus II*, edited by Chris Berry, 128–36. London: BFI/Palgrave MacMillan, 2008.

Harris, Kristine. "Re-makes/Re-models: *The Red Detachment of Women* between Stage and Screen," *The Opera Quarterly*, 26, no. 2–3 (2010): 316–42.

Harrison, James P. *The Communists and Chinese Peasant Rebellions: A Study in the Rewriting of Chinese History*. New York: Atheneum, 1969.

Hayford, Charles W. "*Hibiscus Town*: Revolution, Love and Bean Curd." In *Chinese Films in Focus: 25 New Takes*, edited by Chris Berry, 120–27. London: BFI Publishing, 2003.

He Qiliang. "Between Accommodation and Resistance: Pingtan Storytelling in 1960s Shanghai." *Modern Asian Studies* 48, no. 3 (May 2014): 524–49.

He Weiguo 何衛國. *Hongloumeng yingshi wenhua yingshi wenhua lungao* 紅樓夢影視文化論稿 [Theses on motion culture and TV culture of *Dream of the Red Chamber*]. Beijing: Wenhua yishu chubanshe, 2017.

Heilmann, Sebastian, and Elizabeth J. Perry. "Embracing Uncertainty: Guerrilla Policy Style and Adaptive Governance in China." In *Mao's Invisible Hand: The Political Foundations of Adaptive Governance in China*, edited by Sebastian Heilmann and Elizabeth J. Perry, 1–29. Cambridge, MA: Harvard University Press, 2011.

Hellbeck, Jochen. *Revolution on My Mind: Writing a Diary Under Stalin*. Cambridge, MA: Harvard University Press, 2006.

Holland, Dorothy, William Lachicotte Jr., Debra Skinner, and Carole Cain. *Identity and Agency in Cultural Worlds*. Cambridge, MA: Harvard University Press, 1998.

Hongqi geming zaofan bingtuan 404 zongdui 紅旗革命造反兵團404縱隊 [The 404 column of the red flag revolutionary and rebellious corps]. "Zalan 'gao xingchou' zhidu" 砸爛"高薪酬"制度 [Smash the system of "high remuneration"]. In *Gaoju Mao Zedong sixiang weida hongqi, chedi zalan fangemin xiuzheng zhuyi wenyi heixian* 高舉毛澤東思想偉大紅旗，徹底砸爛反革命修正主義文藝黑線 [Hoist the great red banner of Maoist thought to completely smash the reactionary and revisionist black line of art and literature], edited by Shanghai hongqi dianying zhipianchang hongqi gemin zaofan bingtuan Shanghai haiguan xuanchuan zu 上海紅旗電影製片廠紅旗革命造反兵團上海海關宣傳組 [The customs propaganda team of the revolutionary and rebellious corps at the Shanghai Red Flag Film Studio], 20–21. N.p., 1967.

"Hu Yeqin shi Yueju yuan dangnei touhao zou ziben zhuyi daolu de dangquan pai" 胡野檎是越劇院黨內頭號走資本主義道路的當權派 [Hu Yeqin is the number one capitalist establishment inside the communist party in the Yue opera troupe]. In *Yueju zhanbao* 越劇戰報 [Yue opera war report], edited by Shanghai Yueju yuan bayi gongshe *Yueju zhanbao* bianji bu 上海越劇院八一公社《越劇戰報》編輯部 [Editorial office of Yue opera war report of the August 1 Commune at Shanghai Yue opera troupe], 11–20. N.p., 1967.

Huang Chen 黃晨. "Kongsu 'Siren bang' dui Zheng Junli tongzhi ji qita dianying gongzuozhe de canku pohai" 控訴"四人幫"對鄭君里通知及其他電影工作者的殘酷迫害 [Denouncing the "Gang of Four" for their cruel persecution of Comrade Zheng Junli and other film workers]. In *"Siren bang" shi dianying shiye de sidi* "四人幫"是電影事業的死敵 ["The Gang of Four" are the archenemy of the film industry], 199–207. Beijing: Zhongguo dianying chubanshe, 1979.

Huang Chen 黃晨, and Zheng Dali 鄭大里. *Wo he Junli* 我和君里 [Junli and I]. Shanghai: Shanghai wenhua chubanshe, 2013.

Huang Yin 黃音. "Yiye riji" 一頁日記 [One page of a diary]. *Dazhong dianying* 大眾電影 [Mass Film], no. 9 (1957): 28–29.

Huang Yuanqi 黃元起. "*Wu Xun lishi diaocha ji* suo tishi de zhishi fangfa" 《武訓歷史調查記》所提示的治史方法 [The approach of historical studies as proposed by *The Investigation Report of the History of Wu Xun*]. *Xin shixue tongxun* 新史學通訊 [Newsletter of New Historical Studies] 1, no. 6 (September 15, 1951): 1–2.

Huang Zongying 黃宗英. *Huang Zongying wenji di 1 juan: cun zhi tianxia* 黃宗英文集第1卷：存之天下 [The collected writings of Huang Zongying, vol. 1: Conserve (Zhao Dan's paintings) in the world]. Shenzhen: Haitian chubanshe, 2017.

Hui, Kwok Wai (Xu Guohui 許國惠). "Revolution, Commercialism and Chineseness: Opera Films in Socialist Shanghai and Capitalist-Colonial Hong Kong, 1949–1966." PhD diss., University of Chicago, 2013.

Hui, Kwok Wai (Xu Guohui 許國惠). "Shangye yu zhengzhi: lengzhan shiqi Xianggang zuopai dui xin Zhongguo xiqu dianying haibao de zai chuangzao" 商業與政治：冷戰時期香港左派對新中國戲曲電影海報的再創造 [Business and politics: The left-wingers' remaking of opera film posters made in new China during the Cold War era]. In *Shunliu yu niliu: chongxie Xianggang dianying shi* 順流與逆流：重寫香港電影史 [Current and counter current: Rewriting the film history of Hong Kong], edited by Poshek Fu (Fu Baoshi 傅葆石) and Su Tao 蘇濤, 119–45. Beijing: Beijing daxue chubanshe, 2020.

Hung Chang-tai. "Reeducating a Blind Storyteller: Han Qixiang and the Chinese Storytelling Campaign." *Modern China* 19, no. 4 (October 1993): 395–426.

"*Hunshi mowing*"—*Zhao Dan* "混世魔王"—趙丹 [Zhao Dan, "a fiend in human shape"]. Unpublished.

Iovene, Paola. "Chinese Operas on Stage and Screen: A Short Introduction." *The Opera Quarterly* 26, no. 2–3 (August 2010): 181–99.

Ji Wenfu 嵇文甫. "Fengjian renwu jiudeng lun—cong *Wuxun zhuan* shilun suo yinqi de lishi renwu pingjia wenti" 封建人物九等論—從武訓傳時論所引起的歷史人物評價問題 [On nine ranks of people in feudal (society)—The issue of appraising historical figures stemming from the current discussions of *The Life of Wu Xun*]. *Xin shixue tongxun* 新史學通訊 [Newsletter of New Historical Studies] 1, no. 5 (1951): 1–2.

Jiang Jin. *Women Playing Men: Yue Opera and Social Change in Twentieth-Century Shanghai*. Seattle: University of Washington Press, 2009.

Jin Danyuan 金丹元. *Xin Zhongguo dianying meixue shi, 1949–2009* 新中國電影美學史 1949–2009 [A history of film aesthetics in new China, 1949–2009]. Beijing: Shenghuo dushu xinzhi sanlian shudian, 2013.

Jin Taipin 金肽頻. *Anqing xin wenhua biannian 1915–2015: pinglun juan* 安慶新文化編年 1915–2015：評論卷 [The one-hundredth anniversary of Anqing new culture, 1915–2015: Commentaries]. Hefei: Anhui wenyi chubanshe, 2016.

Johnson, Matthew D. "Beneath the Propaganda State: Official and Unofficial Cultural Landscapes in Shanghai, 1949–1965." In *Maoism at the Grassroots: Everyday Life in*

China's Era of High Socialism, edited by Jeremy Brown and Matthew D. Johnson, 199–229. Cambridge, MA: Harvard University Press, 2015.

Johnson, Matthew D. "Cinema and Propaganda during the Great Leap Forward." In *Visualizing Modern China: Image, History, and Memory, 1750–Present*, edited by James A. Cook, Joshua Goldstein, Matthew D. Johnson, and Sigrid Schmalzer, 195–211. Lanham, MD: Lexington Books, 2014.

Johnson, Matthew D. "Propaganda and Censorship in Chinese Cinema." In *A Companion to Chinese Cinema*, edited by Yingjin Zhang, 153–78. Malden, MA: Wiley-Blackwell, 2012.

Johnston, Timothy. *Being Soviet: Identity, Rumour, and Everyday Life under Stalin, 1939–1953*. Oxford: Oxford University Press, 2011.

Kahn, Harold, and Albert Feuerwerker. "The Ideology of Scholarship: China's New Historiography." *The China Quarterly*, no. 22 (April–June 1965): 1–13.

Kaikonen, Marja. "*Quyi*: Will It Survive?" In *The Eternal Storyteller: Oral Literature in Modern China*, edited by Vibeke Børdahl, 62–68. Richmond, Surrey: Curzon Press, 1999.

Kassymbekova, Botakoz. *Despite Cultures: Early Soviet Rule in Tajikistan*. Pittsburgh: University of Pittsburgh Press, 2016.

Kotkin, Stephen. *Magnetic Mountain: Stalinism as a Civilization*. Berkeley: University of California Press, 1997.

Kuoshu, Harry H. *Lightness of Being in China: Adaptation and Discursive Figuration in Cinema and Theater*. New York: Peter Lang, 1999.

Laolaoxia 老老夏. "Huanxi yuanjia Chen Liting he Zhao Dan" 歡喜冤家陳鯉庭和趙丹 [Chen Liting and Zhao Dan: A quarrelsome and loving duo]. *Shanghai caifeng* 上海采風 [Folk Art Collection in Shanghai], no. 5 (2010): 26–33.

Lau, Frederick. "Forever Red: The Invention of Solo dizi Music in Post-1949." *British Journal of Ethnomusicology* 5 (1996): 113–31.

Law Kar, and Frank Bren. *Hong Kong Cinema: A Cross-Cultural View*. Lanham, MA: The Scarecrow Press, 2004.

Lee Haiyan. *Revolution of the Heart: A Genealogy of Love in China, 1900–1950*. Stanford: Stanford University Press, 2007.

Lee, Leo Ou-fan. "The Tradition of Modern Chinese Cinema: Some Preliminary Explorations and Hypotheses." In *Perspectives on Chinese Cinema*, edited by Chris Berry, 6–20. London: BFI Publishing, 1991.

Lefort, Claude. *The Political Forms of Modern Society: Bureaucracy, Democracy, Totalitarianism*. Cambridge, MA: The MIT Press, 1986.

Lewis, Greg. "The History, Myth, and Memory of Maoist Chinese Cinema, 1949–1966." *Asian Cinema* 16, no. 1 (March 2005): 162–83.

Leyda, Jay. *Dianying: An Account of Films and the Film Audience in China*. Cambridge, MA: The MIT Press, 1972.

Li Hsiao-t'i. *Opera, Society, and Politics in Modern China*. Cambridge, MA: Harvard University Press, 2019.

Li Huaiyin. *Reinventing Modern China: Imagination and Authenticity in Chinese Historical Writing*. Honolulu: University of Hawai'i Press, 2013.

Li Hui 李輝. *Zhao Dan zishu* 趙丹自述 [Zhao Dan in his own words]. Zhengzhou: Daxiang chubanshe, 2003.

Li Jing 李菁. *Wangshi bu jimo Koushu jingxuan ji—2006-2008* 往事不寂寞《口述》精選集—2006-2008 [The past is not lonesome: The best of *Oral Accounts*—2006-2008]. Beijing: Shenghuo dushu sanlian shudian, 2009.

Li Jiuru 李九如. "'Xin shenghuo yundong xianfeng dui': *Tiyu huanghou* yu 20 shiji 30 niandai chuqi de xiandaixing shenti huayu" "新生活運動先鋒隊":《體育皇后》與20世紀30年代初期的現代性身體話語 [*Queen of Sports*: The body discourse in 1930s]. *Dangdai dianying* 當代電影 [Contemporary Cinema], no. 7 (2014): 86–92.

Li Miao 李淼. *Yunnan shaoshu minzu ticai dianying yanjiu: bianjiang xiangxiang, minzu renting yu wenhua jiangou* 雲南少數民族題材電影研究:邊疆想像、民族認同與文化建構 [Studies on minorities films in Yunnan: The imagination of the frontier, ethnic identities, and cultural construction]. Kunming: Yunnan daxue chubanshe, 2016.

Li Moran 李默然. "Deng Shichang xingxiang de chuangzao" 鄧世昌形象的創造 [The creation of the image of Deng Shichang]. *Dianying yishu* 電影藝術 [Cinematic Arts], no. 3 (1962): 54–57.

Li Yiming 李奕明. "Xie Jin dianying zai Zhongguo dianying shi shang de diwei" 謝晉電影在中國電影史上的地位 [The standing of Xie Jin's films in Chinese film history]. In *Lun Xie Jin dianying* 論謝晉電影 [On Xie Jin's films], edited by Zhongguo dianying jia xiehui 中國電影家協會 [China Film Association], 69–90. Beijing: Zhongguo dianying chubanshe, 1998.

Li Zhen 李鎮. *Zheng Junli quanji di 3 juan* 鄭君里全集 第3卷 [Zheng Junli's anthology, vol. 3]. Shanghai: Shanghai wenhua chubanshe, 2016.

Li Zhen 李鎮. *Zheng Junli quanji di 6 juan* 鄭君里全集 第6卷 [Zheng Junli's anthology, vol. 6]. Shanghai: Shanghai wenhua chubanshe, 2016.

Li Zhen 李鎮. *Zheng Junli quanji di 7 juan* 鄭君里全集 第7卷 [Zheng Junli's anthology, vol. 7]. Shanghai: Shanghai wenhua chubanshe, 2016.

Lian Xiufeng 連秀鳳. "Cengjing canghai nanwei shui—pouxi Wu Yonggang de dianying meixue guan" 曾經滄海難為水—剖析吳永剛的電影美學觀 [Having ever seen a vast ocean, one may not content himself with a pond of water: An analysis of Wu Yonggang's ideas of cinematic aesthetics]. MA thesis, Beijing dianying xueyuan, 1992.

Liangkai 良凱. "'Chengfeng polang' gaipai caishe yingpian" "乘風破浪"改拍彩色影片 [*Brave the Wind and Waves* will be shot as a color film]. *Xinmin wanbao* 新民晚報 [Xinmin Evening News], May 5, 1957.

Lifton, Robert Jay. *Thought Reform and the Psychology of Totalism: A Study of "Brainwashing" in China.* Chapel Hill: The University of North Carolina Press, 1989.

Lin Ting 林霆. *Bei guixun de xushi: shiqi nian nongye hezuohua ticai xiaoshuo yanjiu* 被規訓的敘事:十七年農業合作化題材小說研究 [The disciplined narrative: A study on novels about the rural collectivization movement in the seventeen years (of the PRC)]. Taiyuan: Beiyue wenyi chubanshe, 2014.

Link, Perry. "The Crocodile Bird: Xiangsheng in the Early 1950s." In *Dilemmas of Victory: The Early Years of the People's Republic of China*, edited by Jeremy Brown and Paul G. Pickowicz, 207–31. Cambridge, MA: Harvard University Press, 2007.

Link, Perry. *Evening Chats in Beijing: Probing China's Predicament.* New York: W. W. Norton & Company, 1992.

Lishi jiaoxue bianji bu 《歷史教學》編輯部 [The editorial office of History Teaching]. "1951 nian de Lishi jiaoxue" 1951年的《歷史教學》 [History Teaching in 1951]. Lishi jiaoxue 歷史教學 [History Teaching], no. 1 (2011): 70–72.

Liu Chenghan 劉成漢 (Lau Shing Hon). "Zhongguo neidi zai dianying zai Xianggang—zongjie pian" 中國內地電影在香港—總結篇 [Mainland-made films in Hong Kong—A summary]. In Shanyao zai tongyi xingkong—Zhongguo neidi dianying zai Xianggang 閃耀在同一星空—中國內地電影在香港 [Shining in the same starry sky—Mainland-made films in Hong Kong], edited by Zhu Hong 朱虹, 283–84. Kunming: Yunnan renmin chubanshe, 2005.

Liu Shu 劉澍. "Dang yinhai zaoyu bingshan—Wu Xun zhuan de xiaoshi yu Lu Xun zhuan de yaowang" 當銀海遭遇冰山—《武訓傳》的消失與《魯迅傳》的夭亡 [When the silver sea meets the iceberg: The disappearance of The Life of Wu Xun and the demise of The Life of Lu Xun]. Tongzhou gongjin 同舟共進 [Advancing in the Same Boat], no. 7 (2009): 64–66.

Liu Shu 劉澍. "Liuguang yicai de 22 da mingxing" 流光溢彩的22大明星 [The shimmering twenty-two great stars]. Dazhong dianying 大眾電影 [Mass Film], no. 12 (2005): 31–35.

Liu Xiao. "Red Detachment of Women: Revolutionary Melodrama and Alternative Socialist Imaginations." Differences: A Journal of Feminist Cultural Studies 26, no. 3 (2015): 116–41.

Loh Wai-fong. "From Romantic Love to Class Struggle: Reflections on the Film Liu Sanjie." In Popular Chinese Literature and Performing Arts in the People's Republic China, 1949–1979, edited by Bonnie S. McDougall, 165–76. Berkeley: University of California Press, 1984.

Lü Huang 呂鑌, and Li Gangbing 李鋼兵. "Chaoyue shenti de kunjing: cong Tiyu huanghou, Nülan wuhao he Sha'ou kan Zhongguo tiyu gushipian zhongde nüxing" 超越身體的困境：從《體育皇后》、《女籃5號》和《沙鷗》看中國體育故事片中的女性 [The plight of overstepping the body: Seeing the female in Chinese sports films through Queen of Sports (1934), Woman Basketball Player No. 5 (1957), and Sha Ou (1981)]. Fünu yanjiu luncong 婦女研究論叢 [Essays on Women's Studies], no. 4 (2009): 66–72.

Lu Shoujun 陸壽鈞. Haishang yingren 海上影人 [Filmmakers in Shanghai]. Shanghai: Shanghai shudian chubanshe, 2013.

Lu Xiaoning. "Zhang Ruifang: Modelling the Socialist Red Star." In Chinese Film Stars, edited by Mary Farquhar and Yingjin Zhang, 97–107. London: Routledge, 2010.

Lu Xiaoning. Moulding the Socialist Subject: Cinema and Chinese Modernity (1949–1966). Leiden: Brill, 2020.

Luo Yijun 羅藝軍. "Xie Jin, wode tonglu ren" 謝晉，我的同路人 [Xie Jin, my fellow traveler]. In Lun Xie Jin dianying 論謝晉電影 [On Xie Jin's films], edited by Zhongguo dianying jia xiehui 中國電影家協會 [China Film Association], 3–50. Beijing: Zhongguo dianying chubanshe, 1998.

Ma Ning. "Spatiality and Subjectivity in Xie Jin's Film Melodrama of the New Period." In New Chinese Cinemas: Forms, Identities, Politics, edited by Nick Browne, Paul G. Pickowicz, Vivian Sobchack, and Esther Yau, 15–39. Cambridge: Cambridge University Press, 1994.

Marchetti, Gina. "Two Stage Sisters: The Blossoming of a Revolutionary Aesthetic." In Transnational Chinese Cinemas: Identity, Nationhood, Gender, edited by Sheldon Hsiao-peng Lu, 59–80. Honolulu: University of Hawai'i Press, 1997.

Mazur, Mary G. *Wu Han: Historian: Son of China's Times*. Lanham, MD: Lexington Books, 2011.

McGrath, Jason. "Communists Have More Fun! The Dialectics of Fulfillment in Cinema of the People's Republic of China." *World Picture* 3 (Summer 2009): 1–18.

McGrath, Jason. "Cultural Revolution Model Opera Films and the Realist Tradition in Chinese Cinema." *The Opera Quarterly* 26, no. 2–3 (September 2010): 343–76.

Meisner, Maurice. *Mao Zedong: A Political and Intellectual Portrait*. Malden, MA: Polity, 2007.

Meng Liye 孟犁野. *Xin Zhongguo dianying yishu shi, 1949–1965* 新中國電影藝術史 1949–1965 [A history of film in new China, 1949–1965]. Beijing: Zhongguo dianying chubanshe, 2011.

Meng Yue 孟悦, and Dai Jinhua 戴錦華. *Fuchu lishi dibiao—xiandai funü wenxue yanjiu* 浮出歷史地表—現代婦女文學研究 [Emerging from the earth's surface: Studies on contemporary women's literature]. Zhengzhou: Henan renmin chubanshe, 1988.

Neri, Corrado. "Sun Yu and the Early Americanization of Chinese Cinema." In *Media, Popular Culture, and the American Century*, edited by Kingsley Bolton and Jan Olsson, 227–48. New Barnet, UK: John Libbey Publishing, 2011.

Minyi 民宜. "Chengfeng polang waijing rizhi pianduan"《乘風破浪》外景日誌片段 [Selected daily records about location shooting of *Brave the Wind and Waves*]. *Dazhong dianying* 大眾電影 [Mass Film], no. 15 (1957): 26–28.

Mitchell, Timothy. "Everyday Metaphors of Power." *Theory & Society* 19, no. 5 (October 1990): 545–77.

Ng, Kenny K. K. "Inhibition vs. Exhibition: Political Censorship of Chinese and Foreign Cinemas in Postwar Hong Kong." *Journal of Chinese Cinemas* 2, no. 1 (2008): 23–35.

Pan Yihong. "Crafting the 'New Woman' in China's Left-Wing Cinema of the 1930s: Sun Yu's Three Films." *Frontier of History in China* 6, no. 2 (2011): 264–84.

Pang Laikwan. *The Art of Cloning: Creative Production during China's Cultural Revolution*. London: Verso, 2017.

Pepper, Suzanne. *Radicalism and Education Reform in 20th-Century China: The Search for an Ideal Development Model*. Cambridge: Cambridge University Press, 2010.

Pickowicz, Paul G. *China on Film: A Century of Exploration, Confrontation, and Controversy*. Lanham, MD: Rowman & Littlefield, 2012.

Plaks, Andrew H. "Towards a Critical Theory of Chinese Narrative." In *Chinese Narrative: Critical and Theoretical Essays*, edited by Andrew H. Plaks, 309–52. Princeton, NJ: Princeton University Press, 1977.

Ogden, Suzanne. "From Patronage to Profits: The Changing Relationship of Chinese Intellectuals with the Party-state." In *Chinese Intellectuals between State and Market*, edited by Edward Gu and Merle Goldman, 111–37. London: Routledge, 2004.

Qiaiboshi 奇愛博士. "Xianggang zuopai chuanqi—'Chang Feng Xin'de gushi" 香港左派傳奇——"長鳳新"的故事 [The legend of Hong Kong's left-wing (film companies)]—The stories of Great War, Phoenix, and United Film Corporation]. *Dazhong dianying* 大眾電影 [Mass Film], no. 18 (2015): 86–91.

Qiuyun 秋耘. "Chongkan *Song Jingshi*" 重看《宋景詩》 [Watching *Song Jingshi* for the second time]. *Renmin ribao* 人民日報 [People's Daily], June 13, 1957.

Qizhi 啟之. *Mao Zedong shidai de renmin dianying, 1949–1966 nian* 毛澤東時代的人民電影, 1949–1966年 [The people's cinema in the Mao Zedong era, 1949–1966]. Taipei: Xiuwei zixun keji gufen youxian gongsi, 2010.

Rebull, Anne. "Locating Theatricality on Stage and Screen: Rescuing Performance Practice and the Phenomenon of *Fifteen Strings of Cash* (*Shiwu guan*, 1956)." *CHINOPERL: Journal of Chinese Oral and Performing Literature* 36, no. 1 (July 2017): 46–71.

Ren Hui 任晦. "Cong *Nülan wuhao* xiangdao de yixie wenti 從《女籃5號》想起的一些問題 [Some thoughts provoked by (watching) *Woman Basketball Player No. 5*]. *Renmin ribao* 人民日報 [People's Daily], January 3, 1958.

Ren Zhonglun 任仲倫. "Lun Xie Jin dianying" 論謝晉電影 [On Xie Jin's films]. In *Lun Xie Jin dianying* 論謝晉電影 [On Xie Jin's films], edited by Zhongguo dianying jia xiehui 中國電影家協會 [China Film Association], 3–18. Beijing: Zhongguo dianying chubanshe, 1998.

Roberts, Rosemary A. *Maoist Model Theatre: The Semiotics of Gender and Sexuality in the Chinese Cultural Revolution (1966–1976)*. Leiden: Brill, 2010.

Rong Mengyuan 榮孟源. *Lishi renwu pingjia wenti* 歷史人物的評價問題 [Issues of evaluating historical figures]. Shanghai: Huadong renmin chubanshe, 1954.

Rothman, William. *The 'I' of the Camera: Essays in Film Criticism, History, and Aesthetics*. Cambridge: Cambridge University Press. 2003.

Ryans, Tony. "Breakthroughs and Setbacks: The Origins of the New Chinese Cinema." In *Perspectives on Chinese Cinema*, edited by Chris Berry, 104–13. London: BFI Publishing, 1991.

Ryans, Tony. "The Second Generation." In *Electric Shadows: A Century of Chinese Cinema*, edited by James Bell, 16–27. London: British Film Institute, 2014.

Semsel, George S. "Interviews." In *Chinese Film: The State of the Art in the People's Republic*, edited by George Stephen Semsel, 107–78. New York: Praeger, 1987.

Shanghai hongqi dianying zhipian chang hongqi geming zaofan bingtuan 217 zongdui 上海紅旗電影製片廠紅旗革命造反兵團217縱隊 [The 217 column of the red flag film studio revolutionary and rebellious corps]. "Dadao xiuzheng zhuyi de 'sanming zhuyi' he 'sangao zhengce'" 打倒修正主義的 "三名主義" 和 "三高政策" [Down with the revisionist "three principles of famous" and "policy of three highs"]. In *Gaoju Mao Zedong sixiang weida hongqi, chedi zalan fangemin xiuzheng zhuyi wenyi heixian* 高舉毛澤東思想偉大紅旗，徹底砸爛反革命修正主義文藝黑線 [Hoist the great red banner of Maoist thought to completely smash the reactionary and revisionist black line of art and literature], edited by Shanghai hongqi dianying zhipianchang hongqi gemin zaofan bingtuan Shanghai haiguan xuanchuan zu 上海紅旗電影製片廠紅旗革命造反兵團上海海關宣傳組 [The customs propaganda team of the revolutionary and rebellious corps at the Shanghai Red Flag Film Studio], 18–20. N.p., 1967.

Shanghai hongqi dianying zhipianchang hongqi geming zaofan bingtuan xuanchuan zu 上海紅旗電影製片廠紅旗革命造反兵團宣傳組 [The propaganda team of the revolutionary and rebellious corps at the Shanghai Red Flag Film Studio]. "Gaoju Mao Zedong sixiang weida hongqi, chedi zalan fangemin xiuzheng zhuyi wenyi heixian" 高舉毛澤東思想偉大紅旗 徹底砸爛反革命修正主義文藝黑線 [Hoist the great red banner of Maoist thoughts to completely smash the reactionary and revisionist black line of arts and literature]. In *Gaoju Mao Zedong sixiang weida hongqi, chedi zalan fangemin xiuzheng zhuyi wenyi heixian* 高舉毛澤東思想偉大紅旗 徹底砸爛反革命修正主義文藝黑線 [Hoist the great red banner of Maoist thought to completely smash the reactionary and revisionist black line of arts and literature], edited by Shanghai hongqi dianying zhipianchang hongqi gemin zaofan bingtuan Shanghai haiguan xuanchuan zu 上海市紅旗電影製片廠紅旗革命造反兵團上海海關宣傳組 [The customs propaganda team of the revolutionary and rebellious corps at the Shanghai Red Flag Film Studio], 3–6. N.p., 1967.

Shangyue bayi gongshe changying 上越八一公社長纓. [The long spear of the August 1 commune at Shanghai Yue opera troupe]. "Yueju *Honglou meng* bixu chedi pipan" 越劇《紅樓夢》必須徹底批判 [We must thoroughly criticize *Dream of the Red Chamber*, the Yue opera play]. In *Yueju zhanbao* 越劇戰報 [Yue opera war report], edited by Shanghai Yueju yuan bayi gongshe *Yueju zhanbao* bianji bu 上海越劇院八一公社《越劇戰報》編輯部 [Editorial office of Yue opera war report of the August 1 commune at Shanghai Yue opera troupe], 8–11. N.p., 1967.

Shao Wenyan 邵雯豔. *Huayu dianying yu Zhongguo xiqu* 華語電影與中國戲曲 [Sinophone films and Chinese operas]. Shanghai: Fudan daxue chubanshe, 2013.

Shaw, Tony, and Denise J. Youngblood. *Cinematic Cold War: The American and Soviet Struggle for Hearts and Minds*. Lawrence: University Press of Kansas, 2010.

Shen Ji 沈寂. *Huashuo dianying* 話說電影 [The story about motion pictures]. Shanghai: Shanghai sanlian shudian, 2008.

Shen Ji 沈寂. *Shen Ji renwu suoyi* 沈寂人物瑣憶 [Shen Ji's memories of figures (in the past)]. Shanghai: Shanghai shehui kexueyuan chubanshe, 2017.

Shen Ji 沈寂. "Yinhai yizhu" 銀海遺珠 [The unrecognized treasure in the silver ocean]. In *Xu Changlin wenji: yige dianying gongzuozhe de shouji* 徐昌霖文集：一個電影工作者的手記 [The collected writings of Xu Changlin: Notes of a film worker], edited by Xu Changlin 徐昌霖, 1–6. Shanghai: Wenhui chubanshe, 2010.

Shen Ji 沈寂. *Zuoye xingcheng—wo yanzhong de yingren pengyou* 昨夜星辰 我眼中的影人朋友 [Yestreen's stars: Friends in the world of film in my eyes]. Shanghai: Shanghai renmin chubanshe, 2005.

Shen Pengnian 沈鵬年. *Xingyun liushui jiwang erji (xia)* 行雲流水記往二集（下） [Remembering the past (like) floating clouds and flowing water, vol. 2, bk. 2]. Shanghai: Shanghai sanlian shudian, 2011.

Shen, Vivian. *The Origins of Leftwing Cinema in China, 1932–37*. London: Routledge, 2005.

Shen Yun 沈芸. *Zhongguo dianying chanye shi* 中國電影產業史 [History of the Chinese film industry]. Beijing: Zhongguo dianying chubanshe, 2005.

Shi Hui 石揮. *Shi Hui tanyi lu wuhai yehang* 石揮談藝錄 霧海夜航 [Shi Hui on arts—Navigating at night on a foggy ocean]. Beijing: Beijing lianhe chuban gongsi, 2017.

Shlapentokh, Vladimir. *Public and Private Life of the Soviet People: Changing Values in Post-Stalin Russia*. New York: Oxford University Press, 1989.

Shuicao 水草. "Nongmin qunzhong relie huanying guochan yingpian" 農民群眾熱烈歡迎國產影片 [Rural viewers warmly greet domestically produced films]. *Dianying yishu* 電影藝術 [Cinematic Arts], no. 6 (1960): 47–48.

Shuman, Amanda. "No Longer 'Sick': Visualizing 'Victorious' Athletes in 1950s Chinese Films." *Historical Social Research* 43, no. 2 (2018): 220–50.

Silbergeld, Jerome. *Contradictions: Artistic Life, the Socialist State, and the Chinese Painter Li Huasheng*. Seattle: University of Washington Press, 1993.

Smith, Aminda M. *Thought Reform and China's Dangerous Classes: Reeducation, Resistance, and the People*. Lanham, MA: Rowman & Littlefield, 2012.

Song Song 宋嵩. "Song Jingshi jiqi yansheng wenben de chuangzuo" 《宋景詩》及其衍生文本的創作 [Song Jingshi and the creation of its derivative texts]. *Wenyi bao* 文藝報 [Literature and Arts Paper], June 24, 2016.

Song Xiaobin 宋小濱. *Jiali jiawai hua Xie Jin* 家裡家外話謝晉 [On Xie Jin both in and outside his family]. Beijing: Zhongguo shehui chubanshe, 2013.

Song Zhao 宋昭. *Mama de yisheng: Wang Ping zhuan* 媽媽的一生—王蘋傳 [My mom's life—Wang Ping's biography]. Beijing: Zhongguo dianying chubanshe, 2006.

Stacey, Jackie. "Feminine Fascinations: Forms of Identification in Star/Audience Relations." In *Stardom: Industry of Desire*, edited by Christine Gledhill, 141–63. London: Routledge, 1991.

Sun Yu 孫瑜. "Jiangshang xing—chuangzuo *Chengfeng polang* xia shenghuo suiji" 江上行—創作《乘風破浪》下生活隨記 [Travelling on the river—Random notes on experiencing the lives of (the ship's crew) to make *Brave the Wind and Waves*]. *Dazhong dianying* 大眾電影 [Mass Film], no. 9 (1957): 26–27.

Sun Yu 孫瑜. "Zunzhong dianying de yishu chuantong" 尊重電影的歷史傳統 [Respect film's historical tradition]. *Wenhui bao* 文匯報 [Wenhui Daily], November 11, 1956.

"Sun Yu shi shenme house" 孫瑜是什麼貨色 [What on earth is Sun Yu]. *Hongqi zhanbao* 紅旗戰報 [Red Flag Battlefield Report], no. 6 (1967): 8.

Tan Qiuwen 檀秋文. *Zhongguo dianying ren koushu lishi yinhai chenfu lu Luo Yijun koushu lishi* 中國電影人口述歷史 銀海沉浮錄 羅藝軍口述歷史 [Oral history of Chinese filmmakers, the record of ups and downs, Luo Yijun's oral history]. Beijing: Zhongguo dianying chubanshe, 2015.

Tang Xiaodan 湯曉丹. *Chenmo shijin: Tang Xiaodan dianying riji xia* 沉默是金:湯曉丹電影日記下 [Silence is golden: Tan Xiaodan's diary about film, bk. 3]. Beijing: Shangwu yinshuguan, 2016.

Taylor, Jeremy E. *Rethinking Transnational Chinese Cinemas: The Amoy-Dialect Film Industry in Cold War Asia*. London: Routledge, 2011.

Tian Han 田漢. "Suzao yingxiong renwu de chubu chengjiu—kan jibu yingpian de ganxiang" 塑造英雄人物的初步成就—看幾部影片的感想 [Preliminary accomplishments in creating historical characters—Thoughts on viewing a number of films]. *Dianying yishu* 電影藝術 [Cinematic Arts], no. 7 (1960): 14–16.

Tian Yiye 田一野. "Choupai lishi jupian *Lu Xun zhuan* shimo" 籌拍歷史巨片《魯迅傳》始末 [The whole story of planning and preparing for the epic film *The Life of Lu Xun*]. *Dazhong dianying* 大眾電影 [Mass Film], no. 8 (1985): 10–11.

Tsipursky, Gleb. *Socialist Fun: Youth, Consumption, and State-Sponsored Popular Culture in the Soviet Union, 1945–1970*. Pittsburgh: University of Pittsburgh Press, 2016.

Tung, Timothy. "The Work of Xie Jin: A Personal Letter to the Editor." In *Film and Politics in the Third World*, edited by John D. H. Downing, 199–207. New York: Praeger, 1987.

Tyszka, Krzysztof. "'Homo Sovieticus' Two Decades Later." *Polish Sociological Review*, no. 168 (2009): 507–22.

U, Eddy. *Creating the Intellectual: Chinese Communism and the Rise of a Classification.* Berkeley: University of California Press, 2019.

Von Geldern, James. "Conclusion: Epic Revisionism and the Crafting of a Soviet Public." In *Epic Revisionism: Russian History and Literature as Stalinist Propaganda*, edited by Kevin M. F. Platt and David Brandenberger, 325–40. Madison: The University of Wisconsin Press, 2006.

Wagner, Rudolf. *The Contemporary Chinese Historical Drama: Four Studies.* Berkeley: University of California Press, 1990.

Wang Hui 汪暉. "Zhengzhi daode jiqi zhihuan de mimi—Xie Jin dianying fenxi" 政治與道德及其置換的秘密—謝晉電影分析 [Politics, morality, and the secret of their displacement—An analysis of Xie Jin's films]. In *Lun Xie Jin dianying* 論謝晉電影 [On Xie Jin's films], edited by Zhongguo dianying jia xiehui 中國電影家協會 [China Film Association], 178–205. Beijing: Zhongguo dianying chubanshe, 1998.

Wang Qingjia 王晴佳 (Q. Edward Wang). *Renxie de lishi bixu shi rende lishi ma* 人寫的歷史必須是人的歷史嗎 [Does history written by humans have to be history about humans]. Shanghai: Shanghai renmin chubanshe, 2020.

Wang Shaoguang. "The Politics of Private Time: Changing Leisure Patterns in Urban China." In *Urban Spaces in Contemporary China: The Potential for Autonomy and Community in Post-Mao China*, edited by Deborah S. Davis, Richard Kraus, Barry Naughton, and Elizabeth J. Perry, 149–72. Cambridge: Cambridge University Press, 1995.

Wang Wei 王維. *Zhongguo wenxue jie "jiantao" yanjiu (1949–1955)* 中國文學界"檢討"研究 (1949–1955) [A study on the "confession" in the literary circles in China (1949–1955)]. Beijing: Qunyan chubanshe, 2015.

Wang, Zheng. *Finding Women in the State: A Socialist Feminist Revolution in the People's Republic of China, 1949–1964.* Berkeley: University of California Press, 2017.

Wang Zhulou 王竹樓. "Youguan Song Jingshi de ziliao" 有關於宋景詩的資料 [Materials concerning Song Jingshi]. *Renmin ribao* 人民日報 [People's Daily], September 17, 1951.

Wang Zhuoyi. *Revolutionary Cycles in Chinese Cinema, 1951–1979.* London: Palgrave MacMillan, 2014.

Watson, Rubie S. "Memory, History, and Opposition under State Socialism: An Introduction." In *Memory, History, and Opposition under State Socialism*, edited by Rubie S. Watson, 1–20. Santa Fe, NM: School of American Research Press, 1994.

Weigelin-Schwiedrzik, Susanne. "Back to the Past: Chinese Intellectuals in Search of Historical Legitimacy (1957–1965)." *Berliner China-Hefte/Chinese History and Society* 31 (2006): 3–23.

Windscript, Shan. "How to Write a Diary in Mao's New China: Guidebooks in the Crafting of Socialist Subjectivities." *Modern China* 47, no. 4 (2021): 412–40.

Witke, Roxanne. *Comrade Chiang Ch'ing.* Boston, MA: Little, Brown and Company, 1977.

Wu Couchun 吳湊春. *Dangdai Zhongguo zhuanji pian chuangzuo xianxiang piping* 當代中國傳記片創作現象批評 [Criticism of the phenomena of making biographical films in contemporary China]. Guangzhou: Jinan daxue chubanshe, 2013.

Wu Han 吳晗. "Lishi de zhenshi yu yishu de zhenshi" 歷史的真實與藝術的真實 [The historical reality and the artistic realness]. *Xiju bao* 戲劇報 [The Drama Journal], no. 20 (1959): 5–9.

Wu Han 吳晗. "Lun lishi renwu pingjia" 論歷史人物評價 [On the evaluation of historical figures]. *Renmin ribao* 人民日報 [People's Daily], March 23, 1962.

Wu Jun 伍俊. *Lianhua yingye gongsi fazhan beijing xia de Sun Yu zaoqi dianying (1930–1937)* 聯華影業公司發展背景下的孫瑜早期電影（1930–1937）[Sun Yu's early films in the developmental years of the United Photoplay Service (1930–1937)]. Shanghai: Shanghai jiaotong daxue chubanshe, 2018.

Wu Yigong 吳貽弓. *Shanghai dianying zhi* 上海電影志 [The chronicle of film in Shanghai]. Shanghai: Shanghai shehui kexueyuan, 1999.

Wu Yin 吳茵. *Huishou hua dangnian* 回首話當年 [Looking back at the past]. Beijing: Zhongguo dianying chubanshe, 1993.

Wu Yonggang 吳永剛. "Chunfeng jiedong yougan" 春風解凍有感 [Some thoughts (inspired by) thawing by the spring breeze]. *Xinmin wanbao* 新民晚報 [Xinmin Evening News], May 5, 1957.

Wu Yonggang 吳永剛. "Shennü wancheng zhihou" 神女完成之後 [After completing *The Goddess*]. *Lianhua huabao* 聯華畫報 [UPS Pictorial] 5, no. 1 (1935): 2–3.

Wu Yonggang 吳永剛. "Zhenglun buneng daiti yishu" 政論不能代替藝術 [Political commentary should not usurp arts)] *Wenhui bao* 文匯報 [Wenhui Daily], December 7, 1956.

Wu Ze 吳澤. *Lishi renwu de pingpan wenti—wei kaizhan Wu Xun pipan er shilun* 歷史人物的評判問題—為展開武訓批判而試論 [The issue of evaluating historical figures—A tentative treatise for unfolding (the movement) of criticizing Wu Xun]. Shanghai: Tangdi chubanshe, 1951.

Xia Yu 夏瑜. *Yaoyuan de ai—Chen Liting zhuan* 遙遠的愛—陳鯉庭傳 [Remote love: The biography of Chen Liting]. Beijing: Zhongguo dianying chubanshe, 2008.

Xiaer Taisong 夏爾·泰松 (Charles Tesson) et al. *Jiuba li de dushi ren* 酒吧裡的讀詩人 [Poem readers in bars]. Kaifeng: Henan daxue chubanshe, 2019.

"Xianggang *Xinsheng wanbao* zaiwen zanshang wo Yueju yingpian *Biyu zan*" 香港《新生晚報》載文讚賞我越劇影片《碧玉簪》[Hong Kong Xinsheng Evening publishes an essay to praise our Yue opera film, *The Jade Hairpin*]. *Cankao xiaoxi* 參考消息 [Reference News], April 25, 1963.

Xie Jin 謝晉. "Cong daoyan de ganshou dao guanzhong de ganshou—*Hongse niangzi jun* daoyan sanji" 從導演的感受到觀眾的感受—《紅色娘子軍》導演散記 [From the director's feelings to the audience's experiences—Some random notes on directing *Red Detachment of Women*]. *Renmin ribao* 人民日報 [People's Daily], August 23, 1961.

Xie Jin 謝晉. "Yao shenme yang de juben" 要什麼樣的劇本 [What screenplays do (we) want]. *Guangming ribao* 光明日報 [Guangming Daily], March 11, 1962.

Xu Dunle 許敦樂. *Kenguang tuoying* 墾光拓影 [Cultivating light and shadow]. Hong Kong: MCCM Creations, 2005.

Xu Lanjun. "The Southern Film Corporation, Opera Films, and the PRC's Cultural Diplomacy in Cold War Asia, 1950s and 1960s." *Modern Chinese Literature and Culture* 29, no. 1 (Spring 2017): 239–82.

Xu Sangchu 徐桑楚. *Tabian qingshan ren weilao* 踏遍青山人未老 [Crossing all mountains adds nothing to my years]. Beijing: Zhongguo dianying chubanshe, 2006.

Xu Suling 徐蘇靈. "Shitan xiqu yishu pian de yixie wenti" 試談戲曲片的一些問題 [On some issues of the opera art film]. *Zhongguo dianying* 中國電影 [China Cinema], no. 2 (1956): 41–45.

Xu Tao 徐韜. "*Sou shuyuan* daoyan chanshu" 《搜書院》導演闡述 [The director's statement on *Searching a School*]. In *Dianying daoyan chanshu ji* 電影導演闡述集 [Anthology of the directors' statements], edited by Zuolin 佐臨 et al., 38–46. Beijing: Zhongguo dianying chubanshe, 1959.

Xu Yuan 許元. "Yueju dianying fazhan shi kaolun" 越劇電影發展史考論 [Investigation and analysis of the history of Yue opera films]. In *Xiju xue di 5 ji* 戲劇學 第5輯 [Studies on drama, number 5], edited by Shanghai xiju xueyuan xiju xue yanjiu zhongxin 上海戲劇學院戲劇學研究中心 [Research center of drama studies at the Shanghai Theater Academy], 43–66. Shanghai: Wenhua yishu chubanshe, 2017.

Xu Yulan 徐玉蘭, and Dong Yu 董煜. *Renru baiyu xi ru lan* 人如白玉戲如蘭 [The person is like white jade, and the play orchid]. Shanghai: Shanghai shiji chuban gufen youxian gongsi, 2013.

Yang Futian 楊福田. "*Dianying yishu* dui guoqing xianli yingpian de pingjie" 《電影藝術》對國慶獻禮影片的評介 [*Film art*'s evaluation of and review of films to celebrate the national day]. *Dushu* 讀書 [Reading], no. 19 (1959): 39–40.

Yang, Mayfair Mei-hui. "From Gender Erasure to Gender Difference: State Feminism, Consumer Sexuality, and Women's Public Sphere in China." In *Spaces of Their Own: Women's Public Sphere in Transnational China*, edited by Mayfair Mei-hui Yang, 35–67. Minneapolis: University of Minnesota Press, 1999.

Yang Panpan 楊槃槃. "Meng zhu chaosheng qu—'Lengzhan' geju xia de Chaoyu xiqu pian" 夢逐潮聲去——"冷戰"格局下的潮語戲曲片 [The dream is gone with the noise of the tide—The Teochew opera film in the Cold War]. *Dangdai dianying* 當代電影 [Contemporary Cinema], no. 7 (2017): 140–43.

Yao Wen-yuan (Yao Wenyuan 姚文元). *On the Counter-Revolutionary Double-Dealer Chou Yang*. Beijing: Foreign Languages Press, 1967.

Yau, Ching-mei Esther. "Compromised Liberation: The Politics of Class in Chinese Cinema of the Early 1950s." In *The Hidden Foundation: Cinema and the Question of Class*, edited by David E. James and Rick Berg, 138–71. Minneapolis: University of Minnesota Press, 1996.

Yau, Ching-mei Esther. "Filmic Discourse on Women in Chinese Cinema (1949–65): Art, Ideology and Social Relations." PhD diss., University of California, Los Angeles, 1990.

Yekelchyk, Serhy. *Stalin's Citizens: Everyday Politics in the Wake of Total War*. Oxford: Oxford University Press, 2014.

Ye Ming 葉明. "Wu Yonggang daoyan yishu de daolu" 吳永剛導演藝術的道路 [The path of Wu Yonggang's directorial arts]. In *Wode tansuo he zhuiqiu* 我的探索和追求 [My exploration and pursuits], edited by Wu Yonggang 吳永剛, 1–12. Beijing: Zhongguo dianying chubanshe, 1986.

Ye Shuyu 葉舒瑜 (Yap Soo Ei). "Lengzhan yu Xianggang de Changcheng, Fenghuang, Xinlian—yi 1945-1967 nian wei kaocha shiduan" 冷戰與香港的長城、鳳凰、新聯—以1945-1967年為考察時段 [A study of the Hong Kong leftist film companies during the Cold War (1945-1967)]. MA thesis, National University of Singapore, 2011.

Ye Yuan 葉元. "Luetan lishi ju de xugou" 略談歷史劇的虛構 [Briefly on the fictionalization of historical films]. *Dianying yishu* 電影藝術 [Cinematic Arts], no. 2 (1979): 44–48.

Ye Zhou 葉周. "Yidai ren de Lu Xun meng" 一代人的魯迅夢 [A generation's dream of Lu Xun]. In *Wenmai chuancheng de jianxing zhe: Ye Yiqun bainian danchen jinian wenji* 文脈傳承的踐行者：葉以群百年誕辰紀念文集 [The practitioner of inheriting the literary heritage: An anthology (to commemorate) Ye Yiqun's one-hundredth birthday], edited by Ye Zhou 葉周, 209–12. Shanghai: Shanghai sanlian shudian, 2011.

Yijun 藝軍. "Ping 'Nülan 5 hao'" 評"女籃5號" [Review of "*Woman Basketball Player No. 5*"]. In *Zhongguo dianying pinglun ji di 2 ji* 中國電影評論集第2集 [Collection of reviews of Chinese films, bk. 2], edited by Zhongguo dianying chubanshe 中國電影出版社, 46–52. Beijing: Zhongguo dianying chubanshe, 1959.

Yi Quan 易荃. "Shangying chang junzuo xiaozu ru yuhou chunsun" 上影廠劇作小組如雨後春筍 [Playwriting teams in Shanghai-based film studios spring up like mushrooms]. *Dianying yishu* 電影藝術 [Cinematic Arts], no. A2 (1956): 58.

Yin Hong 尹鴻, and Ling Yan 凌燕. *Xin Zhongguo dianying shi (1949–2000)* 新中國電影史（1949–2000） [A history of film in new China (1949–2000)]. Changsha: Hunan meishu chubanshe, 2002.

Ying Dabai 應大白. *Ying Yunwei* 應雲衛 [Ying Yunwei]. Chongqing: Chongqing chubanshe, 2007.

"Yingdang zhongshi dianying *Wu Xun* zhuan de taolun" 應該重視電影《武訓傳》的討論 [(We) must emphasize the discussion of the film *The Life of Wu Xun*]. *Renmin ribao* 人民日報 [People's Daily], May 20, 1951.

Ying Yuwei 應雲衛, and Liu Qiong 劉瓊. "*Song Shijie* daoyan chanshu" 《宋士杰》闡述 [The directors' statement on *Song Shijie*]. In *Dianying daoyan chanshu ji* 電影導演闡述集 [Anthology of the directors' statements], edited by Zuolin 佐臨 et al., 29–37. Beijing: Zhongguo dianying chubanshe, 1959.

"Yishu pian fang weixing zuotanhui shang de baogao" 藝術片放衛星座談會上的報告 [A talk at the symposium on achieving prominent success in (producing) feature films]. In *Zhongguo dianying yanjiu ziliao, 1949–1979 zhong* 中國電影研究資料：1949–1979 中 [Research materials of Chinese film, 1949–1979, bk. 2], edited by Wu Di 吳迪, 214–17. Beijing: Wenhua yishu chubanshe, 2006.

Yu Huanqing 余煥卿. "Guanyu jianguo hou nongzhan shi yanjiu de pinglun wenti—yu Huang Minlan tongzhi shangque" 關於建國後農戰史研究的評價問題—與黃敏蘭同志商榷 [On the issue of how to evaluate the research about peasant war after the establishment of the PRC—A discussion with comrade Huang Minlan]. *Shixue lilun* 史學理論 [Historical Theories], no. 2 (1996): 11–17; 35.

Yu Ji 余紀. "Jiefang de sixiang yu sixiang de jiefang" 解放的思想與思想的解放 [The emancipatory thoughts and thought emancipation]. In *Lun Xie Jin dianying* 論謝晉電影 [On Xie Jin's films], edited by Zhongguo dianying jia xiehui 中國電影家協會 [China Film Association], 106–12. Beijing: Zhongguo dianying chubanshe, 1998.

Yu Ling 于伶. "Yonggang, yongbie le!" 永剛，永別了！ [Yonggang, farewell!]. In *Zhongguo dianying nianjian 1983* 中國電影年鑒1983 [Chinese film yearbook, 1983], edited by Zhongguo dianying jia xiehui 中國電影家協會 [China Film Association], 124. Beijing: Zhongguo dianying chubanshe, 1984.

Yu Miin-ling (Yu Minling 余敏伶). *Xingsu "xinren": Zhonggong xuanchuan yu Sulian jingyan* 形塑"新人"：中共宣傳與蘇聯經驗 [Shaping the new man: CCP propaganda and Soviet experiences]. Taipei: Zhongyang yanjiu yuan jindaishi yanjiu suo, 2015.

Yu Qiuyu 余秋雨. "Xu" 序 [Preface]. In *Lun Xie Jin dianying* 論謝晉電影 [On Xie Jin's films], edited by Zhongguo dianying jia xiehui 中國電影家協會 [China Film Association], 1–2. Beijing: Zhongguo dianying chubanshe, 1998.

Yu, Sabrina Qiong. "Vulnerable Chinese Stars: From *Xizi* to Film Worker." In *A Companion to Chinese Cinema*, edited by Yingjin Zhang, 218–38. Malden, MA: Wiley-Blackwell.

Yuan Xuefen 袁雪芬 et al. "He Xianggang tongbao xiangchu de rizi" 和香港同胞相處的日子 [(Our) days with the Hong Kong compatriots]. *Xiju bao* 戲劇報 [The Drama Journal], no. 4 (1961): 13–14.

"Yueju Honglou meng qingqian 50 zai" 越劇紅樓夢情牽50載 [The Yue operatic [play] of *Dream of the Red Chamber*: Sentiment that lingers for half a century]. Shanghai TV Station, March 15, 2008.

Yurchak, Alexei. *Everything Was Forever, Until It Was No More: The Last Soviet Generation.* Princeton: Princeton University Press, 2005.

"Zai dianying chuangzuo zhong gaoju zhengzhi shuaiqi, jianchi gongnongbing wenyi fangxiang" 在電影創作中高舉政治帥旗，堅持工農兵文藝方向 [(We must) hoist the commander's flag of politics and adhere to the focus of literary and artistic creations for the workers, peasants, and soldiers]. *Dazhong dianying* 大眾電影 [Mass Film], no. 12 (1958): 21.

Zeitlin, Judith T. "Operatic Ghosts on Screen: The Case of *A Test of Love* (1958)." *The Opera Quarterly* 26, no. 2–3 (August 2010): 220–55.

Zhang Junxiang 張駿祥. "Wutai yishu jilu pian xiang shenme fangxiang fazhan" 舞臺藝術紀錄片向什麼方向發展 [To what direction are documentaries of stage arts steered in]. In *Lun xiqu dianying* 論戲曲電影 [On opera film], 10–17. Beijing: Zhongguo dianying chubanshe, 1958.

Zhang Kaiyuan 章開沅. *Xinhai gemin yu jindai shehui* 辛亥革命與近代社會 [The 1911 revolution and the modern society]. Wuhan: Huazhong shifan daxue chubanshe, 2011.

Zhang Mingtang 張銘堂. "Xie Jin dianying zhimi" 謝晉電影之謎 [The enigma of Xie Jin's films]. In *Lun Xie Jin dianying* 論謝晉電影 [On Xie Jin's films], edited by Zhongguo dianying jia xiehui 中國電影家協會 [China Film Association], 35–68. Beijing: Zhongguo dianying chubanshe, 1998.

Zhang Shuoguo 張碩果. "1950 niandai zaoqi Shanghai de dianying wenhua lunzheng yu gaizao—cong 'wenyi ke bukeyi wei xiao zichan jieji fuwu' taolun dao 'wenyi zhengfeng xuexi yundong'" 1950年代早期上海的電影文化論爭與改造—從"文藝可不可以為小資產階級服務"討論到"文藝整風學習運動" [Debates and reform of film culture in early 1950s Shanghai—From "whether literature and arts can serve the petty bourgeoisie" to "the movement of reform and studies of literature and arts"]. In *Zhizao "guomin": 1950–1970 niandai de richang shenghuo yu wenyi shijian* 製造"國民"：1950–1970年代的日常生活與文藝實踐 [Creating the "national citizenry": The day-to-day life and practice of literature and arts, the 1950s–1970s], edited by Luo Xiaoming 羅小茗, 267–90. Shanghai: Shanghai shudian chubanshe, 2011.

Zhang, Xudong. *The Modernism in the Era of Reforms: Cultural Fever, Avant-Garde Fiction, and the New Chinese Cinema.* Durham, NC: Duke University Press, 1997.

Zhang, Yingjin. *Chinese National Cinema*. London: Routledge, 2004.

Zhang, Yingjin. "From 'Minority Film' to 'Minority Discourse': Questions of Nationhood and Ethnicity in Chinese Cinema." *Cinema Journal* 36, no. 3 (Spring 1997): 79–90.

Zhang, Yingjin. "Zhao Dan: Spectrality of Martyrdom and Stardom." In *Chinese Film Stars*, edited by Mary Farquhar and Yingjin Zhang, 86–96. London: Routledge, 2010.

Zhang, Yingjin and Zhiwei Xiao. *Encyclopedia of Chinese Film*. London: Routledge, 1998.

Zhang Yue 章越. "Kan gushi pian 'Hasen yu Jiamila'" 看故事片"哈森與加米拉" [Watching the feature film *Hasen and Jiamila*]. *Renmin ribao* 人民日報 [People's Daily], August 2, 1955.

Zhang, Zhen. *An Amorous History of the Silver Screen: Shanghai Cinema, 1896–1937*. Chicago: University of Chicago Press, 2006.

Zhao Changju 趙長聚, and Tong Zi'an. "Zhao Dan yu Wu Xun" 趙丹與武訓 [Zhao Dan and Wu Xun]. *Chun Qiu* 春秋 [Spring and Autumn], no. 3 (1995): 38–39.

Zhao Dan 趙丹. "Guande tai juti, wenyi mei xiwang" 管得太具體，文藝沒希望 [There is no hope for literature and the arts if they are regulated too specifically]. *Renmin ribao* 人民日報 [People's Daily], October 10, 1980.

Zhao Dan 趙丹, and Qu Baiyin 瞿白音. "Shi Hui 'gun' de yishu he tade 'caineng'" 石揮"滾"的藝術和他的"才能" [Shi Hui's arts of "rolling-out" and his "talents"]. In *Hanwei dang dui dianying shiye de lingdao xubian* 捍衛黨對電影事業的領導續編 [Defending the party's leadership in the film industry, supplementary volumes], 33–39. Beijing: Zhongguo dianying chubanshe, 1958.

Zhao Jingbo 趙景勃, and Ran Changjian 冉常建. *Wutai yu yinmu zhijain: xiqu dianying de huigu yu jiangshu* 舞臺與銀幕之間：戲曲電影的回顧與講述 [Between the stage and the screen: A review and narrative of opera films]. Beijing: Zhongguo wenlian chubanshe, 2007.

Zhao, Mi. "From Singing Girl to Revolutionary Artist: Female Entertainers Remembering China's Socialist Past (1949–The Present)." *Twentieth-Century China* 39, no. 2 (May 2014): 166–90.

Zhao Qing 趙青. *Wode diedie Zhao Dan* 我的爹爹趙丹 [My father Zhao Dan]. Beijing: Zhongguo dianying chubanshe, 2005.

Zhao Qizhi 趙憩之. "*Wu Xun lishi diaocha ji* yu xin shixue" 武訓歷史調查記與新史學 [*The investigation report of the history of Wu Xun* and new historiography]. *Lishi jiaoxue* 歷史教學 [History Teaching], no. 4 (October 1951): 114–16.

Zhao Weifang 趙衛防, and Zhang Wenyan 張文燕. "Jianguo hou juyou neidi Beijing de Xianggang dianying gongsi chengli chutan" 建國後具有內地背景的香港電影公司成立新探 [A new study on the establishment of Hong Kong film companies with Mainland background after the founding of New China]. *Shanghai daxue xuebao (shehui kexue ban)* 上海大學學報（社會科學版） [Journal of Shanghai University (Social Sciences Edition)] 29, no. 6 (November 2012): 20–30.

Zheng Boqi 鄭伯奇. *Liangqi ji* 兩栖集 [The anthology of the amphibious]. Shanghai: Shanghai shudian chubanshe, 1987.

Zheng Junli 鄭君里. *Huawai yin* 畫外音 [Offscreen Voice]. Beijing: Zhognguo dianying chubanshe, 1979.

Zheng Junli 鄭君里. "Tantan Song Jingshi—shidai Beijing he lishi pingjia" 談談宋景詩—時代背景和歷史評價 [On Song Jingshi—The historical background and (his) evaluation in history]. *Zhongguo qingnian bao* 中國青年報 [China Youth Daily], May 31, 1957.

Zheng Junli 鄭君里. "Women zai tansuo qianjin—guanyu 'Song Jingshi' de xiugai" 我們在探索前進—關於"宋景詩"的修改 [We're exploring and making progress—On the revision of Song Jingshi]. *Zhongguo dianying* 中國電影 [China Cinema], no. 3 (1957): 13–18.

Zheng Rui 鄭睿. "Makesi zhuyi shiguan guanzhao xia de Zhongguo zaoqi dianying shi xiezuo—Xiandai Zhongguo dianying shilue de lishi yanjiu fangfa" 馬克思主義史觀觀照下的中國早期電影史學寫作—《現代中國電影史略》的歷史研究方法 [The historical writing of early Chinese film history inspired by Marxist historiography—The methodology of historical studies in *Brief History of Contemporary China*]. *Dangdai dianying* 當代電影 [Contemporary Cinema], no. 2 (2016): 144–46.

Zhong Dianfei 鍾惦棐. "Xie Jin dianying shisi" 謝晉電影十思 [Ten thoughts on Xie Jin's films]. In *Lun Xie Jin dianying* 論謝晉電影 [On Xie Jin's films], edited by Zhongguo dianying jia xiehui 中國電影家協會 [China Film Association], 98–105. Beijing: Zhongguo dianying chubanshe, 1998.

Zhong Shu 鍾恕. "Caise gushi pian *Chengfeng polang* shezhi fengguang" 彩色故事片《乘風破浪》攝製風光 [Anecdotes of the shooting of *Brave the Wind and Waves*, the color feature film]. *Dazhong dianying* 大眾電影 [Mass Film], no. 23 (1957): 34–35.

Zhongguo dianying nianjian she 中國電影年鑒社 [The publishing house for the Chinese film yearbook]. *Zhongguo dianying nianjian 2002* 中國電影年鑒2002 [Chinese film yearbook, 2002]. Beijing: Zhongguo dianying nianjian she, 2002.

"Zhongshi xiqu gaige gongzuo" 重視戲曲改革工作 [Emphasize the reform of the (traditional) opera]. *Renmin ribao* 人民日報 [People's Daily], May 7, 1951.

Zhongshu Huang 中叔皇. "Zai 'Minzhu jiuhao' lun shang" 在"民主九號"輪上 [On *The People 9*]. 大眾電影 [Mass Film], no. 9 (1957): 27–28.

Zhou Bin 周斌. *Yingshi xiju sibian lu* 影視戲劇思辨錄 [An intellectual inquiry into film, TV, and theater]. Shanghai: Dongang chuban zhongxin, 2019.

Zhou Xia 周夏, Chen Mo 陳墨, and Qizhi 啟之. *Haishang yingzong (Shanghai juan)* 海上影蹤（上海卷）[The trace of film in Shanghai (the volume of Shanghai)]. Beijing: Minzu chubanshe, 2011.

Zhou Yang 周揚. "Fan renmin, Fan lishi de sixiang he fan xianshi zhuyi de yishu dianying *Wu Xun zhuan* pipan" 反人民、反歷史的思想和反現實主義的藝術 電影《武訓傳》批判 [(A work) against the people, against historicist thoughts, and against realist art: A criticism of the film *The Life of Wu Xun*]. *Renmin ribao* 人民日報 [People's Daily], August 8, 1951.

Zhou Yiping 周一平. *20 shiji houbanqi Zhongguo shixue shi shang* 20世紀後半期中國史學史上 [The history of Chinese historiography in the second half of the 20th century, part one]. Shanghai: Shanghai shudian chubanshe, 2017.

Zhu Anping 朱安平. "*Qingshan lian*: 'jiadang' zhong qiusuo" 《青山戀》："夾檔"中求索 [*Love in the Green Mountains*: Exploration between two opinions]. *Dazhong dianying* 大眾電影 [Mass Film], no. 22 (2013): 38–40.

Zhu Anping 朱安平. "*Wutai jiemei* 'taiwai youtai'" 《舞臺姐妹》"臺外有臺" [*Stage Sisters*, a stage outside the stage]. *Dazhong dianying* 大眾電影 [Mass Film], no. 2 (2006): 36–39.

Zhu Dake 朱大可. "Xie Jin dianying moshi de quexian" 謝晉電影模式的缺陷 [The flaw in Xie Jin's cinematic mode]. In *Lun Xie Jin dianying* 論謝晉電影 [On Xie Jin's films], edited by Zhongguo dianying jia xiehui 中國電影家協會 [China Film Association], 91–93. Beijing: Zhongguo dianying chubanshe, 1998.

Zhu Hong 朱虹. *Shanyao zai tongyi xingkong—Zhongguo neidi dianying zai Xianggang* 閃耀在同一星空—中國內地電影在香港 [Shining in the same starry sky—Mainland-made films in Hong Kong]. Kunming: Yunnan renmin chubanshe, 2005.

Žižek, Slavoj. *The Sublime Object of Ideology*. London: Verso, 1989.

Index

Anti-Rightist Movement, 10, 16, 21, 49–50, 53, 76, 91, 109, 117–18, 135

Beijing Opera, 39, 73, 95–96, 101, 103, 113
biographical film, 4, 10, 15, 18, 21, 23, 26, 28, 35, 42, 79, 87, 139
Brave the Wind and Waves (*Chengfeng polang*), 10, 66–89, 139

Cai Ben, 93, 102
censorship, 3, 14, 17, 19, 91, 98, 100, 136, 139
Chen Baichen, 12, 26–28, 32, 59
Chen Huangmei, 14, 35–36, 41, 75, 77, 97, 100–104, 124, 127–30, 133
Chen Liting, 5, 46, 49, 56–60, 64, 129, 135
cinema of attractions, 96, 100, 106
Cinematic Cold War, 11, 17, 90–93, 98–103, 110, 113
class view, 18, 20–26, 32–38, 91, 108, 110, 129
comedy, 67–68, 76–79, 114
confession, 36, 41, 46, 54, 61–66
Cultural Revolution, 1, 6–7, 10–14, 19, 21–22, 27, 39–42, 45–55, 61–64, 90, 92, 94, 97, 104–8, 113, 115, 120, 128, 130, 132, 134, 137–39
Cultural Thaw, 87, 92, 126

degendering, 68, 84–86
director-centeredness (director-centrism), 3, 14, 56, 76
documentary artistic film, 72

Dream of the Red Chamber (*Honglou meng*), 105–7

entanglement, 15, 20, 141

Great Leap Forward, 16, 22, 39, 41, 50–51, 55, 72, 77, 100, 104, 139

Hibiscus Town (*Furong zhen*), 115, 134
historical film, 10, 18. *See also* biographical film
historicism, 18, 20–26, 28, 32–36, 38–39
Huang Chen, 11, 50, 138–39
humanism, 10, 93, 108–10, 113, 131
Hundred Flowers, 68, 71, 76, 78, 118

Jian Bozan, 34, 36, 39
Jiang Qing, 16, 23, 26–28, 32, 50, 53–54, 64, 138–39
Jin Caifeng, 106–7, 111

leftwing (Hong Kong), 16, 91–92, 98, 100, 102–3, 113
Leyda, Jay, 38, 58, 67, 122
Liang Shanbo and Zhu Yingtai (*Liang Shanbo yu Zhu Yingtai*), 77, 91, 99–100, 113
Lin Zexu, 10, 15, 18, 21, 34–41, 54, 57, 62, 78
Liu Qiong, 49, 94–95, 101, 116, 119
Love in the Green Mountains (*Qingshan lian*), 52, 55–56

Index

Mao Zedong, 19, 22–23, 27, 53
Marriage Between a Fairy and Man (Tianxian pei), 99, 102, 140
martyr, 1, 42, 44–47, 64, 118, 138–39
melodrama, 17, 114–15, 122, 125, 131–37, 140. See also Xie Jin mode of cinema

opera films (*xiqu dianying*), 5, 10, 16–17, 77, 89–113, 140
orientalism, 97

peasant warfare, 10, 15, 19, 26, 28–29, 32, 36
propaganda, 2, 6–7, 32–33, 51, 73, 91–92, 100, 103, 119, 122, 139
public space, 21–22, 42. See also public sphere
public sphere, 21, 39. See also public space

Qin Yi, 116, 119
Queen of Sports (Tiyu huanghou), 10, 16, 79–86

Red Detachment of Women (Hongse niangzi jun), 115, 120–27, 131, 133–36
resistance/accommodation paradigm, 1, 6–9, 13, 44, 65, 138, 140
Rightist, 5, 50, 63, 92, 109, 112. See also Anti-Rightist Movement

second-generation directors, 66–67, 75, 88, 92–94
Sentinel under the Neon Lights (Nihongdeng xia de shaobing), 133
Shanghai Film Bureau, 71, 76, 78, 82, 93, 102, 122, 127, 135
Shanghai Jiangnan Film Studio, 5, 71–72, 75
Shanghai Pegasus Film Studio, 5, 50, 102, 126, 129, 133
Shanghai Petrel Film Studio, 5, 101, 107
Shen Fu, 35, 135
Shen Ji, 71, 117
Shi Hui, 7, 33, 50, 71, 99, 117–18
Song Jingshi, 15, 18, 20–21, 26, 29–32, 38, 42, 59, 71, 91

Stage Sisters (Wutai jiemei), 87, 115, 126–36
stardom, 5, 10, 15–16, 43–48, 50–53, 55–57, 60, 62, 64–65, 119, 139
subjectivity, 2, 8–9, 11, 13–16, 42–47, 69, 93, 137–38, 141. See also subjectivizing practice
subjectivizing practice, 8–9, 13–14, 16, 42–44, 46, 89, 93, 138, 141. See also subjectivity
Sun Yu, 2, 4–5, 10–11, 16–17, 48, 56, 66–89, 93, 135, 139

The Goddess (Shennü), 10, 92–93, 108, 110–12
The Investigation Report of the History of Wu Xun, 23, 29
The Investigation Report on the History of Song Jingshi, 26–28
The Jade Hairpin (Biyu zan), 16, 93–94, 100, 103, 105–13
The Life of Lu Xun (Lu Xun zhuan), 35, 45, 53, 55, 57–61, 64
The Life of Wu Xun (Wu Xun zhuan), 4, 10, 15, 19–20, 22–23, 25–26, 28, 33, 41, 44, 46–49, 53, 62–63, 66–67, 72, 77, 79
Tian Han, 39–41, 58

Woman Basketball Player No. 5 (Nülan wuhao), 77, 115–20, 125–26, 131–36
Wu Han, 22, 34, 36, 38–39
Wu Yonggang, 2, 5, 10–11, 16–17, 90, 92–95, 107–13, 139–40

Xia Yan, 14, 41, 52, 58, 60–62, 88, 91, 94, 100–110, 113, 120, 127–28, 130–31, 133, 136
Xie Jin, 2, 5, 10–11, 17, 71, 77, 114–37, 139–40
Xie Jin mode of cinema, 10, 17, 115, 131–36. See also melodrama, Xie Jin
Xu Dunle, 99–100
Xu Yulan, 104

Yang Xiaozhong, 49, 93, 135
Ying Yunwei, 5, 49, 93, 95–96

Yu Ling, 48, 58, 109, 111
Yue opera, 4, 94–95, 103–6, 113, 127

Zhang Chunqiao, 61, 128–29, 132
Zhao Dan, 1–2, 5, 10, 12, 28, 35–36, 38, 41, 43–66, 72, 135, 139
Zheng Junli, 2, 5, 7, 10–11, 15–16, 18, 21, 29, 32–38, 40–42, 48–50, 66, 138–39
Zhou Enlai, 16, 36, 52–54, 117, 128, 130, 136
Zhou Yang, 22–23, 26, 48, 53, 58–59